French Beans and Food Scares

French Beans
and Food Scares

Culture and Commerce in an Anxious Age

Susanne Freidberg

OXFORD

UNIVERSITY PRESS

2004

OXFORD
UNIVERSITY PRESS

Oxford   New York
Auckland   Bangkok   Buenos Aires   Cape Town   Chennai
Dar es Salaam   Delhi   Hong Kong   Istanbul   Karachi   Kolkata
Kuala Lumpur   Madrid   Melbourne   Mexico City   Mumbai   Nairobi
São Paulo   Shanghai   Taipei   Tokyo   Toronto

Copyright © 2004 by Oxford University Press, Inc.

Published by Oxford University Press, Inc.
198 Madison Avenue, New York, New York 10016

www.oup.com

Oxford is a registered trademark of Oxford University Press

Library of Congress Cataloging-in-Publication Data
Freidberg, Susanne Elizabeth.
French beans and food scares : culture and commerce in an anxious age / Susanne Freidberg.
p.   cm.
Includes bibliographical references (p.   ).
ISBN 978-0-19-516961-4 (pbk)
1. Produce trade—Government policy—England.   2. Horticultural products industry—
Government policy—England.   3. Produce trade—Government policy—France.   4. Horticultural
products industry—Government policy—France.   5. Produce trade—Government policy—
Africa.   6. Horticultural products industry—Government policy—Africa.   7. Produce trade—
Government policy—United States.   8. Horticultural products industry—Government policy—
United States.   9. Produce trade—Government policy—Developing countries.   10. Horticultural
products industry—Government policy—Developing countries.   11. Food adulteration and
inspection—International cooperation.   12. Horticultural products—Inspection—International
cooperation.   I. Title.
HD9011.7.E5 F74 2004
382'.41'094—dc22
2003023133

5 7 9 8 6 4

Printed in the United States of America
on acid-free paper

Preface

From the time I first had the idea to write this book until I submitted the manuscript in mid-2003, mad cow disease seemed to most Americans a distant and exotic danger. Certainly the United States had a few late twentieth-century food scares: E-*coli* in hamburgers and apple juice; hepatitis on Guatemalan berries; scattered salmonella outbreaks. But these episodes passed quickly from the public eye, as individual companies issued apologies and recalls, and the government slapped temporary bans on suspect imports. These scares caused nothing near the level of public outrage and political controversy that followed the British government's 1996 announcement that, contrary to previous claims, the brain-eating bovine disease known as BSE might actually endanger humans too. Americans, for the most part, continued to trust their own government's claim that the United States' food supply was the safest in the world. They did not demand dramatic changes in laws or food industry practices, and did not get them.

One result was that European food politics and policies in the post–mad cow era appeared, to many Americans, stranger than ever. Not even the British could be considered as allies when it came to negotiations over, say, trade in genetically modified crops. Another result was that Americans could more easily ignore the broader implications of their collective power to demand safe, high-quality food. Supermarkets provided them with relatively little information about where their food came from, just as the media provided relatively little coverage of the questions raised by the mad cow crises in other countries—questions that had important consequences for the places and people featured in this book.

These were questions about how, for example, to make an increasingly complex food supply more traceable and transparent without wiping out small producers and traditional production methods; about the true costs of cheap groceries; about the ethics of supporting farmers at home versus those in former colonies; about exactly what it takes to build trust in the face of inevitable foodborne risks. All these concerns received so little attention from the American media that I often wondered, while writing, whether this book would even make sense in the country of its publication.

Two days before Christmas 2003, a crazy-eyed Holstein exposed the broken fence around fortress America. The United States' first mad cow, found on a Washington State dairy farm, surprised no one familiar with the country's historically lax methods for keeping BSE at bay. If anything, it was remarkable that the disease had not appeared sooner. Within days, more than forty countries had closed their markets to U.S. beef, despite the Department of Agriculture's rapid announcement of new slaughterhouse and BSE testing policies and despite its public relations emphasis on the cow's Canadian origins. Within weeks, it was clear that these new BSE policies, still much less rigorous than those in Europe and Japan, would not likely win back international customers anytime soon. On the home front, it was equally clear that food producers and retailers desperately wanted to avoid letting the discovery of one mad cow turn into anything more than that. They did not want the event to build support for country-of-origin food labeling, or to raise questions about the cozy relationship between agribusiness and the USDA. In short, they wanted to avert everything that mad cow had unleashed on the other side of the Atlantic, several years before.

The beef industry, at least, took heart from evidence that Americans were eating hamburgers at about their usual rate. Again, this was very different from what happened in Europe, but perhaps not surprising. After all, only one mad cow had been found, and election year media coverage had quickly pushed her story off the front pages. But her death pulled the United States into the bigger story about how different societies perceive and respond to the dangers born of an ever more globalized food supply and about how their responses have, in turn, potentially global consequences. As this book went to press, that bigger story remained far from finished.

I owe thanks to the many people who helped bring this book into the world. First, I am grateful for the fellowships provided by the National Science Foundation's Geography and Regional Science and Cultural Anthropology Programs, the Walter and Constance Burke Foundation, and the Nelson A. Rockefeller Center at Dartmouth College. These institutions' financial support enabled me to conduct field research on two continents and four countries. I am also deeply grateful for the financial support provided by the Radcliffe Institute for Advanced Studies' Bunting Fellowship Program, which made possible a year's leave in 2000–2001.

In Burkina Faso, where the idea for this book first hatched, I most emphatically thank Fatimata Toe and Jérémie Koulibaly, who worked with me both during my dissertation fieldwork in 1993–1994 and again in 2000. I could not have hoped for wiser, more professional or more companionable research assistants. I am thankful also to the staff at IFD (ORSTOM) in both Bobo-Dioulasso and Ouagadougou, as well as at the American Cultural Center, for permitting me access to their libraries and computers. Not least, I am grateful to the family and staff at l'Auberge, for their warm hospitality and cool veranda. In Zambia, a country much less familiar to me than Burkina Faso, I owe thanks to Guy Scott, who helped me to find, see, and figure out a great deal that I wouldn't have otherwise. My research there also benefited from visits to the Institute of Economic and Social Research.

In France and Great Britain, I thank Arouna Ouedraogo for sharing his time, ideas, and office space on both sides of the Channel. I also thank his colleagues at the Ivry-sur-Seine branch of the Institut National de Recherche Agronome, who never questioned why a study of *l'haricot vert* would require so many extended visits or such disparate lines of inquiry. I feel especially fortunate to have gotten to know Martin Bruegel who, besides becoming a good friend, helped me think more like a historian. Conversations with Claire Marris, similarly, sent me down new and fruitful research paths. Monique Boulesteix proved a skilled and swift transcriber of my many interviews in French, as well as a historian of central Paris in her own right. In the U.K., I owe thanks to Bill Vorley and Tom Fox at the International Institute for Environment and Development; to Vicky Hird at Sustain; and to Tim Lang, Geoff Tansey, Felicity Lawrence, John Vidal, Danny Miller, Mick Blowfield, Catherine Dolan, and Alex Hughes. All these individuals' insights into British food politics and the workings of British supermarkets proved hugely helpful. Fond thanks as well to Maurice Bloch, for moral support and a cross-Channel perspective on green bean appreciation. Lastly, I am grateful to those many people who made every trip to Paris feel like a homecoming, including the greengrocer on Rue Saint Jacques, and the staff at Fish, Chez George, and Café de l'Industrie.

At the University of California at Berkeley, I want first to thank Gill Hart, who provided timely and spot-on advice when I was developing the original proposal for this project. Thanks as well to my dissertation advisor Michael Watts, for inspiring and guiding the initial research in West Africa, and to Michael Johns, for appreciating good stories. At Harvard, my first stop after Berkeley, I am enormously grateful to Skip Gates, Karen Dalton and the staff at the W. E. B. Du Bois Institute, where a fellowship position proved invaluable. Elsewhere on campus, I am thankful to the staff at the Bunting Institute, for all their help during my year there, and to Woody Watson, Calestous Juma, and Pauline Peters, for their advice and encouragement.

At the other end of Cambridge, I owe equally huge thanks to Deborah Fitzgerald for all-around support and, in particular, for lending me the MIT office where I finished the first draft of this book and concocted ideas for the next one. I also appreciate the friendly help provided by the administrative staff of

MIT's Science, Technology, and Society Program. Not least, I am grateful to all those who worked at the various Cambridge establishments where I wrote much of the manuscript, among them Peet's and Darwin's. Special thanks to those who humored, sustained, and sometimes saved me from my late-night scribbling at Casablanca, in particular Mick Lay, Anil Pillay, Shannon Plank, Servio Garcia, Jeff Warner, Jesse Steiger, and Eric Cross.

At Dartmouth, I owe thanks to the Geography Department colleagues who supported this project in all kinds of ways: Richard Wright and Frank Magilligan, for permitting and indeed encouraging frequent and far-flung research trips; Mona Domosh, for (among many other things) introducing me to worlds of geography I never learned about at Berkeley; Chris Sneddon and Pam Martin, for their comments on a draft of the manuscript; and Ben Forest, for saving me from disaster more times than I care to remember. I am also grateful to Kelly White, Geography's local hero, for extraordinary administrative help.

Others at and around Dartmouth who helped make this book both possible and pleasurable include Christianne Hardy Wohlforth and others at the John D. Dickey Center for International Understanding, which sponsored a stimulating manuscript review seminar; Linda Fowler who, on behalf of the Rockefeller Center, offered consistently generous support; Jodie Davi, who made the maps; David Barreda, Annie Kneedler, and Leah Horowitz, who all participated in the research; Alice Hartley, who took photographs; Anna McCall Taylor and Katie Greenwood, who moved many boxes; and Richard Sealey, who brought drama and hilarity to small town life.

At Oxford, I owe thanks to Clifford Mills, for taking on a book quite unlike the rest of his repertoire, and to John Rauschenberg, Rebecca Johns-Danes, and James Cook, for pushing the manuscript through the pipeline with minimal delays and angst.

Here the geography of my debts scatters. Among the people whose ideas, comments, and camaraderie enriched this book I want to thank Elizabeth Barham, Simon Batterbury, Lisa Disch, Judy Carney, Sam Chang, Fred Cooper, Margaret Fitzsimmons, Gail Hollander, Tad Mutersbaugh, Mark O'Malley, Jesse Ribot, Mahir Saul, Erica Schoenberger, and Marilyn Strathern. I am especially grateful to Julie Guthman, Elizabeth Dunn, and Bruce Braun, for their detailed and thoughtful comments on the manuscript.

One person who never read a word of the manuscript but who nonetheless helped me to finish it was the late Margot Silin. She started off as my landlady but became like family, and I only wish I could have given her a copy of the completed book. I also want to thank the real family: my siblings Jill and Mark Freidberg, for never letting me assume that school had all the answers, and my parents Colleen and Stan Freidberg, for giving me the confidence and freedom to go asking questions elsewhere.

Finally, I am grateful to the many unnamed individuals in Burkina Faso, Zambia, France, and Britain who responded to those questions and whose words and ideas fill this book. In telling me about their work, they took not only time but also, in some cases, risks. As participants in this thing we call globalization, they helped me appreciate complexity and humanity in places where both are often overlooked. They gave me hope where I did not expect to find it.

Contents

1
The Global Green Bean and Other Tales of Madness   *3*

2
Feeding the Nation: The Making of Modern Food Provisioning   *33*

3
Burkina Faso: Rural Development and Patronage   *61*

4
Zambia: Settler Colonialism and Corporate Paternalism   *93*

5
France: Expertise and Friendship   *127*

6
Britain: Brands and Standards   *167*

Conclusion   *211*

Notes   *223*

Works Cited   *235*

Index   *261*

French Beans and Food Scares

1

The Global Green Bean
and Other Tales of Madness

Scene I: The Ouagadougou International Airport, Burkina Faso, West Africa

The manager of the airport green bean packhouse arrived before dawn, and she may not sleep until well after midnight. It depends, she says, on whether tonight's Paris-bound cargo plane arrives and leaves on time. Often the flights run hours behind schedule, and in the meantime someone has to watch over the day's 15-ton shipment of green beans. She does not seem fazed by the hours, or by the general disarray of the packhouse. But then, she was hired because her Parisian boss needed someone who was never fazed, and he figured a Burkinabé woman would work harder than the nightclubbing French man she replaced. Her boss also needed someone who would keep a close eye on the 100-some women who inspect and re-pack the beans that arrived in cardboard cartons each morning from the villages. She tells them to make sure that "the peasants" have not hidden the wrinkled, fat or otherwise imperfect beans at the bottom of the cartons. If so, the cartons must be sent back, and the peasants reprimanded. The peasants get angry when this happens; they don't see why other people won't eat the same beans they do. "But they don't understand," she says, "if our French clients want quality, we must send them quality." Only the perfect may go to Paris.

Scene II: A business park near Heathrow Airport, London.

By early evening most of the fresh produce import firm's employees have gone home. The company's "technologist," however, works late, getting ready for a visit to one of his company's suppliers, a high-value horticultural export company in Africa. He is going to prepare for another visit later in the year, when he will accompany buyers from a major British supermarket chain. He must help the export company's manger, himself a British national, get ready for "the presentation." This is

Figure 1.1.
Burkina Faso's finest: green
beans ready for sale at the
Parisian wholesale market.
Photo by Christophe Maître.

*one of his main responsibilities as technologist: to make sure that sup-
pliers understand and comply with the supermarkets' rigorous codes of
good practice. The Zambian company's facilities must be spotless, he explains; its grounds groomed, its lower-level managers prepped. He will
also arrange a tour of the housing, childcare, and clinics the company
provides its workers. Perhaps a safari, too, because it's good to keep the
buyers busy and entertained. Above all, he must make sure that the
company has documentation ready to answer any questions the supermarket buyers might ask. He refers to them as "the 25-year-olds." They
tend to be recent university graduates, and not likely to stay long in
their current positions. Typically they know little about Africa. "But they
like paper," the technologist says, so this will be provided.*

The last years of the 20th century were tough times for selling food to Europeans. The competition was fierce, the rules uncertain, and the retail markets picky. It was not just that huge supermarket chains had come to dominate

food retailing, and to demand products conforming to ever-higher standards of convenience and aesthetic quality; these trends were common across the industrialized world. In addition, they demanded that the suppliers of those products—farmers and manufacturers, but also a range of intermediaries—meet standards of hygiene and accountability that were unimaginable twenty, even ten years earlier. The supermarkets wanted assurances that none of their products would set off another food scare; too many had already shaken European consumers' faith in the supermarkets' increasingly globalized offerings.

On the supermarket shelves, these assurances might appear as new labels or packaging, if they appeared at all. What consumers largely did not see was the work that went into providing them with food as certifiably pure as it was pretty. This work took place on farms and in packhouses; in consultants' offices and corporate boardrooms; in activists' meetings and chemical analysts' laboratories. It demanded long flights, short deadlines, and nonstop vigilance. Above all, the work of assuring the overall goodness of globalized food required all kinds of people and things to deal with each other in new ways, and often across great distances. In this sense, it transformed the social relationships of food provisioning on both an interpersonal and transcontinental scale.

This book explores how these changes took shape within two fresh vegetable trades, or commodity networks, linking two Sub-Saharan African countries to their former European colonial powers. The francophone network brings Burkina Faso's green beans to France, while the anglophone network brings an assortment of prepackaged fresh vegetables from Zambia to the United Kingdom. Broadly similar in some ways, they differ radically in others, including the ways that they experienced Europe's late twentieth-century food scares. By exploring the history of these differences and how they are sustained and transformed in specific places, practices, and social institutions, I hope to illuminate the relationship between culture and power in globalized food provisioning. More specifically, I want to show that the power to demand goodness in food—as defined by cultural norms of what makes food safe, natural, moral, and appetizing—has introduced new forms of domination and vulnerability into postcolonial food commodity networks.

So this is not primarily a book about food scares, despite the title. Mad cows and microbes enter into the story only occasionally, and usually just as specters that other actors strive to keep offstage. Nonetheless, the story has to start with food scares, particularly those that struck Europe between the late 1980s and 2001, to see why they unleashed events and restructuring processes that touched the far reaches of the global food economy. At the simplest, food scares are episodes of "acute collective anxiety," set off by reported risks of invisible food-borne pathogens and resulting, typically, in plunging sales of the suspect products (Beardsworth 1990; Miller and Reilly 1995). Although popular anxieties about tainted food are by no means new, modern food scares owe their political potency to 19th century developments in mass media, mass food marketing, and scientific measures of food purity and danger (Paulus 1974; French and Phillips 2000). This potency, however, has little to do with *proven* danger; none of the diseases implicated in Europe's late 20th century food scares had yet sickened or killed anywhere near as many people as, say, obesity or smoking (Lang and Rayner 2001). Rather, what alarms people is the evidence that the risks hidden in an increasingly industrialized and internationalized food supply are neither well understood by science nor well regulated by government.[1]

Fear and Loathing, 1988–2001

The alarms went off earliest and most embarrassingly in Britain. In 1988, salmonella felled 120 members of the House of Lords within three days, as well as prominent guests at two financial district banquets. Salmonella is an old and familiar food-borne germ, and one that adapted exceedingly well to the crowded and antibiotic-rich conditions of modern livestock farming. When the Junior Minister of Health admitted on television that salmonella now infected "most of the egg production in this country," the egg market promptly collapsed, despite denials by the poultry industry and the food and agriculture ministry (MAFF). Soon afterward, the discovery of listeria-tainted pâté and soft cheese set off similar shockwaves, especially when subsequent research indicated that the bacteria infected a full 25 percent of Britain's supermarket deli case foods (Shears, Zollers, et al. 2001; Mitchell and Greatorex 1993, 18).

The bacterial scares of the late 1980s proved to be only unsettling foretastes of a much more serious crisis which was already spreading through Britain's cattle population. Mad cow disease, or bovine spongiform encephalopathy (BSE), was first detected in 1986. No one knew its cause, but brain autopsies suggested links to scrapie, a degenerative brain syndrome long found in sheep. The government therefore banned sheep meal in livestock feed, but assumed that since scrapie did not endanger human health, neither did BSE.

MAFF maintained this stance for several years, even as BSE reached epidemic levels—it had been detected in one-third of the country's herds by 1993—and even as brain-eating diseases appeared in other mammals such as zoo antelope and housecats. But government efforts to reassure consumers about the safety of British beef, such as when Agriculture Minister John Gummer had his four-year-old granddaughter eat a hamburger on television, wore increasingly thin. Indeed, by the time the government admitted on March 20, 1996, to a possible link between BSE and several recent incidents of Creuztfeldt

Jacob Disease (CJD) in young hamburger-eating humans (CJD previously only struck the elderly, and very rarely), it simply confirmed widely held fears. It did not help that some scientists forecast that BSE-infected beef would cause 5,000 to 10 million cases of this "new variant" CJD in the United Kingdom within 15 years (Powell and Leiss 1997, 8; Ratzan 1998, chapter 12).

The European Union slapped an immediate and indefinite embargo on all British beef products, and its mainland governments subsequently blamed their own relatively few BSE cases on British feed and cattle exports. Like the British press, continental Europeans also blamed BSE on Thatcher-era meat industry deregulation, which had allowed slaughterhouses to render carcasses destined for animal feed at temperatures too low, it turned out, to kill BSE. But the continent soon had to contend with its own homegrown scares: reports that French government officials had overlooked rampant trafficking in banned animals and feedstuffs; that Belgian chickens had consumed feeds adulterated with dioxin-rich used motor oil; that foul-smelling Coca-Cola was leaving hundreds nauseated (Jaillette 2000; Mamère and Narbonne 2001).[2]

Finally came the 2001 outbreak of hoof-and-mouth disease, which struck several countries but hit the United Kingdom first and by far the hardest. Although the disease does not affect humans, it generated, if anything, even more profound popular revulsion and anguish than the mad cow crisis. The massive and controversial preventative destruction of millions of healthy animals—the alternative policy of vaccination was rejected because it would have cost the livestock industry its US market[3]—devastated already struggling agricultural and tourism-based rural economies. It also generated awful images: countryside infernos, fueled by tens of thousands of carcasses; prized pet lambs bound for slaughter; inconsolable farmers, quarantined on their properties. This time, critics blamed supermarkets as well as government, on the grounds that their long-distance shipping of animals between farms and centralized slaughterhouses had contributed to the speed and breadth of the epidemic (Monbiot 2001).

To varying degrees, Europe's food scares undermined public trust in government food regulators and their scientific methods of risk assessment (Cowan 1998; Levidow and Marris 2001; Wynne 2001). The scares also energized a wide range of oppositional and alternative "agro-food" movements. Opposition to genetically modified organisms (GMOs) spread fast and lasted, uniting French goat farmers and British "greens" (among others) against the common enemies of corporate (and specifically American) agribusiness. Similarly, the Slow Food movement that began in France and Italy (where else?) quickly mushroomed into an intercontinental celebration of local cuisine (Petrini 2003). But other movements mobilized around issues only indirectly related to food, such as countryside preservation and animal welfare. Diverse in methods, goals, and

The Global Green Bean and Other Tales of Madness

ideology, agro-food activists shared profound doubts about the "progress" achieved by industrialized food provisioning.

Yet why and how would all these events affect regions of Africa where farming was anything but industrialized? First, because the food scares fueled concerns about "emerging plagues" and the places they emerged from. Even before the 1996 BSE crisis, centuries-old images of Africa as a disease-ridden "hot zone" gained renewed currency with the spread of HIV/AIDS, two Ebola virus outbreaks, and popular media predictions of African anarchy (Garrett 1994; Preston 1994; Kaplan 1994). Perhaps not surprisingly, in August 1997 London's *Independent* newspaper made a front-page story out of "the growing body of scientific evidence" that BSE itself had come from Africa and had arrived in the United Kingdom via imported meat and bonemeal (Arthur 1997). Although the African origins theory of BSE did not gain much momentum, broader concerns about African contagions led to a series of EU bans on African food-stuffs in the late 1990s, due to possible though never proven dangers. Scattered cholera outbreaks in East Africa, for example, led to a ban on the entire region's fish; Madagascar's meat was barred due to lack of proper hygiene documen-tation (Mahende 1997; Andriatiana 1998; "EU Bans Kenya Fish" 1998). At a time when EU politicians were under pressure to show commitment to policing Eu-rope's food borders better, banning dubious commodities from the "dark con-tinent" might well have seemed like an obvious (and politically easy) step in that direction.

The bans, however, were temporary. Over the long run, EU regulatory reforms, undertaken with minimal input from sub-Saharan African countries, would have much more disadvantageous consequences for those countries' food exporters, especially smaller ones. Although these reforms were not prompted by food scares alone (one of the objectives of European unification was to facilitate trade through the creation of a common, or "harmonized" body of food laws) the scares made it politically imperative for European lawmakers to harmonize at least some food safety laws upward, rather than towards the "lowest common denominator" anticipated several years earlier (Millstone 1991; Shears, Zollers, et al. 2001). The harmonization of pesticide residue laws, in particular, effectively banned many of the cheaper, out-of-patent pesticides suit-able for tropical agriculture—pesticides, African farmers would note, that Eur-opeans had previously encouraged them to use (Chan and King 2000). Similarly, the European Commission standard for aflatoxin, a carcinogenic toxin naturally occurring in peanuts and some grains, promised to cost African exporters $670 million in lost revenue annually (Otsuki, Wilson, et al. 2001). Not least, the requirement that all European food businesses move towards full "traceability" appeared likely to discourage fresh produce importers from maintaining suppliers whose operations lacked the necessary record-keeping and communication technologies.

It is worth remembering that the European Commission was not the only government body to set food and crop hygiene standards that effectively barred certain imports; similar regulations have kept France's raw cheese out of the United States and American apples out of Japan.[4] With the formation of the World Trade Organization (WTO) in 1994, the defense of consumer health and safety became one of the few permissible "non-tariff trade barriers," and one that wealthy WTO member states have invoked repeatedly.[5] Europe's food safety policies, however, had the greatest effect on Africa, simply because Europe is the biggest overseas market for most African food commodities.

That said, to focus only on regulatory reforms would be to miss the real story of how African green bean farmers came to feel the fallout of Europe's mad cow crisis. More broadly, it would not explain why and how the wealthy world's food anxieties have transformed work in the globalized food economy in profound and varied ways. This is because the real work of moving food around the globe takes place in commodity networks that link specific people and places and things, and that deal with laws and standards—as they deal with events such as food scares—in specific ways. This specificity owes partly to different material conditions and structures of food production and distribution, as early studies of food "commodity chains" demonstrated (Friedland, Barton, et al. 1981). In addition, and as the events of the late 20th century made clear, food is a commodity extraordinarily freighted with meanings, and these shape the "social life" of food well before it arrives on the plate (Appadurai 1986). Such meanings, in fact, inform not only the distinctive practices characterizing specific food commodity networks, but also the politics and policy debates surrounding food globalization more generally.

Culture and Nature in Transnational Commodity Networks

This book's investigation of food commerce begins from two basic premises. The first, drawing on "cultural economy" analysis, assumes that economic practices are not merely "embedded" in social and cultural contexts. Rather, the economic and cultural are mutually constitutive, both over time and in place. To refer to a cultural economy, then, is simply to acknowledge that a particular set of economic practices, categories and measures of value (for example, market exchange, gourmet food, commodity grades and standards) are informed by particular cultural meanings and representations, and vice versa.[6]

In the context of contemporary transcontinental food trades, this first premise immediately raises a question: exactly where and how does culture take shape?

Traditional ethnographies of commerce provide no immediate answer, because most focus on markets and diasporas where shared cultural identity, whether rooted in ethnicity, religion, or hometown, provides the preexisting basis for trust and cooperation.[7] The francophone and anglophone green bean networks, however, rely on the ambivalent relationships and commonalities established under colonial rule. In the francophone network, many transactions take place between people who have little in common besides the colonial language (or some of it) and an interest in getting their products to market. The anglophone network, meanwhile, connects a smaller, more socially homogeneous and indeed more tribal set of corporate managers, technologists, and white settler farmers. But radically different local political, economic, technical, and social conditions in rural Zambia and London have complicated corporate supermarkets' efforts to impose their own organizational culture overseas.[8]

Culture within transnational settings, therefore, refers not to one society's taken-for-granted customs, nor to a single organization's learned discourses and behaviors. Instead, it describes the norms, practices, and social institutions shaping, and shaped by, relations between actors in the commodity network. It is culture that revolves around commerce, but encompasses many activities besides the basic negotiations and transactions of commodity trade. Its public norms of product quality and professional conduct may be dictated by particular institutions (regulatory agencies, supermarkets) or societal ideals (the supposed superiority of French taste), but actors' beliefs and behaviors may be more eclectic and less consistent, depending on where they are and who (or what) they are dealing with at the time. Perhaps most importantly, the breadth of many transnational commodity networks—their passage through different places and institutions—subjects them to diverse, potentially contradictory normative influences, as well as practical contingencies that demand improvisation and compromise. Thus, whatever makes them culturally distinctive may also be internally inconsistent, contested, and unstable.

So the second basic premise here is that food differs fundamentally from other commodities, due to the very nature of its production and consumption—in other words, the biophysical processes involved in agriculture and eating and the uncertainties and risks associated with both (Goodman and Redclift 1991; Fine 1994). Food's unique nature has made it uniquely central to human social life (in gardens and markets as well as homes and restaurants) and therefore a carrier of historically constructed meanings both intimate and geopolitical (Mintz 1986; Weismantel 1993). These meanings in turn enter into food markets at a variety of levels. Different groups and societies' ideas of food purity and danger, of the "proper meal" and the proper treatment of farmland and livestock, of government's responsibility to protect producers and consumers from food risks—all these norms influence not simply market supply and demand but also food trade politics and the governance of food commodity networks. One consequence, apparent to would-be free-traders from the 18th century onwards, is that food is never free of the meanings that make it the subject of bread riots, trade wars, and media scares.[9]

Beyond the distinctive nature of food in general, the natural qualities of specific foodstuffs (such as the perishability of green beans, or the bacterial content of certain dairy products) clearly matter. They condition how such products can be traded, transformed, and otherwise handled, as well as how they are assigned monetary, social, and symbolic value in different societies and markets. These natural qualities are of course themselves subject to change over time, whether through evolution or purposeful modification. The point here is that they are woven into the cultural fabric of food commodity networks.

This is one of several reasons why actor-network theory (ANT) has proven useful to many studies of food commerce.[10] In contrast to traditional social network analysis (Mitchell 1969), ANT assumes that nature (like other nonhuman things) is not just an environment or resource for human activity but also itself an agent, participating in the "collective action" of networks in diverse and not always predictable or controllable ways (Murdoch 1997). In the world of food and agriculture, one kind of nature that has defied human control is the prion, the brain-eating protein that causes BSE (Fitzsimmons and Goodman 1998). But any farmer could provide many more mundane examples. Farmers and food traders in agrarian societies have historically dealt with nature's vagaries partly through what is often described as the "moral economy"—that is, through relations of reciprocity and trust, born of and reinforced by mutually recognized norms of justice (Scott 1976; Watts 1983).

Technological and institutional forms of risk protection (such as cold storage and crop insurance) have perhaps made personal trust less necessary to markets dealing in relatively stable, standardized food commodities (soybeans, pork bellies), especially when all parties have access to such protections. But what about the many networks that deal in high value, highly perishable food commodities, and that span not only oceans and weather systems but also great differentials of socioeconomic security and technology access? The case studies in this book show how the innovations that make long-distance food trades technically feasible have not rendered personal trust unimportant. Rather, they have made it matter in different places and relationships.

This shifting geography of trust owes at least partly to the uneven "space-time compression" brought about by transportation and communication advances (Harvey 1989). Here again, actor-network theory highlights how actors' power to overcome time and distance constraints through "technological intermediaries" is unequally distributed within and between networks (Bridge 1997). The fax machines and refrigerated cargo flights that link green bean exporters in the Burkina Faso capital with Parisian vegetable importers, for example, have not "compressed" the few dozen or hundred kilometers that the green beans must travel between farm and airport; they have not fixed the potholes or the dilapidated lorries. The time pressures of transcontinental fresh vegetable trading have made certain distances, if anything, more problematic and stressful for everyone involved. They have also made punctuality and empathy all the more important as measures of trustworthy behavior. In Zambia, the managers of export firms face equally acute time pressures whenever their supermarket clients conduct unannounced, at-a-distance audits. Intended to check up on supply chain "traceability," these audits require managers to assemble detailed, on-farm production records and fax them to their clients within a matter of hours. It can be a stressful task in a country where the phone lines are often jammed or down, but also one that displays the commitment and managerial expertise that the U.K. supermarkets demand.

I provide these examples to clarify how the history, material conditions, and social life of transnational food commodity networks all help to maintain their cultural distinctiveness, even in the face of worldwide economic liberalization and regulatory harmonization. This distinctiveness is not peripheral or doomed; rather, it is central to any understanding of how global forces play out in specific places and commodity networks, and how in turn such forces draw guidance and legitimacy—for example, on matters of food purity—from specific cultural norms and practices. As in other realms of cultural analysis, therefore, qualitative methods have much to offer the study of the transnational food commodity networks. But this methodological choice raises two questions. First, what can case studies of two networks dealing in minor fresh vegetable commodities tell us about broader forces and trends? Second and more practically, when networks reach from sub-Saharan farms to London supermarkets, where does fieldwork begin and end? The following account of the research that went into this book—what questions motivated it, where I conducted it and, not least, what problems I encountered en route—provides a preliminary answer to these questions.

From Market Gardens to Global Markets

Doctoral research in southwestern Burkina Faso from mid-1993 to mid-1994 introduced me to some of the actors in the transnational francophone green bean trade and provided ideas and contacts that I later used to study it. The research itself focused on the social and environmental history of market gardening (or truck farming, but without trucks) in and around the city of Bobo-Dioulasso (Freidberg 1996a). There, men in hinterland villages have cultivated dry season "European" vegetables (lettuce, cabbage, carrots, green beans) since the early days of French colonial rule. Once a form of forced labor, market gardening is now a recognized and, under certain conditions, well-respected profession. The vegetables themselves, once produced primarily for the local European population, have become an appreciated part of the region's foodways (Freidberg 2003). Between the village gardens and urban marketplaces, women wholesalers provide intermediary services: buying and reselling, transport, and credit for both gardeners and customers.

In the early 1990s these actors were feeling the effects of World Bank-imposed economic austerity measures, and gardeners in particular faced the additional problems of declining soil fertility and riverbank erosion. These conditions made the inherent uncertainties and risks of local fresh vegetable marketing (weather, pests, glutted markets) even more difficult to manage, and made trust relations all the more important on all sides. It was clear from my conversations with women wholesalers and gardeners that these relations were not necessarily egalitarian (due to the wholesalers' superior control of cash and information) or conflict-free. Like commercial intermediaries around the world, the wholesalers as a group were often resented and characterized as parasites or thieves. But their services were also obviously indispensable, and relationships between individual wholesalers and gardeners sometimes endured across generations.

As I spent time in the villages and marketplaces around Bobo-Dioulasso, I learned about another, quite different group of intermediaries who were buying hinterland produce. A handful of businessmen, self-described agro-entrepreneurs, had recently begun contracting with villagers to grow premium quality green beans, which they shipped out of the Bobo-Dioulasso airport on overnight flights to Paris. The country had actually exported green beans since the late 1960s, but most were produced on relatively large foreign-financed irrigation schemes and flown out of the airport in the capital city, Ouagadougou. For many years, in fact, no sub-Saharan African country exported more green beans than Burkina Faso, except Kenya. But by the early 1990s, Burkina Faso faced much more competition, as well as more pressure to increase its exports—one reason for the green bean flights out of Bobo-Dioulasso's airport. The pressure was due to three distinct, but related, conditions facing Burkina Faso and other "least developed" countries at the end of the 20th century. These deserve brief mention because they help to show why Burkina Faso's green bean trade represents broader tendencies in food globalization.

First, these countries needed relatively high-value "non-traditional" commodities to replace revenue lost in slumping world markets for "traditional" exports such as cotton and copper, Burkina Faso's and Zambia's primary sources of foreign exchange (Little and Dolan 2000). Even the World Bank, which had long encouraged African countries to exploit their comparative advantage in one or two export commodities, conceded that world markets no longer supported this approach to export-led development (World Bank 1989).

Second, they needed to provide their own commercial farmers with alternatives to producing food for domestic markets, where they could not easily compete with subsidized American and European farm products. Although the United States and the EU had committed to reducing their agricultural subsidies when the WTO was formed in 1994, strong farm lobbies assured that neither acted quickly on this front (McMichael 2000). Farmers in poor countries could not afford to wait.

Third, despite persistent agricultural protectionism in the global North, the World Bank and bilateral donors required aid recipients such as Burkina Faso to open up their own economies to free trade and private enterprise. The Bank argued that although trade liberalization might be painful initially, it would ultimately encourage indigenous entrepreneurship. It was particularly supportive of the contract farming arrangements characteristic of fresh fruit and vegetable (FFV) export enterprises in Burkina Faso and Kenya (among other countries) because at least in principle they linked the entrepreneur's capital and connections with the small farmer's cheap and industrious family labor force (Watts 1994b, Jaffee 1995a).

The Burkinabé green bean exporters I met in the early 1990s, like the gardeners and local market traders, understood very well how liberalization affected their lives and livelihoods. Fuel, fertilizer, and schooling became more expensive; factory workers lost jobs; local people cut back on purchases of fresh vegetables and other non-necessary foodstuffs. The exporters, however, hoped that free market policies would eventually benefit them. After all, not only were they adapting to the realities of modern globalized trade, they were also catering to modern, globalized tastes. Health-conscious, well-traveled consumers in West Europe, as in North America, now expected to find year-round variety in the fresh produce aisles, and at least some of them would pay a premium to have hand-picked green beans at Christmas (Cook 1994; Friedland 1994b). Although Burkina Faso lacked Kenya's long growing season and Morocco's proximity to Europe, the exporters still believed that overseas markets offered niches for anyone who worked hard enough to find them. And even though for years Burkina Faso's only FFV export commodities had been green beans and mangoes, shipped almost entirely to France, the exporters hoped to diversify both product lines and markets.

Similar aspirations fueled the emergence of trans-hemispheric fresh food commodity networks around the globe (Islam 1990; Friedland 1994a; Jaffee

1995b). Several linked new green bean production zones in francophone Africa—Senegal, Mali, Madagascar—to the French market. Supported by an assortment of financial and technological aid packages and feeding the wealthy world's growing appetite for value-added freshness, these networks appeared to many observers as evidence of a new stage in the globalized food economy (Friedmann 1982, 1993). Some, like the World Bank, saw new opportunities for export-led development (Jaffee and Gordon 1993); others saw only new forms of exploitation and risk, including the risks posed by heavy pesticide use on export farms.[11] What seemed indisputable was that these new South-North FFV networks had been made possible by the kinds of technological innovations and trans-hemispheric capital flows that characterized late 20th century economic globalization.

That said, these innovations and investments did not have globally uniform effects. If the technological improvements and productivity increases in the Chilean fruit industry represented a "miracle," the miracle of Burkina Faso's green bean export business was simply that it had survived despite chronic mishap and indiscipline (Barrientos 1999). The aforementioned bad roads were hardly the only problem. Water pumps broke down, Air Afrique's cargo flights arrived hours late or not at all, fertilizer went missing, growers refused to harvest if it interfered with a funeral or other local social obligation. Beans grew intolerably fat on the vine (this takes only one day) or wilted by the side of the road (this takes only several hours). Under such conditions, could entrepreneurial ambition and dirt-cheap labor continue to earn Burkina Faso's green beans a place in an increasingly crowded market?

By the late 1990s, European responses to the BSE crisis and other food scares raised additional doubts. European governments had equipped livestock with "passports" and created new, tough-talking food safety agencies. France had defied a WTO ruling on the safety of American hormone-fed beef, opting to pay sanctions rather than accept imports. The United Kingdom's top supermarkets, meanwhile, demanded that *all* their suppliers comply with strict standards of hygiene, traceability, and social welfare. Although the supermarkets had been legally required to demonstrate "due diligence" in matters of food quality and safety since 1990, after the mad cow scare they competed to impress consumers by not just meeting but indeed exceeding government regulations (Marsden et al. 2000).

The U.K. supermarkets' reformist zeal had dramatic consequences in Kenya, sub-Saharan Africa's biggest exporter of green beans and related commodities. In the 1980s, Kenya's smallholders, often organized in cooperatives, took on more and more of the country's fresh vegetable export production— nearly 75 percent by 1992. They helped to make Kenya one of the World Bank's favorite "success stories" of non-traditional export development (Harris 1992;

Jaffee and Gordon 1993). But during the mid-1990s, as U.K. supermarkets consolidated their control over their overseas supply chains, they looked increasingly to "source" Kenyan fresh produce from large, vertically integrated, and typically white-owned company farms. In their view, large operations could provide better facilities and more services than smallholder cooperatives, could be more easily audited, and could more reliably meet stringent safety and quality standards, as well as high-volume orders (Harris-Pascal, Humphrey, et al. 1998; Dolan, Humphrey, et al. 1999). By the end of the decade, seven such firms controlled 75 percent of the country's FFV export production.

But did the back-to-the-plantation shift in Kenya foretell a more general trend in FFV networks between Africa and Europe? Institutional economists might answer this question by way of "global value chain" analysis. They would first examine the changing regulatory environment and demands of European food retailing, and in particular retailers' demand for invisible qualities such as purity, "ethics," and "sustainability." They would find that the regulatory environment, meaning the EU, was largely harmonized, and that all the major European supermarket chains were signing onto industry-wide initiatives to assure the safety and quality of imported produce.[12] Second, they would consider whether different networks could relay to African suppliers the necessary information about new laws and quality standards—information that, for standards measuring qualities such as "ethics," is quite complex. Lastly, they would assess the competency of suppliers to respond to that information (Humphrey and Schmitz 2001; Stevens 2001). According to this sort of analysis, the green bean commodity network between Burkina Faso and France would appear a chaotic mess, and an even more likely candidate for rapid restructuring than its Kenya-U.K. counterpart.

A cultural economy analysis, however, would raise a series of doubts, starting from the observation that these networks remain largely faithful to colonial ties (see tables 1.1 and 1.2).

French colonialism left behind a very different landscape of export agriculture in Sahelian West Africa, one where FFV plantations, especially those run by European settlers or foreign corporations, were relatively scarce and often economically or politically unviable (Mackintosh 1989). The region's postcolonial governments continue to focus rural development programs on smallholder agriculture, and French bilateral aid encourages them to do so. Under these conditions, where would French importers and retailers find large, vertically integrated green bean suppliers—if that was even what they wanted?

This raises the next question. Even a quick read of French food retailing history indicates that the country's consumers did not traditionally expect the same displays of authoritative quality control from their supermarkets that British consumers expected from theirs. French consumers had different ideas

Table 1.1

Top ten vegetable and fruit imports from ACP member
countries[1] into France in 2000 (thousand U.S. dollars):

Morocco	334,535
Ivory Coast	171,796
Madagascar	59,756
Cameroon	53,770
Kenya	36,677
Tunisia	36,328
Algeria	13,765
Senegal	7,994
Zimbabwe	6,133
Burkina Faso	4,538

Source: *2000 World Trade Annual*

[1]African, Caribbean, and Pacific Group of States

about where to find such authority (on the farm or at the outdoor market) and
what it would look like (Lazareff 1998; Larmet 1999). How might this history
continue to inform French supermarkets' approaches to quality control, especially vis-à-vis their suppliers?

Last, the many and widely recognized (indeed, caricatured) differences
between British and French foodways are apparent in different national markets
for not only specific varieties of imported produce from Africa (the Brits, with
their historically polyglot cuisine, import more "Asian" vegetables such as baby
corn, the French import more green beans) but also specific kinds of processing

Table 1.2

Top ten vegetable and fruit imports from ACP member
countries[1] into U.K. in 2000 (thousand U.S. dollars)

Kenya	98,695
St. Lucia	48,356
Jamaica	39,767
Belize	34,282
Cameroon	31,856
Morocco	29,516
St. Vincent	28,005
Suriname	27,677
Dominica	18,432
Zimbabwe	18,049

Source: *2000 World Trade Annual*.

[1]African, Caribbean, and Pacific Group of States

The Global Green Bean and Other Tales of Madness

17

(the Brits prefer their beans trimmed and pre-packed, the French prefer theirs naked) (RAP Market Information Bulletin 1995; COLEACP 2001). These differences in national demand for green beans and baby corn do not translate into huge differences in dollar terms; these are, after all, very minor commodities. But they reflect differences in taste that, however natural they may now seem, have in fact been cultivated over time and within particular cultural economies. How have British and French food intermediaries, together with their African suppliers, helped to create and sustain such differences?

All these questions indicated that a research project comparing the Burkina Faso-France green bean commodity network with one linking an anglophone African FFV exporter to Britain would provide useful information about the future viability of development strategies based on high-value fresh food export production. Such a research project also offered an opportunity to explore how cultural constructs of food goodness had, over time, both shaped and been shaped by economic globalization.

On the Commodity Trails

So where to start? Even the unprocessed, unadorned Burkinabé green bean travels a long path between Sahelian farm and Parisian plate, and I planned to compare two such paths. In addition, I knew that the people whose work most interested me—exporters, importers, and other key decision-making intermediaries—were not only widely scattered but also not always easy to identify, much less meet. Fortunately, by the late 1990s many geographers and other social scientists were not only calling for "multi-site" research, but also writing about how they had conducted it, and how in particular they had gotten access to corporate "elites." They emphasized the value of mixed methodologies and sources (to balance the partiality of elite interviews, and the partiality of ethnographic observation), the need to make contacts one-by-one and, not least, the role of luck in helping to "connect the dots" in complex and sometimes secretive networks.[13]

With this advice in mind, I started fieldwork in the summer of 1999 at a market where I knew I would find plenty of transnational green bean traders. The Marché Internationale de Rungis, located on the outskirts of Paris near the Orly airport, is one of the world's largest fresh food wholesale markets and the destination for most green beans from francophone Africa (the rest go to Marseille). A vast concrete space of warehouses, loading docks and truck parking lots, Rungis sells to everyone from Parisian greengrocers and restaurateurs to overseas exotic food distributors. Most of the actual exchange of produce occurs in the early morning hours, but importers do much of their business later in the day and over the phone.

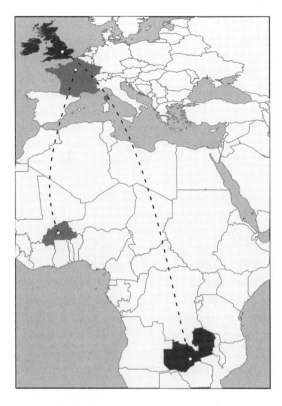

Figure 1.2.
The francophone and anglophone commodity networks

At Rungis I interviewed nearly all the FFV importers who worked in Africa and who were willing to speak to me (21 total) plus an assortment of wholesalers, transporters, and representatives of the importers' trade association. Luck came in handy immediately: I discovered that the son of French family I had known in Burkina Faso now worked for one of the Rungis green bean importers, and was able to put me in contact with several others. As in Burkina Faso I wanted to know about importers' professional histories, about how their work and commercial relationships had changed over time, and why they thought it had changed (food scares, as it turned out, did not top their list of reasons). I was particularly interested in the practical and social value that importers attached to relationships with different kinds of suppliers, customers and competitors.

Although the office interviews hardly resembled traditional participant observation, the long-distance phone calls that frequently interrupted the discussion provided insights into how importers conducted transactions and handled day-to-day crises. In fact some were remarkably indifferent about what I heard or witnessed, and their openness grew over time (I conducted research at Rungis during three consecutive summers, plus one brief winter visit). Partly, I think, this indifference reflected the relative invisibility of Rungis—certainly compared to the intensely scrutinized British supermarkets—in the eyes of the French media and academy. It may have reflected the traders' belief that any threats to their businesses could not possibly come in the form of a young American female academic. In any case, I also had many casual conversations with tradespeople (who are overwhelming male) both on the wholesale floors and in one of the main Rungis bars. These were useful for what they revealed about the practical knowledge and beliefs that Rungis traders used to assess both products and people.

Six months later, I returned to Burkina Faso during the green bean "high" season (January–March). Once I had met with the president of the fresh produce exporters' association, all the then-active members of the association (ten men and one woman) were willing to speak to me. These interviews followed the same general themes as those in Rungis, but this time I wanted to know about exporters' relations with growers, French importers (the men in Rungis) and each other. Given that several French importers had blamed Burkina Faso's relatively poor export performance in recent years on the Burkinabé exporters, I was particularly interested to hear how the exporters themselves characterized the situation.

I also interviewed members and presidents of growers' cooperatives, spoke with representatives of the agencies providing aid to the green bean export sector, and visited several informants from my earlier research. Lastly, I frequently visited the main packhouse at the Ouagadougou airport, where a few hundred workers (mostly young women) sort and pack beans for night flights. Thanks to the friendly Burkinabé woman manager there, I was able to spend as much time as I wanted on the packhouse floor, talking with the workers and learning how they sort good beans from rejects. This kind of access was unexpected and, as it turns out, unrepeated. In the anglophone network, such an apparent lack of concern about sanitation and public relations would have been considered dangerous and unprofessional.

For the anglophone African case study, I had originally chosen Zimbabwe, which once had one of the continent's most dynamic horticultural industries. But political violence and land occupations in mid-2000 made farm visits in Zimbabwe look less feasible, if not impossible, so I went to Zambia instead. In some ways it turned out to be a better case study to compare with Burkina Faso. The two countries have nearly the same population and per capita income (ten million and $320, respectively); both are landlocked, post-socialist, and dependent on a very narrow range of export commodities. This does not mean that either are "typical" francophone or anglophone FFV exporters. The social organization of Burkina Faso's export sector, for example, reflects geographic and historical conditions very different from those in Senegal and Morocco, while Zambia has historically depended more on its mineral resources and less on white settler agriculture than Kenya or pre-2002 Zimbabwe. The labels "francophone" and "anglophone" signal the importance of particular colonial experiences and places—and enduring postcolonial linkages—more than they describe a standard type of export economy or trade relationship.

Some of the biggest contrasts between Burkina Faso and Zambia lie in their agro-ecology (Burkina Faso has less water and a shorter growing season) and in the very shape of their FFV export economies. Whereas Burkina Faso's exporting lies in the hands of several small (in some cases one-man) operations, Zambia's is entirely controlled by two large companies, both of which export a relatively wide range of vegetables snowpeas, baby corn, baby squash, peppers, and of course green beans), most of them pre-packed, as well as roses.[14] These companies are financed by foreign corporate capital and run by men of European descent; all the exporters in Burkina Faso are black Burkinabé nationals, and financed by a combination of informal credit, bank loans, and creative uses of foreign aid monies. Nearly all growers in Burkina Faso (who are predominantly, but not entirely, male) cultivate less than a hectare, using household and sometimes hired labor. In Zambia, nearly all production takes place on plantations of thirty to thousands of hectares, owned by the export companies themselves or by a handful of white commercial farmers, who are known as the industry's "outgrowers." The labor force is predominantly female, except for technical and managerial positions. Finally, Burkina Faso's vegetable exports declined in the last years of the twentieth century, while Zambia's boomed.

In Zambia, I interviewed the top and middle-level managers of the two companies, as well as several of their outgrowers. I also spoke informally with some of the lower-level employees of these companies, most of whom are black Zambians, and with some of the many consultants and non-governmental organization (NGO) workers involved in upgrading and promoting the country's booming horticultural sector. I was particularly interested in how these different actors perceived and were reacting to British supermarkets' efforts to assure not only good hygiene but also social welfare in their African supply regions. Because the British media had previously portrayed the industry in a highly unfavorable light (drawing on reportage in Kenya and Zimbabwe), the Zambian export company managers were determined not only to appear friendly and forthcoming, but also to control where I went and who I talked to. Their watchfulness did not prove insurmountable—I found people to talk to—but it meant that I could not, for example, observe packhouse operations without a manager at my side. Ultimately, the managers' careful image control proved to be one of the most instructive aspects of the Zambian fieldwork, and one that I found elsewhere in the anglophone network.

The Global Green Bean and Other Tales of Madness

From Zambia I went to Britain for the first of several relatively short visits between mid-2000 and mid-2002. My initial contacts were with the Zambian export companies' import agents in London, whose own firms supply fresh produce to the United Kingdom's top supermarkets. Although such agents play nominally the same intermediary role as the French importers, their relationships with their supermarket customers are both more intimate and, in some ways, more subordinate. The importers I met were therefore well-situated to talk about the power dynamics of supermarket "category management" (discussed in chapter 6). They also helped me to identify other importers who worked in Africa, as well as supermarket produce managers and technologists.

My field visits to the United Kingdom came at a time when Britain's top supermarkets had been undergoing intense scrutiny and criticism. The media, activist NGOs, and even at times the government accused the "food giants" of destroying neighborhood shopping districts, contributing to the spread of foot-and-mouth disease, and above all exerting "armlock" control (Tony Blair's term) over suppliers both at home and abroad. Not surprisingly, then, the British supermarket personnel were keen to talk about the good that their companies' high standards had accomplished (for suppliers as well as consumers), the efforts they'd made to accommodate "stakeholders" (particularly NGOs), and the power of the media to influence a public who knew very little about food or farming.

This intense concern about the media and public image, which resurfaced repeatedly in the anglophone network, was one reason that I began exploring the relationships between British supermarkets and different kinds of civil society actors. In addition, current events in the United Kingdom indicated that the supermarkets were just one target in a broader movement—national in scope but certain to have transnational effects—to overhaul the way Britain fed itself. NGOs of every stripe had joined in campaigns for better nutrition, farm animal welfare, countryside preservation, and trade justice (among others), and a few of them were using the media very effectively to convince government and the supermarkets not only to listen but also change their policies. Although it was not always apparent how specific reforms would play out in supermarkets' African FFV supply regions, it was clear that both the media and the NGOs influenced how commercial intermediaries conducted and thought about their work in those regions. In other words, these civil society actors were participating in the "governance" of the anglophone commodity network—and Britain's food supply more generally—in ways that had no parallel in France or, for that matter, the United States.[15]

Curious about this dynamic, I spoke with representatives of some of the NGOs most active in campaigns to reform supermarket "sourcing" practices. I also spoke with food writers, journalists, and advocacy-minded academics, and attended the 2001 annual conference of the Soil Association. Initially I was primarily interested in the NGO's campaign strategies, their relationships with the media and the supermarkets and, not least, the possible tensions between the "development" NGOs (such as Christian Aid and Oxfam), who wanted Britain's globalized food supply made fairer, and the "green" and "countryside" NGOs (such as the Soil Association), who wanted it "relocalized" as much as possible. But the picture became more complicated. As veteran food activists pointed out, Britain's food movement was neither new nor, in the country's history of social activism, unique in its use of the media to demand that brand-name corporations "do the right thing." Indeed, it was a familiar dance on all sides, but one that had gained momentum as the supermarkets competed to offer consumers increasingly comprehensive forms of goodness.

Each stage of this research project had its challenges. Some were logistical, others analytical. Some of these challenges highlighted the practical limits of research on social interactions that take place in private spaces and across great distances. In other cases, comparative and historical analysis helped make the perplexing less so. A brief discussion of these challenges will help clarify what kinds of questions this book attempts to answer, and how.

The most immediate challenge in each site was getting access as quickly as possible to the necessary people and places. Except for Burkina Faso, I went to each site with few or no contacts, and little time—anywhere from a few days to several weeks—to make them. I also did not have time to learn all the local languages (I know English and French and conversational Dioula, one of the languages spoken in southern Burkina Faso). As it turned out, the sites and

Table 1.3
A Study in Contrasts

Measures	Burkina Faso	Zambia	France	U.K.
GNP per capita, U.S.$	210	300	24,090	24,430
Total population (*millions*)	11,535	10,421	59,238	59,634
Rural population as % total	82	60	24	11
Agricultural labor force as % total labor force	92	69	4	2
Total land, thousands of hectares	27,360	74,339	55,010	24,088
Irrigated land, thousands of hectares	25	46	2,000	108
Agricultural trade balance, millions of U.S.$	9.8	−13.5	10,166	−9,193
Agriculture as % of total GDP	34.5	27.3	2.9	1.0
Per capita dietary energy supply, kcal/day	2,320	1,900	3,580	3,300
Per capita dietary protein supply, g/day	68	47	116	98

Source: FAOSTAT, *World Bank World Development Indicators* 2002.

The Global Green Bean and Other Tales of Madness

social interactions I wanted most to understand were all thoroughly anglophone and francophone. In addition, most of the intermediaries proved surprisingly accommodating, at least as far as putting aside time for an interview. Some were actually eager to meet because, I later realized, they thought I might be useful to them. By contrast, it was difficult if not impossible to get unrestricted access to many key workplaces along the commodity networks, especially on the anglophone side. This meant that I could not confirm, for example, whether the Zambian export company managers kept records and monitored packhouse hygiene as assiduously as they claimed; I could not actually observe their meetings with British clients. Key informants helped fill in certain holes, but their comments could not substitute for direct observation.

This leads to the second and obviously related challenge: how to get accurate information in networks where secrecy and even deception are standard tools of the trade, and where at least some actors worry about publicity of any sort. Statements promising confidentiality do not necessarily reassure people who (as in the francophone network) are accustomed to broken promises or who (in Zambia) work in a community so small and intimate that no one is truly anonymous. Past experiences in Zambia also fostered fears that I might be a corporate spy or, worse, an undercover "BBC agent."

Even if they did not care much about confidentiality, many people quite understandably wanted to portray themselves positively, and so talked much more readily about others' faults and wrongdoings than about their own. At best, they might concede that injustices "happen" in their milieu, that mistakes get made—but not by them. So, for example, exporters in Burkina Faso talked at length about the duplicity of growers and importers, but blamed their own collective reputation for shady dealings on an unscrupulous, unnamed few. In Zambia, export company managers claimed that they rejected their outgrowers' produce only when quality was sub-standard; outgrowers claimed that the quality standard itself varied according to how badly British supermarkets needed Zambian *mangetout peas*.

The basic problem of getting the whole story is hardly unique to research on food commodity networks. But in this case the transnational and comparative framework helped to make sense of contradictions and ambiguities. The more important question ultimately became not so much whether certain actors were telling the truth about aspects of their work I could not observe, but rather why their accounts employed specific discourses and emphasized specific activities, problems, and goals—and why their accounts differed or agreed with those of other actors.

That said, the following chapters feature plenty of statements that are highly ambiguous, contradictory, and in some cases probably just false. They are part of the story. They help to illustrate how globalization, at the level of workaday practices and social relationships, not only depends on certain forms of secrecy, but also on intermediaries' tolerance for situations that are often confusing and politically or morally uneasy. This is perhaps especially true in the many commodity networks (not only those dealing in food) that are supposed to "develop" poor countries but which depend on their labor staying extremely cheap, and thus poor. The individuals interviewed for this book do not necessarily think about their work in terms of this paradox, but neither are they naïve about how particular inequities might appear to outsiders. More generally, even if they are not concerned about protecting a company image, they need to find in their work a meaning they can live with.

The most interesting challenge was how to make sense of the normative themes, or ideals, expressed repeatedly both within the transnational commodity networks themselves and by the equally distinctive French and British "agrofood" movements. At the broadest level, these themes describe not only what makes food good in different ways (pure, natural, appetizing, worth paying extra for) but also what kinds of knowledge, labor, and social relations can and should assure food's goodness. Practically, these themes inform the conventions within each network—that is, the methods used by intermediaries to assess and market valued but not immediately apparent food qualities, such as taste (Sylvander 1995). But as ideals they are also often invoked to express opposition to existing practices and nostalgia for past ones. And like the term "quality" itself, they are often taken for granted as true or valuable in a particular cultural context, even if in another context, such as a different commodity network, they are not valued much at all. While comparative analysis helped to illuminate the normative "black boxes" circulating through both the anglophone and francophone networks (Latour and Woolgar 1979), it also made clear that I would need to examine a far broader set of historical developments than those that forged particular postcolonial ties between Africa and Europe.

For example, intermediaries throughout the francophone network placed great value on the sociability of commercial exchange. This was apparent not only in observed exchanges but also, and even more forcefully, in the intermediaries' descriptions of commercial transactions and relationships. They emphasized the pleasures of regular (and ideally face-to-face) contact with suppliers and buyers; the expected, even ritualized, bargaining; the favors inevitably asked of them. Many of these accounts, especially coming from French importers, described a romanticized past rather than current day-to-day business, most of which they conduct over the phone in airless offices. Many were also self-flattering, reflecting the underlying assumption that sacrifices made for one's suppliers and customers were not just 'traditional' but also morally worthy.

Francophone fresh produce merchants are obviously not alone in appreciating the sociability of market exchange. Farmers' markets and other local food initiatives have flourished in many highly industrialized countries—including Britain—partly because they offer a conviviality missing from the average supermarket, and partly because they have become associated with better (fresher, healthier, tastier, perhaps less expensive and more "ethical") food.[16] In other words, local food devotees share the francophone intermediaries' faith in conventions of quality assurance based on relations of familiarity and trust. But while there are important parallels between consumers' fondness for farmers' markets and the francophone intermediaries' ideals of friendship, we should not conflate them. As the Burkinabé exporters would quickly point out, solid and useful commercial friendships, whether forged in the villages or in Paris, demand ongoing investment, a capacity to adapt to diverse social situations, and a willingness to take losses. Compared to consumers' typically casual acquaintances with local retailers, they are not easy relationships.

Closely coupled with the francophone network's ideal of sociable commerce is a notion the Greeks called *mētis*. It describes the situated, practically acquired skills and knowledge needed for all kinds of activities dealing with constantly changing conditions, from glassmaking to airplane piloting to agricultural production and trade (Scott 1998, 313–315). Actors throughout the francophone network acknowledge the *mētis* of the peasant (even if they do not always believe the peasants put it to proper use); they also value the commercial savvy and product knowledge acquired through years in the wholesale market.

On one level, the same would likely be true of any food commodity network peopled by farmers and intermediaries who have learned mostly through experience rather than formal education. In fact, as James Scott suggests in *Seeing Like a State* (1998), food provisioning activities throughout history have depended on the *mētis* of producers and intermediaries. Only in modern times have governments (and other powerful actors) attempted to replace the peasants' localized knowledge with the codified principles of "scientific" agriculture, and the market traders' savvy with "rational" systems of mass food retailing.

On another level, the meaning and value of *mētis* within the francophone green bean commodity network is quite specific. This is because French foodways, as a set of ideals, institutions, and more or less frequent practices, do not just recognize but indeed enshrine many kinds of local knowledge related to food provisioning. *Mētis* is legally protected by the French system of geographic appellations (Barham 2003), performed by market vendors and four-star chefs, celebrated in the country's tradition of gastronomic tourism, and defended by the *Confederation Paysanne*'s José Bové and other opponents of "McDonaldization." As chapter 5 discusses at greater length, the fact that industrial-scale farms and supermarkets now dominate France's food economy has not made the ideal of specialized, localized food knowledge any less important to French cultural identity.

How did the twinned ideals of *metis* and sociable commerce become so important to French foodways, and why do they continue to resonate among intermediaries in a postcolonial francophone commodity network? Intermediaries' own accounts provide some clues, but I think the historical answer to these questions lies in France's overlapping projects of empire and nation building in the 19th and early 20th century. These projects depended on the commercial and cultural ties between countrysides and the capital city—that is, on the roads and rail lines built, the commodities shipped, the regional recipes documented, and the values assimilated by peasants. They depended also on rural development policies that sought to "modernize" the keepers of agrarian *mētis,* namely the peasants of France and West Africa. This path was not necessarily more benign than the land expropriation and settler colonialism undertaken in British East and southern Africa (as well as in French Algeria), but rather one that appeared cheaper and less politically destabilizing. Chapters 2, 3, and 5 explores the policies and discourses of France's empire and nation-building projects, and considers their formative role in both domestic and transnational food cultural economies. Together these chapters show not only why the ideals of *mētis* and sociability continue to shape French norms of food goodness, but also why and how transnational food intermediaries depend on and defend these ideals.

Very different norms define goodness and professionalism in the anglophone commodity network. Here the intermediaries identify themselves not as traders or entrepreneurs, but as managers or technologists working for firms that have moved beyond the unpredictable, unstable trading environment in favor of the efficiencies and consistencies offered by supply chain management. To assess both suppliers and their goods, intermediaries employ codified standards of quality and "best practice," including the all-important practice of traceability. Intermediaries are expected to continue checking up on standards compliance through audits, conducted via ostensibly objective procedural and human actors (checklists, third party certification agencies) (Hughes forthcoming). Together, standards, audits, and traceability are supposed to demonstrate that a supply chain is well managed at all levels, and that the brand-name retailer controlling the chain is therefore acting responsibly (and responsively) towards consumers, shareholders and stakeholders. Ideally, this responsible conduct will win the retailer (and thus its suppliers) a greater share of an intensely competitive market. At the least, it should help win over the few but very valuable consumers who will go farther and pay extra for organic, fairly-traded, or otherwise certifiably good food.

At first glance, these managerial practices and the normative assumptions that go with them appear simply and generically corporate. After all, whether the label says "Gap" or "Tesco," any major consumer goods retailer these days will expect suppliers to adhere to codes of standards and undergo audits; they in turn will seek to demonstrate transparency and accountability. For that matter, many large public institutions—government agencies, universities, foundations—are expected to do the same. The late 20th century "audit explosion," while perhaps most thoroughly studied in the United Kingdom, has spread across borders and sectors, helped along by the now-globalized turn towards neoliberal governance (Power 1997; Strathern 2000a). Standardized quality and best practice codes, moreover, have helped all kinds of producers and retailers—not just those dealing in food—to globalize their goods (Du Toit 2001; Tanaka and Busch 2003). Like internationally recognized technical grades that define an extra-fine green bean as one measuring six millimeters or less in diameter, standards simply assure the world's customers that they are getting the qualities they want and pay for ("environmentally friendly," "cruelty-free") even if they cannot see them.

When supermarket or FFV export firm managers employ the now-standard tools and lingo of corporate accountability, however, they do so in specific settings and relationships, and in order to address specific concerns. Even the relatively few corporations involved in this network do not agree on exactly what accountability means or who they must be accountable to. The differences are apparent not just among corporate retailers (some have implemented "ethical sourcing" standards more aggressively than others) but also between the retailers and the Zambian export firms. Even though the latter's expatriate managers, as individuals, have much in common with their British clients, they must contend with radically different local socioeconomic and political conditions. Faced with massive unemployment, one of the world's highest rates of HIV/AIDS infection, and the seizure of white-owned commercial farms in neighboring Zimbabwe, the Zambia-based managers are understandably as keen to demonstrate "social responsibility" as are their British supermarket clients. But they do not necessarily agree on how to go about it, or who should pay. Chapter 4 explores these tensions in light of Zambia's colonial history of foreign corporate enterprise and white settler farming. Along with Chapter 6, it also examines how suppliers' and supermarkets' different priorities play out in close but highly lopsided supply-chain "partnerships."

What is most striking about the standards that the top British supermarkets expect of their African fresh vegetable suppliers is their scope and detail. They cover realms of supplier performance that most consumers, according to supermarket managers themselves, probably do not think about while shopping for a package of *mangetout* peas, such as on-farm wetlands and wildlife management, and packhouse gender equity. Moreover, suppliers must provide concrete evidence of their performance in these realms—evidence that can be quickly assessed even by auditors unfamiliar with the local environmental and social conditions.

Chapter 6 explores the reasons behind the U.K. supermarkets' increasingly systematic efforts to demonstrate accountability. Certainly, government regulatory reforms such as the 1990 Food Safety Act provided important incentives for rigorous traceability, as well as for food safety standards well above government baseline regulations.[17] But judging from the accounts of importers and middle managers, the supermarkets' collective superego, on a day-to-day basis, is much more preoccupied (indeed, extraordinarily preoccupied) by the media and by the NGOs that use the media to push for ever more extensive reforms in supermarket behavior.

Why would this be so? Is it simply because the British press is extraordinarily aggressive and hounds supermarkets, politicians, and movie stars with equal audacity? Perhaps, but this raises the question of why supermarkets, like politicians and movie stars, command the kind of public presence that makes them good story material. In addition, why have the supermarkets become a target for numerous NGO reform campaigns? Chapter 6 examines the political, economic and social dynamics behind these campaigns, as well as their effects on supermarket governance. But it starts from the premise that the relationship between the supermarkets and the reformers, as well as the results of their campaigns (namely the codified standards), must be understood in light of a long history of campaigns to clean up and moralize corporate food power. Chapter 2's discussion of the 19th century anti-adulteration movement explores this history.

Portrayed as a set of simplified themes, the cultural norms of the francophone and anglophone commodity networks appear diametrically opposed. In one, intermediaries value embedded trust relations and experiential knowledge, and see them as the best assurance of quality in an intrinsically volatile commercial and natural environment. In the other, intermediaries value the management tools, technical skills, and corporate "partnerships" that, in their view, reduce volatility to a minimum and allow them to market goods possessing an ever broader range of value-adding qualities.

To a certain extent, intermediaries in both networks endorse this dichotomy by using familiar stereotypes to describe both themselves and each other: the cold, excessively rational (or alternatively, professional and forward-looking) "Anglo-Saxons," versus the careless, immoral (or alternatively, passionate and humane) French (and francophone Africans).[18] These stereotypes (and others even more vast, such as "the Africans") are not meaningless; later chapters consider how these and other stereotypes need not be accurate to be useful to commercial intermediaries. But it will also become clear that neat, dichotomous characterizations do not begin to describe the way people actually work. Anglophone corporate managers, for example, depend on trust and subjective assessments of quality all the time. French importers, meanwhile, must increasingly do the bidding of French supermarket chains, which sometimes means severing longtime relationships with less competent suppliers.

These are just two of many possible examples illustrating how intermediaries in the anglophone and francophone networks, for all their differences, confront some of the same challenges. In fact, only by recognizing these commonalities can we appreciate why cultural analysis is so important to understanding the politics and technologies of globalized food. Two broader points, in particular, emerge from these case studies. First, both illustrate how power is being exerted in new ways through old, and formerly colonial relationships between global North and South. The field of postcolonial studies has not, by and large, taken much interest in contemporary African economies except to note how they have been gutted by corrupt and violent postcolonial states (Mbembé 2001) and subjected to the neo-imperial power of the World Bank and International Monetary Fund (Sidaway 2002). Nonetheless, the field's insights into how certain kinds of colonial power worked—or did not work—pertain directly to the transnational commodity networks featured in this book.

In particular, postcolonial scholarship considers the power contained in the so-called civilizing mission. Relying more on the collection and production of knowledge than overt violence, this power operated on the details of daily life—on how people washed, dressed, ate—through a range of social relationships and "micro-technologies" (Foucault, Burchell, et al. 1991, Abrahamsen 2003).[19] It was couched in discourses of progress and social uplift. Partly in order to make colonial rule more efficient and stable, it intended to make colonial subjects identify with a larger civilization, though typically without the citizen's rights (Mamdani 1996). Ultimately, of course, this proved an unsustainable project, but it left its mark on the identities of both colonized and colonizer, and on their relationships with one another (Stoler and Cooper 1997).

Later chapters will show how a similar form of power came to operate, albeit in different ways, through the social relationships of two postcolonial commodity networks. Mobilized to contain anxieties and consolidate new tastes in the global North (not just Britain and France), this power has brought the North's consumers more and more choices and assurances of food quality. But it is also transforming the material conditions and social relations of "quality" food provisioning in some of the world's poorest countries. Exactly how livelihoods in different regions will be affected over the longer term is an empirical question, and one that I hope this book will encourage others to pursue.

Second, and related, intermediaries in both networks are not just witnessing but participating in multiple struggles—some waged at the level of national and international social movements, others at the level of village disputes—to define *where* goodness in food lies. Although often framed as a geographic, ecological, or technical question—should the food supply be global or localized, produced "organically" or "scientifically"—it is fundamentally a social one. It is about who should participate in food provisioning and through what kinds of relationships. And to the extent that such relationships bring mutual obligations to actors in different places—including, ultimately, consumers—the question of where food should come from is also a question about whose food provisioning livelihoods we should care about (Smith 1998). This book does not pretend to provide definitive answers, only to show why the question matters.

2

Feeding the Nation

The Making of Modern Food Provisioning

The concentration of trade in the hands of powerful merchant companies has had menacing consequences for public health. When a harmful substance is added to a food, under the pretext of improving or preserving it, an entire country, even the whole of Europe, is threatened. Not by acute poisoning, which is rare and limited, but by troubles that develop slowly and can compromise the health and lifespan of an entire generation. Big corporate capital is involved, and when one points out the danger posed, they do not hesitate to claim that one is ruining national trade.[1]

In the late 20th century, a time when many Europeans protested against the corporate conquest of their food shops and farmlands, the sentiments expressed above were no doubt commonplace. The quotation, however, dates back to the 1889 International Hygiene Conference in Paris. Then as now, scientific and technological innovations and the expanding reach of "merchant companies" were stretching the geographic and biological limits of food supply, and sowing controversy along the way. On one hand, food was getting cheaper, more abundant, and more varied, especially in cities. On the other hand, food was coming from farther away and passing through more hands, and national governments could not assure that it was safe or truthfully marketed. As the conference-goers acknowledged, national borders were not stopping either epidemics or the trade in "falsified products."

The period between the mid-19th and early 20th centuries bears further examination not simply because it saw anxieties and controversies over food remarkably similar to those of the turn-of-the millennium period. In addition, events and developments of this era set the stage for contemporary food globalization through diverse and culturally distinctive commodity networks. With Europe's colonization of Africa came the establishment of enduring relationships of trade, aid, and investment in African food production. With the emergence of the bureaucratic welfare state, corporate food processing and retailing, and new food sciences and technologies, it became possible to provide the mass market with reasonably safe and wholesome food; with growing consumer awareness and activism, it became both economically and politically necessary. With the emergence of an urban bourgeois society devoted to gastronomy—the "science of taste"—both the French state and French farmers realized food's power as an expression of natural and national distinction—a distinction that strengthened national consciousness around food on both sides of the Channel.

In short, this era saw what turned out to be a number of pivotal debates and struggles over how to define and best provide for food safety and quality. It was also an era when metropolitan elites looked to their expanding overseas empires not just to enrich national economies but also to consolidate nationhood. How were these two historical processes intertwined? How, in other words, were empire and Epicureanism not just comtemporaneous, but intimately related within the broader project of nation building? This question is important for understanding the parallels and striking differences between the postcolonial commodity networks examined in later chapters. This chapter starts with a broad claim: Namely, that the same conditions of speeding-up capitalism and rapid technological innovation that encouraged colonial expansion also enabled and demanded the consolidation of national foodways. Ambition and anxiety fueled both developments, but they played out differently in different places. Three empirical questions, which necessarily take the story some distance from the subject of contemporary green bean trading, follow from this claim. First, precisely how did rapid economic, technical, and social changes generate anxieties about food purity and quality? Second, how did such anxieties influence the development of new food institutions and technologies, and how in turn were these put to the task of feeding nations and empires? Third, what kinds of food intermediaries took part in this task?

Feeding the Case for Empire

Steamships, railroads, and the telegraph were just a few of the 19th century technologies that opened up a world of new possibilities for European imperialism (Peters 1996). Together with advances in weaponry and the discovery of quinine to treat malaria, these technologies of circulation ("circulation" became a metaphor for all that was "healthy, progressive [and] constructive" [Thrift 1996, 266]) inspired confidence and competitiveness among Europe's political leaders and visions of profitable new markets among industrialists, merchants, and financiers. They promised to advance the overseas work of scientific and evangelical institutions, and entered into the very discourses of bourgeois society. Not least, the 19th century's technological achievements reinforced ideologies of European superiority and rightful dominance over presumably less-advanced world regions (Headrick 1981; Adas 1989, chapter 4).

That said, this sense of superiority did not translate automatically into support for colonial expansion in Africa.[2] Colonization raised concerns not only because it contradicted principles of free trade but also because it posed risks. For Europe's leaders, a new round of colonial occupation would entail political and economic risks, especially in the many parts of Africa where they knew little about the resources they intended to exploit or the societies they intended to govern. But imperial expansion also raised apprehensions about the health and survival of Europeans and European civilization.[3] Evidence that technology could "compress" the distances between continents and markets did not convince everyone that it could also maintain barriers against contagion and degeneration (Anderson 1996a).

How did food play into these debates, circa mid-19th century? On one side, there were a number of reasons why European colonial expansion might increase the quality and quantity of food available to Europeans, Africans, and indeed the world. (*Might* is the operative term here; reality in most cases fell far short of aspiration.) First, colonization would allow Europeans to circumvent the indigenous elites who controlled the cultivation and trade of food commodities. In theory, expanded and modernized production under European auspices would allow for a more reliable and affordable supply of commodities that, in the case of tropical stimulants (tea, coffee, sugar), were rapidly becoming addictively important parts of European (and especially British) working class diets (Mintz 1986; Walvin 1997). In practice, many colonial administrations continued to rely on indigenous elites to organize export production (see chapter 3).

Second, European settlement in Africa's more temperate regions might provide a partial and temporary solution to the crisis of urban unemployment—and the hunger that went with it—back at home. European settlers could in turn earn their keep by producing food for their colonies as well as for export. This argument figured into Britain's decision to encourage emigration to Kenya's highlands during the depression years of the 1880s; it presumed that the settlers would be skilled and forward-looking farmers, which in many cases they were not.

Third, colonization would allow for systematic botanical and zoological research. Centuries of overseas species collection had of course immensely enriched European foodways with "discoveries" ranging from potatoes to chocolate. By the mid-19th century, scientific, commercial, and social concerns had intensified the search for new and useful species. French natural scientists, in particular, enjoyed government support for their "acclimatization" research, which sought to adapt plant and animal species to foreign environments through controlled breeding and climatic conditions (Lever 1992; Osborne 1994). Even though much of this research focused on adapting tropical species to French climes, France and the other European colonial powers later established experimental gardens throughout Africa and Asia.[4] In some French colonies, the *jardins d'essai* doubled as *potagers* (kitchen gardens), providing vegetables such as green beans for the resident European population (Bonneuil 1991).

Lastly, it could be argued that European colonization would help Africans to eat better, insofar as it brought improved transportation and agricultural methods, and taught presumably superior nutrition, food preparation, and household hygiene.[5] Explorers brought back mixed reports of African's food supply and nutritional status in the mid-19th century. Whereas Livingstone saw much evidence of hunger in slave-trade-wracked southern and central Africa (including present-day Zambia), Binger found the west African market of Bobo-Dioulasso (in Burkina Faso) well-stocked with local grains, vegetables, and shea butter, as well as dates from the Sahara (Livingstone 1858; Binger 1892, 371). Relatively favorable accounts such as Binger's, however, by no means clouded European agronomists' and engineers' visions of never-ending progress in and beyond the African farmstead. As Michael Adas notes, this vision assumed that European technologies would bring not simply material abundance but also, by their very presence, "social uplift" (Adas 1989, 226–230). In reality, French colonialism did not bring Burkina Faso an abundance of anything, except taxes and hunger (Gervais 1987); British rule did little better in southern-central Africa (Vaughan 1987; Moore and Vaughan 1994).

Well before harsh colonial tax and labor policies contributed to famine vulnerability across Africa,[6] Europeans worried about how their own populations would survive there. Quinine could combat malaria, but the causes of high rates of Europeans illness and mortality in tropical climes appeared numerous and mysterious, especially before theories of bacterial transmission gained acceptance in the 1880s (Curtin 1989, 1998). By the mid-19th century, in fact, the decades-old debate over whether Europeans as a "race" could acclimatize to the tropics had swayed towards the naysayers,[7] who argued that degeneration—physical, mental, and social—was inevitable (Anderson 1992). Another (and eventually prevailing) line of thought held that the key to European survival in the tropics lay in "very careful living"—which meant, among other things, very careful eating (Livingstone 1999, 104).[8]

Exactly what Europeans in the tropics should eat was debated throughout the 19th century (and beyond). In general physicians' recommendations shifted from *imitation* (Europeans should adopt the plant-centered diet of the locals, albeit avoiding fresh fruits) to *intervention* (Europeans should introduce into the colonies their own crops, processed foods, and food handling methods).[9] By 1900, this shift reflected not only new concerns about the adequacy and hygiene of local diets—which in many places had already deteriorated under colonial rule—but also the newly viable alternatives to eating like the locals. Advances in food canning brought colonials products such as Liebig's Meat Extract, which was marketed by its inventor (himself a chemist) as ideal nourishment for warfare, expeditions, and other difficult conditions (Finlay 1995; Naylor 2000). The growth of colonial towns brought an assortment of European intermediaries, who opened butcher shops, restaurants, and bakeries promising "Parisian-style" croissants (Peters 2001).

Such businesses appealed to Europeans in the colonies not only because of their claims to superior hygiene but also, as the "Parisian-style" billing suggests, because they offered familiar foods. Demand for such foods, in turn, reflected not only mere homesickness for familiar tastes, because the canned goods and adapted recipes did not necessarily even taste much like food at home.[10] European colonials also bought these foods because they helped to identify who they were and were not. For the French in turn-of-the-century Hanoi, Peters argues, even bad canned French food served "as a marker of their non-Vietnameseness" (Peters 2001, 157); for the British in colonial Lusaka, eating fish and chips, even if made with Zambezi fish and local potatoes, identified them as not "native" (Kallman 1999).

The colonial encounter eroded many borders between colonizers and colonized, and one of them was dietary. If the culinary exchange and experimentation ultimately enriched cuisines in both hemispheres, the initial prospect unsettled those Europeans who saw their own foodways as yet another measure (along with railroads and telegraphs) of their superiority as a civilization and race (Adas 1989, chapter 4). In addition, foodways were among a number of increasingly important sources of national identity that, like empire itself, demanded work and imagination to maintain (Anderson 1991). The same technologies that made empire and national foodways imaginable also exposed their fictions.

National foodways were among the many conceits carried to colonial Africa—and planted there, in the form of green bean gardens, among other things—in that they never described how a nation really ate. I return to this issue later in the chapter. Another great conceit was the premise that the European civilizing mission would improve African food supply. The failures of this mission (And its postcolonial rendition as "development") in Africa are by now well documented in the histories of famines as well as in the grim statistics contrasting African food poverty with European and North American excesses.[11] Relatively little, however, has been said about the original fiction—namely, that European food supply in the mid-to-late 19th century merited imitation. In fact, if the *Heart of Darkness's* Mr. Kurtz had seen what went into his homeland's provisions, he might have said what he said when confronted with the barbarities of colonial rule in the Congo: the horror!

The Age of Adulteration

Months after the publication of Upton Sinclair's *The Jungle* sparked public outrage about hygienic conditions in the United States meatpacking industry, Theodore Roosevelt signed the 1906 Pure Food and Drug Act (Young 1989). The law's swift passage, after decades of resistance from business interests, testified to the potency of food safety as a political and moral issue— indeed, an issue that obviously upset readers far more than the unjust labor conditions that so impassioned Sinclair. Roosevelt's determination to pass food purity legislation, however, also reflected his concern about *The Jungle's* effects on the overseas markets for U.S. foods. More precisely, he was concerned about Britain, a country that imported more U.S. canned meat than any other in the world (French and Phillips 2000).

Britain itself had passed landmark food purity legislation nearly three decades earlier. There, it had taken not one inflammatory novel but rather generations of ghastly exposés to convince politicians of the need for regulation.[12] The cleaning up of country's food supply in the second half of the 19th century also was due to the emergence of large-scale food retailers and brand-name manufacturers, both of which recognized that purity, well marketed, could be highly profitable. Not least, advances in food chemistry and bacteriology reinforced the authority of science not only to detect food impurity but also to define and even develop legal food additives. Together, the state, corporate food businesses, and science rebuilt a public confidence in the safety of the food supply that endured well into the next century, until mad cow disease threw into question the efficacy of long-accepted protective measures.[13]

Food-borne illness is an ancient problem, but one that has historically often gone undiagnosed and unreported, except in the event of mass outbreaks. This makes its history difficult to trace with any precision. In the 19th century, however, rapid changes in the distances, social relations, and technologies of food provisioning made certain dangers more commonplace, especially in highly urbanized Britain. Adulterated food—meaning everything from bread made with contaminated flour, to pickles dyed with copper, to milk thinned with water—became particularly ubiquitous, as did fraudulent food marketing. Although not always health-threatening, the purposefulness of food adulteration and fraud provoked more outrage than seemingly natural or accidental food-borne hazards like bacterial infection or botulism.[14]

Both adulteration and fraud had long been discouraged, if not necessarily prevented, by the relatively short distances and familiar relationships between food producers, merchants, and their customers, as well as by the vigilance of local inspectors and other government authorities. Especially given that shop-keepers often lived behind or above their shops, to sell bad products was to risk not just a business reputation but also one's place in a community (Filby 1934). In early 19th century Britain, however, both social and regulatory deterrents to dishonest food marketing disintegrated. The government abolished food price and quality controls at a time of rapid urbanization, encouraging an equally rapid proliferation of small-scale food businesses. The liberalization of beer retailing in 1830, for example, led to 45,000 new beer shops within eight years (Burnett 1966, 84). Faced with heavy taxes but otherwise minimal government oversight, and selling largely to poor and poorly educated customers, many bakers, brewers, and shopkeepers gave in to the temptation to adulterate their products.

Some of the added ingredients, such as the assortment of starches added to flour, simply cheapened products and diluted their nutritive value. Others, such as the copper used to dye pickles or the red lead used to color cheese rinds, added lethal brightness to otherwise monotonous provisions. Alongside domestically produced bread, milk, and ale, imported tea, coffee, cocoa, and spices ranked among the most commonly adulterated products. The prevalence of adulteration in these goods reflected not their tropical origins nor high government duties, but also their handling. Shipped and stored in bulk, they were blended and packaged by grocers who, as Burnett observes in *Plenty and Want,* faced such intense competition that most would not survive if they did not add sawdust or chalk to their dry goods.

The extent and variety of such practices in the United Kingdom first came to light in 1820 with the publication of Accum's *Treatise on Adulterations of Food and Culinary Poisons* (Accum 1966). A chemist, Accum conducted analyses of household foods and beverages that found adulteration was the norm, not the exception. He also published the names of the establishments where he had collected the tainted goods, making him the immediate enemy of the grocery and milling trades. Accum's scientific career quickly ended after he was charged (under suspicious circumstances) with tearing pages out of library books, but other chemists continued in his footsteps, conducting their own tests on food and publishing grimly-titled exposés referring, for example, to "death in the pot."[15]

In France, food adulteration likely affected a smaller proportion of the population simply because the country remained much more rural.[16] In addition, post-Revolutionary efforts to liberalize urban food trades did not go as far as in Britain; police and other municipal authorities' surveillance of marketplaces and shops continued throughout the 19th century. That said, the inspectors' numbers were few, the food sellers many, and those who cared to look had no trouble finding adulterated bread, milk and chocolate. An 1844 culinary guide told readers that although pure chocolate was nearly impossible to find, they could at least learn to detect common adulterants, such as lentil meal, once they started eating: "You will recognize this fraud if the chocolate leaves a pasty taste in the mouth" (Destaminil 1844, 308). In 1856, the government's Conseil de Salubrité advised consumers to "only use the white salt of Bayonne, because it cannot be mixed with unhealthy substances without changing color, thus indicating fraud."[17]

In Britain, the 1850s marked a turning point in the government's attitude toward food safety regulation, thanks in part to a three-year study sponsored and published by the medical journal *Lancet*. It was the first large-scale food analysis study to use the newly invented microscope, and it found that adulteration had become, if anything, more pervasive since Accum's book was published (Hassall and *Lancet* 1855; Burnett 1966, 191). Like Accum, the *Lancet* series published the names of the offenders. Abridged versions of its articles appeared in newspapers and popular magazines such as *The Times,* the *Illustrated London News,* and *Frazer's Magazine,* and books and pamphlets on adulteration proliferated. Some of the published commentaries provided practical advice for consumers; others aimed to disgust and anger.[18] As *Punch* put it, adulteration was a "villainous" practice committed by rogues and scoundrels.[19] Then as now, singularly awful events—like the "Bradford Incident" in 1958, when tainted lozenges poisoned 200 people, killing 17 (Paulus 1974, 27)—received more attention than adulteration's long-term toll on public health. Although incalculable, it was no doubt serious for children especially, given the extent to which milk was diluted, oatmeal mixed with indigestible "rubble," and candy colored with toxic dyes ranging from red lead to Prussian blue (Burnett 1966, 191–2).

The *Lancet* report turned adulterated food from a largely private worry and occasional news scandal into a scientifically proven and highly public problem. As one writer in the *Quarterly Review* observed, "A gun suddenly fired into a rookery could not cause a greater commotion than did the publication of the names of dishonest tradesmen" (Burnett 1966, 192). In response, the House of Commons formed a special committee to investigate. The health threat was not the only or even the most important concern, judging from the report published by the committee in 1856:

Not only is the public health thus exposed to danger and pecuniary fraud committed on the whole country, but the public morality is tainted and the high commercial character of the country is seriously lowered, both at home and in the eyes of foreign countries.[20]

The prevalence of food adulteration, in other words, cast doubt on the quality of all Britain's products, and at a time when it had more and more products it wanted to sell abroad. Yet even after the special committee concluded that the government needed to act, opposition from laissez-faire politicians and the grocery trade prevented passage of all but the most toothless legislation for nearly twenty years. In the meantime, the pure food movement took shape. Members of the "reform-minded" middle class—judges and clergy, businessmen and women's groups—joined doctors and chemists in demanding tougher laws. So, too, did the early consumer cooperative societies and military leaders who saw adulterated food as debilitating to their troops. Not unlike Britain's late 20th century food movement (as well as the earlier movement against slave-produced sugar [Drescher 1987]), the "anti-adulterators" worked through both the general press and their own publications, among them the *Anti-Adulteration Review* and *Food, Water and Air*, to shape public opinion. Shopkeepers, meanwhile, argued against them in *The Grocer* (Paulus 1974, 29).

Much of the debate over food purity regulation centered on two questions, both of which resurfaced in the late 20th century. First, who would to be held responsible for the composition of foods that passed through many hands? This question particularly concerned retailers, who did not want to be held liable for foods that their suppliers had adulterated. Second, and even more fundamental, what defined adulteration? An 1872 ruling defined it as mixing into food or drink "any injurious or poisonous ingredient or material."[21] But manufacturers and retailers complained that some of their so-called adulterated goods contained only benign and even beneficial additives. The cocoa maker Joseph Fry, for example, argued that arrowroot in cocoa made it less bitter, while the condiment manufacturer Colman made a similar case for the use of turmeric in mustard (French and Phillips 2000, 47).

Ultimately, the 1875 Sale of Food and Drugs Act (SFDA) permitted products with such additives as long as they were marketed as "preparations" rather than *pure* cocoa or mustard. The act also increased the penalties for violations and stepped up government inspections and food quality analysis, and increased the penalties for violations (Collins 1993). Perhaps most importantly for the purposes of this story, the SFDA made grocers liable for the quality of all their products. While this liability drove many small grocers out of business, it drove larger stores to seek out goods that they could trust to be consistently pure and high quality.

France passed its own national anti-adulteration legislation in 1905. It resembled the SFDA in that it affirmed manufacturers' responsibility for the purity of their raw ingredients, and centralized formerly municipal food inspection and analysis services under a new national agency, the Service for the Repression of Fraud ("Le Fraud") (Truhaut and Souverain 1963). Also like the SFDA and other national food purity laws passed in Europe and North America in the early 20th century, it presumed that advances in chemistry and toxicology would enable the government to define and detect adulteration more effectively. Indeed, these laws displayed enormous confidence in the power of science to help assure both free trade and the citizen's right to pure and honest food. As the director of Le Fraud wrote in 1913, "science dominates our new organization . . . and it is science that makes possible the regime of liberty brought by our Revolution" (Roux 1913). Yet while this confidence in the science of food purity spanned international borders, it did not put to rest international debates over the standards of purity. On the contrary: Regulators' scientific methods quite literally magnified differences in the composition of foods and the national and regional foodways they belonged to.[22]

Nor did this confidence in science assuage concerns about how it might be wrongly used either by or against food intermediaries. Again, this was a subject of ongoing debate. On one side, government vigilance was needed precisely because, as one French official noted at an international food hygiene conference in 1908, "the more science progresses, the more ingenious the frauds become."[23] As I discuss again below, French peasant associations (wine makers especially) demanded government protection against such "fraudeurs" who flooded the markets with undetectably adulterated wine and other farm products. On the other side, the French Minister of Agriculture, while agreeing with his counterparts in other countries on the need for international product standards, warned against technocratic definitions of food quality. As he remarked at the same 1908 conference, "Let us not be hypnotized by this gripping expression, 'pure food.' This is about normal purity, but not absolute purity . . . the technician's point of view is by itself too narrow. Merchants have the authority to say, voila, this is what we call wine, milk, butter, chocolate."[24]

Later chapters consider how standards defining not only produce but also producer "goodness" later took on their own authority in Britain, whereas merchants' expertise continued to command greater respect in France. The point here is that even as science appeared to overcome certain obstacles to ever fairer, cleaner, and more international trade in food, it created new ones. The limits of science in this regard are perhaps best illustrated by early forays into food canning, a technology very different from the fresh vegetable commodities discussed in this book, but one that also linked Europe to its colonies.

The basic technique of modern food canning dates back to 1810, when a French confectioner, Nicholas Appert, responded to Napoleon Bonaparte's offer of prize money for the invention of a food preservation method suitable for military provisions. Soon troops on both sides of the channel were eating "appertised" foods, as were explorers to the North Pole and central Africa, and settlers in the American West (Naylor 2000; Bruegel 2002). By the 1850s, British officials saw the potential for canned goods to feed and eventually be produced by their colonies, especially in regions where the local food supplies were considered dubious. It was, in short, the ultimate "imperial technology" (Naylor 2000). The problem was that no one yet understood why Appert's vacuum-sealing preservation technique worked—or why, sometimes, it didn't—because science had not yet discovered bacteria. This meant that outbreaks of food poisoning struck often enough in the military to make soldiers and civilians alike wary of food in cans (Bruegel 2002, 118).

Canned food gave cause for anxiety well after theories of bacterial infection took hold in the 1880s. This was partly because germ theory did not by itself solve the problems of defective cans and improper canning (which were the sources of lead poisoning and botulism), and partly because the industry responsible for the most food poisoning—the meat industry—resisted sanitation reforms (Hardy 1999, 302). The British government therefore turned responsibility for protection against dangerous food bacteria over to consumers. Like the French government, its food safety education focused on housewives and housewives-to-be, and included counsel on how to identify potentially tainted products (Hardy 1999, 303, 305; Bruegel 2002, 20).

Marketing Purity

Despite lingering problems, the overall quality of food supply in the United Kingdom had improved by the early 20th century. Tougher legislation helped, but at least three other broad and related changes deserve brief mention. First, public expectations and buying power rose. Rising literacy rates and an accessible press increased public awareness of the threats that chemists had long warned about. The falling real prices for basic foodstuffs in the United Kingdom between the 1850s and 1880s (due partly to cheap imports, partly to lower taxes) gave consumers more leeway to seek out decent provisions. Overall, the cost of feeding the working class household fell by 30 percent between 1877 and 1887 (Burnett 1966, 132).

Second, well before the passage of the SFDA, large-scale food manufacturers undertook voluntarily reforms. Indeed, as Burnett (1966, 251) observes, it did not take them long to realize the marketing possibilities of pure food:

> By the late (eighteen) fifties "Pure and Unadulterated" had become the stock advertising slogan of dealers anxious to cash in on the newly awakened fears of the public—all too frequently it was the same spirit of commercialism which had prompted adulteration in the first instance which now made it more profitable to offer, usually at a somewhat higher price, a commodity which was "guaranteed pure" and bore the certificate of a doctor or analyst.

As in the government, scientists played an increasingly prominent role in the food industry's purity campaign. An on-site laboratory could help a company ward off suspicions of adulteration or poor hygiene; images of white-coated staff scientists and their sparkling equipment also made good advertising copy (French and Phillips 2000, 28–29). Scientists also helped companies develop new processing methods. Crosse & Blackwell replaced its copper pickling vats with glass-coated iron vats (resulting in brown pickles). Cadburys developed a technique for extracting non-bitter cocoa butter, allowing it to promote its Cocoa Essence powder as a pure product, "unadulterated" by the starches used (legally) by its competitors (Burnett 1966, 252).

Third and perhaps most importantly, the second half of the 19th century saw the emergence of large-scale food retailers, which used economies of scale and new marketing techniques to appeal to consumers' concerns about the purity of food and the honesty of food traders. The first such retailers were the consumer cooperatives, which grew out of the 18th century workers' cooperatives (Furlough and Strikwerda 1999). Especially in France, the cooperatives' political agendas ranged from reformist to radical, but in both countries, efforts to recruit new members emphasized their commitment to honest trade and pure food. The pamphlet *Five Reasons for Joining a Cooperative* (first published in Britain and then translated into five other languages) featured a worker saying, "I want no adulteration or deception . . . I want just prices and measure in the store so that justice and truth will be first realized in small things prior to being realized in larger things."[25] Selling consumers on the pure food itself, however, also required educational campaigns, because many people had become accustomed to the taste and appearance of adulterated goods. England's Rochdale cooperatives conducted lecture tours and distributed pamphlets, explaining the superiority of un-dyed tea and naturally brown flour (Gurney 1996).

In both countries, the cooperatives' commitment to honest food struck a cord with consumers weary of grocers' weighted scales and watered-down milk. Britain had 400 cooperative societies with 100,000 members by 1863, 971 societies with a total membership of 547,000 by 1881, and 1,379 societies with

4.5 million members in 1920 (Gurney 1996, 242). France had 2,301 consumer cooperatives by 1907, and 3,250 by 1913 (Furlough 1991, 62). As cooperatives grew in numbers, they also expanded their importing and processing activities so that they were able to offer shoppers more than the basic staples that had once filled their shelves.

On this front, they faced increasing competition from multiple-branch commercial retailers. In their business strategies if not yet their physical size, these retailers were the true predecessors of contemporary supermarkets. In Britain, the early "multiples" typically entered the grocery business either as imported goods distributors or as neighborhood suppliers of cheap but high quality staples. The tea and dairy company Lipton, for example, sold its own products at the seventy branches it opened in London between 1872 and 1890 (Davis 1966, 173). Sainsbury's, also based in London, initially sold butter, bacon, and eggs, then later added packaged goods.

The chain stores stood out because of their bargain prices; they also looked very different than traditional grocers' shops and consumer cooperatives. Bright lighting emphasized the standardized, hygienic nature of their products, while banners and handbills advertised prices and promotions. Not least, they offered an increasingly wide variety of packaged goods, thereby doing away with the grocer's traditional (and long suspect) role in mixing and measuring, as well as shoppers' ability to touch or smell products before buying them. In this way the chain stores helped redefine not only the grocer's profession—marketing savvy mattered more, and processing skills less—but also the basis for consumers' confidence in the groceries themselves. Product packaging and corporate brand image, in other words, became the standard assurances of quality and hygiene (Jefferys 1954). Chapter 6 discusses how British supermarkets and their store brand products continued to appeal to consumers' expectation of chain store "value for money" throughout the next century.

In France, retail food chains emerged during the same period, but took a different form and affected a smaller proportion of its still predominantly rural population. A few were family-run, such as Felix Potin (Camborde 1997), but the more significant growth in chain store retailing came through the grouping of independent shopkeepers into *succarsales*. The early *succarsales* of the 1860s shared the cooperative vision insofar as they aimed to strengthen small retailers' buying power vis-à-vis monopolistic wholesalers, and thereby offer consumers cheaper goods. But the *succarsales'* rapid growth and consolidation (by the 1880s, four large chains each controlled hundreds of franchises, many of them formerly independent shops [Francois 1927]) raised concerns that they were destroying *le petit commerce,* and all the skills and values it embodied.[26] Critics argued that small shopkeepers not only offered better quality products but also, like peasant farmers, contributed to the social stability of rural communities and indeed the political stability of France as a whole. In a country that had seen plenty of instability throughout the previous century, small shop-keepers offered a service far more valuable than cheap provisions; they were "the best safeguard against anarchy" (Curtil 1933, 125).

The president of the *succarsales'* union, by contrast, argued that decentralized small-scale commerce was itself anarchic, as well as anachronistic. As he argued in a 1927 defense of "rational" food retailing: "The anarchic period of isolated retailers has passed . . . It's their turn to acknowledge the law of association. (But) it's not a question of suppressing small-scale commerce. It's about transforming it . . . in this evolution that will bring the consumer great advantages, neither the dignity nor the material interests (of the small grocer) will suffer; on the contrary" (Francois 1927).

Both critics and supporters of the French chain stores, in other words, endorsed the ideal of the small neighborhood or village grocer; they simply disagreed about the importance of independent ownership. As chapter 5 discusses, the belief that small farmers and shopkeepers should be protected has persisted in contemporary France; one result is that the country's laws have placed more restrictions on large-scale retailers than has Britain (Ducrocq 1996).

Although the chain retailers had overtaken consumer cooperatives in both Britain and France by the beginning of World War I, independent shops and marketplaces continued to sell most of each country's food, and an especially large proportion (in Britain, over 95 percent) of fresh produce (Jefferys 1954). By today's standards, then, national food retail markets were far from concentrated. As in the United States, however, these national markets were governed not only by tougher laws than those of a half century prior, but also by higher consumer standards and a new commercial logic (Fraser 1981; Young 1989). Manufacturers and retailers had recognized that food "purity" was not necessarily an added cost so much as a source of added value. Precisely because purity, like freshness, was a quality that consumers desired but could not necessarily detect, it could be packaged and marketed in endless ways. Both government regulators and brand-name food companies relied on science not just to guide their investigations, policies and innovations, but also to legitimate their efforts in the eyes of the consuming public and its advocates, such as the cooperatives and consumer watchdog groups. For although industrialized food already had its share of skeptics—among them the disciples of vegetarianism[27]—science had so far proven its capacity to expose faults and falsehoods in the food supply, and to find solutions.

The basic institutional framework of modern food safety governance had taken shape in the industrialized world by the early 20th century. The roles of the state, the food industry, and scientific knowledge in assuring the safety and quality of national food supplies were considered more or less credible for decades. These institutions did not put an end to outbreaks of food-borne diseases, or to the longer-term health risks associated with poor nutrition, or to the broader inequities in access to decent food. In Britain especially, the urban working-class diet remained extraordinarily poor in nutrients long after adulteration and acute poisoning ceased to be systematic worries (Burnett 1966, 214). But these chronic problems did not provoke the same degree of moral outrage and doubting. If anything, they appeared curable if the state, corporate food enterprises, and agro-food science continued what they were doing—if, in other words, a more industrialized and internationalized food supply assured ever cheaper and more varied provisions. Only in the late 20th century would a new round of food crises seriously challenge this assumption.

Nourishing the Nation

The destiny of nations depends on how they nourish themselves.
—Brillat-Savarin, *The Physiology of Taste,* 1825

The late 19th and early 20th century developments in food regulation drew on the international exchange of scientific knowledge, and facilitated the expansion of transnational food commerce. They also came at a time when migration, tourism, and the popular media all made foreign cuisines more familiar to each country's urban bourgeoisie. Yet during this era when many aspects of food culture were becoming more cosmopolitan, food was also central to campaigns of nation building. These campaigns sought to develop and protect national and colonial agro-industries, improve the health and productivity of national labor forces, and teach the work, hygiene, and consumption habits that would serve both ends. In Western Europe, these campaigns drew resources and inspiration from both domestic and colonial countrysides, even as they sought to draw more clearly the lines demarcating metropolitan civilization. Together, these campaigns helped to build not just the imagined community of the nation (Anderson 1991), but also the imagined table: that is, the nation's foodways.

"Foodways" here refers to cuisine as well as the many norms and practices that define how a nation shops for, cooks, and consumes its food. The descriptions of these practices rely on vast overgeneralizations and simplifications, and do not necessarily describe how many real people think or act. But that does not mean they have no consequence beyond the realm of tourist guides. On the contrary, conceptions of national foodways pervade the discourses of food marketing (for example, "traditionally" English or French) as well as debates and struggles around food and agricultural trade policy, both past and present.

In the late 20th century, the potency of food as a national symbol became acutely apparent in both Britain and France, albeit in different ways. After mad cow disease struck British beef—the pride of the nation's foodways—members of the countryside and organic food movements joined forces to demand that supermarkets "Buy British" (see chapter 6). In France, the government invoked the nation's appreciation of food—and the land it comes from—to defend its own protectionist farm policies and its opposition to American hormone-fed beef, while the Confederation Paysanne did much the same to justify its attacks on McDonalds and genetically modified crops. Judging from opinion polls as well as a series of nationwide "citizens' forums" on food held in 2001 (see chapter 5) these stances garnered broad support among the French public.

As Mennell's comparative history shows, some of the differences between French and British foodways—in the social significance attached to cooking and dining, for example, or in the dietary patterns of particular socioeconomic groups—can be traced back centuries through historically distinctive social and economic relations between town and country (Mennell 1996). But on both sides of the Channel, cooking and eating patterns developed either regionally or within the elite circles of the court and royal nobility. Foodways did not become a recognized part of *national* cultural identity—in that they were written about, taught, served, and exported as such—until the mid-to-late 19th century. The events during and surrounding this period are worth exploring for two reasons.

First, this period sheds light on some of the norms and ideals that inform both contemporary opposition to "food globalization" in France and, somewhat ironically, the views of the French fresh produce importers who participate in globalization. As chapter 5 discusses, such traders do not hesitate to invoke common characterizations of "the French" and "the Anglo-Saxons" to explain why, for example, French consumers prefer unpackaged French beans and why they appear less concerned about food hygiene than British consumers. Their explanations are not necessarily correct, and obviously overlook the diversity of attitudes toward food found in both France and Britain, which produce traders cannot afford to ignore. Yet their use of national stereotypes is nonetheless significant, especially in conversation with an American researcher. They are statements about one source of the traders' identity—a set of ideas about the "natural" superiority of French foodways that coalesced during a time when much was invested in the idea of French nationhood.

Second, events of the late 19th and early 20th century reveal both parallels and critical differences between the processes that built national French foodways and those that built France's African empire. The parallels are clear in Eugen Weber's *Peasants into Frenchmen,* which chronicles the "modernization" of rural France between 1870 and World War I. Weber shows how expanding transportation networks, school systems, military service and state investment in peasant agriculture all succeeded in pulling "the country of savages" (as Balzac described his rural compatriots) into the national polity and dominant culture of France, as defined by Paris. This "civilizing" of rural France, like rural Africa, entailed education and indoctrination at many levels, and systematic attacks on "backwards" local beliefs and practices. It amounted to internal colonization. But Weber argues that it ultimately achieved its political objective of national integration because economic development brought rural people concrete material gains. By joining the modern world and the French nation, they escaped lives of chronic want and insecurity. Once progress meant better food and warm houses, "old ways died unlamented" (Weber 1976, 492).

As peasants became Frenchmen (and women), so, too, did they become participants in the modern market economy, with all its opportunities and risks. Unlike in England, however, this process did not actually destroy the peasantry. Indeed, the number of small farms in France increased during the mid-19th century, peaking at around 3.5 million in the 1880s (Wright 1964, 6). Some of the reasons for the French Republic's commitment to preserve the economic viability of peasant agriculture (at least until the second half of the 20th century) have deep historical roots. But here I want to suggest that the success of French rural modernization in the late 19th and early 20th century owed a great deal to the idea that not only French *food* was superior to others, but also French *taste* for food. More specifically, this idea held that the quality of French foodways lay in the unique relationship between peasant producers and their lands (or *terroirs*), and in French consumers' unique ability to appreciate that relationship (Barham 2003).

This idea developed through both cultural production and political struggle, in both the city and countryside. The conception of French national foodways that emerged, like the other national traditions "invented" in the late 19th century, responded to the dislocating, potentially destabilizing effects of rapid technological and social change, which were especially apparent in cities (Harvey 1989; McClintock 1995). It offered the French citizenry, in other words, a vision of a national community, but one tied to the much smaller rural communities they remembered or still lived in. More concretely, it was a vision that enabled French peasant associations to secure a relatively privileged place in modern national and international food provisioning. Peasants in francophone West Africa, subjected to a later, cheaper, and much more socially and ecologically destructive colonialization, were incorporated into these circuits of commerce on a weaker political footing and on much more perilous economic terms.

Most French culinary historians agree that French national foodways took root in the gastronomic culture of early 19th century Paris, where fine dining became a bourgeois pastime and a show of distinction. Chefs who once cooked for the aristocracy opened restaurants in droves: In Paris alone, they increased from around a hundred after the Revolution to over 3,000 by the 1820s (Pitte 1999, 473). Chefs also opened restaurants in provincial cities and, later in the century, in London and other foreign capitals (Spang, 2000).

Gastronomes of this era did not just eat out; they also read and discussed the essays, criticism and guides of writers such as the journalist Grimod de la Reyniere and Anthelme Brillat-Savarin (Ferguson 1998). Indeed, these individuals did more to define gastronomy as a modern and specifically French institution than any chef of the era except perhaps Antonin Carême, who also wrote several cookbooks. Carême's *L'Art de la Cuisine Francaise,* like Brillat-Savarin's famous *Physiology de Gout,* emphasized that both cooking and taste were objective, measurable skills. Brillat-Savarin even proposed specific meals that could be used to test diners' "gastronomic class," which he saw as correlated with but not determined by income.[28] With enough time and money to devote to learning the "codes" of gastronomy, in other words, good taste could be cultivated. And Paris offered many places to do just this.

The foods and recipes that Parisian diners consumed came from all over France. Early post-Revolutionary cookbooks linked recipes with regions; suffixes such as *à la provencale* became associated with particular ingredients and preparations. The 1808 *Cours Gastronomique,* a school textbook, included chapters describing the natural history and alimentary abundance of each region. Grimod's 1807 *Almanach des Gourmands* proposed a gastronomic map of France, with food replacing monuments as regional symbols: A jar of mustard would represent Dijon, for example, and a terrine of duck liver would depict Toulouse (Csergo 1999, 504).

By the latter half of the century, tourist guides were touting the inherent Frenchness of eating well, in and beyond the capital. Guides for American and British tourists described a Parisian restaurant meal as the quintessential "French" experience, even though the vast majority of the country's population had never eaten one (Spang 2000). For Parisians touring the provinces, the *Guides Joannes* included regional food specialties on their suggested itineraries.

For Auguste Escoffier, the most famous chef of the late 19th century, the abundance of fine cuisine found within the borders of the Republic was no historical accident. Rather, he wrote, it showed that culinary talent and indeed good taste were integral parts of the national nature.

> French soil is privileged [and capable of] naturally producing in great
> abundance the best vegetables, the best fruits and the best wines of
> the world. France also possesses the finest chickens, the most tender
> meats, and the most delicate and varied poultry. Its maritime situa-

tion gives it the most beautiful fish and crustaceans. It is, therefore, natural that the French become both good cooks and good eaters.[29]

This assertion of natural culinary skill was important to the ongoing effectiveness of claims to a superior national cuisine because more and more of the raw material of French cuisine was not, in fact, native to France. In addition to the many New World and Asian plant species introduced to France centuries earlier (including green beans), 19th-century chefs liberally incorporated imported foods as well as foreign techniques and dishes into their repertoire. Even the much-maligned English cookery contributed *bifteck*. Ultimately the greatness of French cooking, according to gastronomic writers, lay in its skilled handling of ingredients (whatever their origins) and the "Frenchifying" of foreign dishes (Suzanne 1894, 8).

French chefs, especially those who sought their fortunes overseas, had good reason to promote their cooking as an inimitable, uniquely French institution. But so, too, did France's post-Revolutionary regimes. Indeed, once the cuisine formerly enjoyed only by the aristocracy became available for public consumption (among the urban elite, anyway), it became an appealing symbol of the Republic's ideals as well as its riches. Haute cuisine embodied both the sophistication of France's culture and the bounty of its countryside. It celebrated rather than denied regional diversity.

That said, the era's gastronomic writers and chefs assumed that haute cuisine was the product of a specifically *male* genius (Mennell 1996, 203; Trubek 2000, 125). To insure that the science of good cooking and eating reached— and was reproduced—across the nation, girls and women needed to learn a more practical set of kitchen skills. According to one speaker at the 1889 International Hygiene and Demography Congress, the continued superiority of French civilization depended on such schooling, because "it is good cooking which has made people intelligent."[30]

Cooking courses and domestic cookbooks proliferated during the 1890s. In keeping with the era's sanitation and adulteration concerns, they taught women kitchen hygiene and how to spot fraudulent, spoiled, or otherwise hazardous foods at the market. They taught the proper order of modern meals (for example, soup as a first course rather than as a main dish, as had been the peasant tradition) and the importance of thrift (Edwards 1997, 249–250). Although these lessons resembled those taught in British domestic science courses, French courses and cookbooks put considerably more emphasis on both the rules and the regional diversity that defined French cuisine. They expected women to know why *pot au feu* was the "national dish" of France and how to use Carême's sauces to make leftovers attractive. *L'Art du Bien Manger* (Richardin 1914), a text taught in domestic science courses across the country, featured recipes from all the provinces, promotions of name-brand goods from French manufacturers, and a preface on the culinary geography of France (Edwards 1997, 252).

These messages about French national foodways reached a far broader audience than they would have a few decades prior, when relatively few French girls attended school and learned to read, and when many of the people who lived in the provinces celebrated in French cookbooks did not even speak, much less read French. With the introduction of mandatory free primary education in 1881, the Third Republic embarked on a massive school-building campaign in rural areas (Weber 1976, 309). This campaign, as part of the larger process of building French national consciousness, helped to instill awareness of French foodways not just directly (through instruction) but also indirectly, as higher literacy rates increased the readership of the national print media.

Two other late 19th century developments furthered the consolidation of French foodways. First, national military service provided men with a "domestic" education that in some ways paralleled women's. For starters, they learned table manners. In some provinces, Weber notes, people previously "did not take their soup at the table at all: in winter they kept the bowl in their lap and sat as close as possible to the hearth; in summer they moved outside to eat, holding the bowl and squatting on the doorstep or just taking their meal standing up" (Weber 1976, 164). In the military, mealtimes were hardly elegant, but reformist officers such as Hubert Lyautey insisted on the construction of mess halls where men sat at "proper tables" and used plates and glasses (Weber 1976, 301). Soldiers also learned to eat modern French food: white bread, coffee with sugar, and even, with some reluctance, canned meat (Weber 1976, 300; Bruegel 2001, 2002).

Second, the expanding system of rural roads and railroads pulled vast swaths of rural France into circuits of regional, national, and even international commerce.[31] For peasants who had previously traveled to markets no farther than they or their animals could walk, improved transportation brought new incentives to produce as much as possible, and new resources (namely fertilizer) with which to do so. Wild foods that once supplemented the daily fare of soup and dark bread—snails, frogs, mushrooms—took on new value. In fact, Weber suggests such foods may have become scarcer in the peasants' diet even as they became more commonplace in Parisian markets simply because the peasants sold everything they could. The peasant "saved for himself the very scum of his products" (Weber 1976, 144, 134). When their incomes justified eating better, peasants ate more of what they had long craved—notably meat— and more of what they had recently learned to appreciate. The aforementioned sugar, coffee, and white bread became standard provisions in village shops (Weber 1976, 143).

So improvements in transportation brought provincial foods to the city, and city foods to the provinces. But the integration of the nation's foodways involved much more than the increased circulation of goods. Rather, it was part of a much broader and more politically and morally charged transformation of national politics and commerce, with the peasantry—at least the peasantry in France—central to both. For while French imperial rhetoric described the people living in already or soon-to-be colonized overseas regions as among the world's "hundred million Frenchmen" (Heffernan 1994), these people did not benefit from the efforts of national and local politicians to cultivate peasant support through shows of patronage. Within France, both republican leaders and conservative rural landholders invested in the creation of peasant associations, which operated either as *syndicats* (unions) or *mutuelles* (cooperatives). These associations in turn not only funneled resources to individual farm households, but also organized politically across broad regions (Wright 1964). While the peasants' politics remained primarily defensive, they were less and less geographically isolated.

Nor was the French peasantry any longer isolated from the desires, temptations, and risks engendered by the expanding consumer market. Producers of recognized regional or local specialities—uncommon varieties of fruits and vegetables, artisanal goods such as cheese, *fois gras,* and wine—saw improved access to the market as an unparalleled opportunity to better their lives. Although the fruits of rural economic growth did not fall evenly, the new prosperity of a few raised the expectations of many; peasants began to see the products of their land in terms of what products from other lands they might buy (Weber 1976, 227). They had the state to thank for building the infrastructure of this opportunity, but urban gastronomic society had first recognized the value of their goods.

Yet the growth of the mass market posed at least three threats to both opportunity and recognition. The first threat came from overproduction. With greater access to information about Parisian prices and tastes came the greater likelihood that too many fruit farmers and wine makers would rush to supply an ultimately limited demand. The second threat came from the mass market's tendency to associate the regional name of a product with the product, not the region. Thus any cheese resembling the hard yellow cheese of Switzerland's Gruyere and Emmenthal regions could be sold as gruyere or emmenthal; sparkling wine could be sold as champagne (Guy 2001).

The third threat came from the opportunity that the market offered not just for imitation but also, as distances between buyers and sellers increased, adulteration and fraud. As discussed earlier, tougher laws, more rigorous inspections, and a general shift in the corporate culture of food manufacturing and retailing all helped to discourage the adulteration of basic foods like flour and

Feeding the Nation: The Making of Modern Food Provisioning

milk. France, however, did not pass such a law until 1905, and even that did not put an end to an assortment of fraudulent marketing practices, many of which were reported in the *Annales des Falsification*. Cheap anchovies were passed off as gourmet Norwegian anchovies; "fresh" eggs turned out to be from Siberia; fruits from one region were labeled as coming from another.[32]

The merchants who lost business to *fraudeurs* called for measures to protect *le commerce loyal* (honest trade), some of which are discussed in chapter 5. The far more tumultuous battles over the protection of regional specialties, however, occurred in the countryside, and began among wine makers in the Midi region (Stanziani 2003). There, a massive replanting of vineyards after the phylloxera epidemic in the 1880s had resulted in skyrocketing production and plummeting prices and quality (Wright 1964, 27). The widespread sugaring of wine contributed to the problem, as did the trade in falsely labeled imported wines. *La mévente*—selling at a loss—became peasants' new plague, but not one they accepted passively (Hamelle, 1913). As one newspaper remarked at the time, "The Midi did not protest when dealt a storm by inclement nature, but only when the disaster became an act of man."[33]

The protest took the form of a 1907 tax strike and demonstrations that brought together hundreds of thousands of people, many of whom traveled to the events on chartered trains. Their demands were frankly commercial ("we want to sell our wine"), and their "we" explicitly regional; "tout le Midi" joined in the protests, according to observers. Their calls for legislative reform, however, focused on the national government (Weber 1976, 276; Hammelle, 1913). The Midi vintners' protest was just one of several in the wine-making regions that led to the formation of regional and national producers associations and, in 1919, the passage of the laws that became the foundation of France's (and later the EU's) "geographic indications" labels (Wright 1964, 28; Guy 2001).

The best known of these are the *appellation d'origine controllée* (AOC) labels found on wine, but the laws also protect many kinds of cheese and other processed foodstuffs, as well as regional varieties of fresh produce. The AOC regulations were (and remain) strict. Drawing on the French concept of the *terroir,* they require producer groups to demonstrate that their specialty possesses a unique, yet widely recognized quality, and that this quality is itself the product of their *terroir's* unique ecology, history and *savoir-faire* (Barham 2003). Once granted AOC status, producers must accept production ceilings, unannounced inspections and, more generally, what may be (and certainly were initially) unfamiliar levels of surveillance and interference by the state and other outside parties (Barham 2003, 136).

Yet at the level of national foodways, the premise of the AOC was already familiar by the early 20th century. Indeed, the belief that regional specialties were worth recognizing, preserving, and paying extra for was a fundamental part of what it meant to eat *à la francais*. Gastronomes, cookbooks, public schooling, and migratory chefs helped to popularize this basic idea in France and abroad, but it only gained the protection of law after concerted rural struggle. The national foodways that took shape in turn-of-the-century France were not, in this sense, simply a set of myths created about rural foods at a time when rural people were abandoning them. Rather, they were among the victories won by rural producers simultaneously imperiled and empowered by the forces of modern nation building.

In Britain, national foodways have had a very different history (Drummond and Wilbraham 1958; Burnett 1966). By the mid-19th century, most English peasants had become landless laborers, and whether they lived in town or country, their diets held little romance for the bourgeoisie. Nor did cooking hold much prestige, as either a profession or a pastime; Londonites who cared about fine-dining could find plenty of French chefs to cook for them. As Mennell (1996) argues in *All Manners of Food,* the meanings and material circumstances of food provisioning changed in very different ways on opposite sides of the Channel. These distinctive histories help explain why Britain's homegrown national foodways have commanded less renown than French cuisine, but have proven more open to immigrant and foreign influences, especially from India. British politicians proudly proclaimed chicken tikka masala a "national" dish in 2001 (Marshall 2001). The greater pluralism of British foodways is apparent, among other places, in the retailing of "Asian" vegetables such as snow peas and baby corn. In Britain, these have become standard items not just in the shops and markets of urban ethnic neighborhoods (where they can also be found in France) but also in most supermarkets' fresh produce sections (where, in France, they tend to be scarcer). The mad cow and hoof-and-mouth crises did fuel nostalgia for the days before supermarket ubiquity, when Britain's countryside largely fed British towns, and local, seasonal provisions were the norm. But this nostalgia envisions a "green and pleasant" land very different from the *paysage* that characterizes French rural nostalgia, and one that, moreover, disappeared much longer ago (Wiener 1981).

All this is to say that taken-for-granted characterizations of national foodways have their roots in histories of agrarian change—which are always, at some level, histories of relations between city and countryside—and that the decades between mid-19th and the early 20th centuries were a particularly important part of these histories. This era saw the formation of official and commercial institutions for governing food safety and quality, and the emergence of national identities informed in part (though obviously not only) by ideals of food and farming. Although the food scares and controversies of the late 20th century seriously tested the legitimacy of certain institutions and ideals, it is still important to recognize their imprint on the norms and practices of modern food provisioning in France and Britain.

It is equally important to recognize the global, and specifically imperial context in which French and British foodways took shape. The colonization of Africa did more than provide Europeans with new sources of raw materials, new markets, and vast new terrains for scientific experimentation. The experience of agrarian change under colonial rule was brief relative to the *longue durée* of African agricultural history, but long enough to establish lasting relationships and hierarchies on both a local and transnational scale.

As mentioned earlier, Weber's *Peasants into Frenchmen* draws many parallels between rural "modernization" in France and the colonization of Africa. These parallels are most readily apparent in the discourses and policies of French colonialism, but they also apply to the British colonial project. In both rural France and colonial Africa, "development" was supposed to increase rural productivity, domesticate rural nature, and civilize rural peoples. In both places, civilizing meant imparting modern metropolitan beliefs, behaviors, and values, or what the French called *assimilation*. In both places, development-as-modernization was seen as an evolutionary process, but one that, somewhat paradoxically, required the intervention of administrators, engineers, and educators.

The differences between development in rural France versus Africa are more obvious than the similarities. In Africa, development programs modeled on the European experience of modernization produced enclaves of industry and "Westernized" consumption, but otherwise failed to spark the predicted "take-off" in living standards and attitudinal change (Roslow 1960). In fact, such programs failed so utterly that the whole concept of modernization fell into disfavor among African intellectuals within two decades of decolonization.[34] In rural France, change did not always come easily, or without coercion. But, Weber notes, "given time and skins of the same color, assimilation worked" (Weber 1976, 491). Peasants accepted the idea of France and, indeed, profited from their role in it.

This reference to skin color is so casual because it is by now well understood that the colonizers' conception of racial difference informed their assumptions about not only who needed to be civilized and how, but also how much they, the colonizers, were politically and morally obliged to invest in the mission. The modern history of famine makes brutally clear that colonial subjects did not enjoy the same basic food rights as citizens. Britain, the colonial power most overtly concerned about its high moral standing, stood by while millions starved first in Ireland and later Bengal. France, so proud of its own food abundance, tolerated repeated incidents of famine in its African empire.

The right not to starve, which European governments were able to assure their own citizens by the early 19th century, did not extend to the dark-skinned colonies (Sen 1981; Davis 2001).

Nor did the European powers' project to modernize African agriculture merit nearly the commitment of resources that fueled their own rural revolutions. Certain strategic or resource-rich regions, such as Zimbabwe's settler-populated highlands or Ivory Coast's cocoa belt, saw significant investments in infrastructure and agricultural extension, but elsewhere "shoestring" agricultural development prevailed (Berry 1993). Grand visions of social and environmental improvement in the colonies gave way to the more modest goal of extracting commodities while maintaining social order. By the time African farmers, like urban laborers, began making demands of the imperial governments in the 1940s, Europeans were already planning their exit (Cooper 1996). They left behind narrow economies, dependent on a few primary export commodities and ongoing aid, and governments poorly equipped to overcome this dependency.

Much of this book is about the ties that continue to bind France and Britain to their former African colonies. They are ties of trade and investment in agricultural commodities, conducted in the languages and through the transportation networks established under colonial rule. Some of these ties appear to defy market logic, and the following chapters seek to understand them in light of both broad historical conditions and personal affinities. It is worth emphasizing, however, that such postcolonial trade relationships, for all their history, are not secured by any special rights. If anything, they stretched across increasingly shaky political and regulatory terrain in the late 20th century, as the governments of the United Kingdom and France sought to divest themselves of less-strategic obligations to their former African empires, and the WTO demanded the phasing-out of preferential trade arrangements between Europe and its former colonies. Even the World Bank's term for the foodstuffs featured in this book—non-traditional export commodities—signaled a desired break from the trade relationships established between colonizer and colonized.

Ironically, however, the very nature of these commodities pulled African food producers more intimately into the provisioning of European consumers than ever before. Fragile, perishable, and subject to grades and standards far stricter than anything used to assess bushels of cocoa or cotton, these crops demanded not just stable climatic conditions but also constant monitoring, careful handling, and on-call harvesting by a well-disciplined labor force. They were not crops that producers—whether peasant farmers or corporate plantations—could undertake casually, just as French farmers could not casually claim AOC designations for their foodstuffs. Even to get access to the market, export producers in Burkina Faso and Zambia had to demonstrate commitment to very precise standards of quality—standards which provided French consumers with flawless green beans in January and British consumers with pre-packaged "baby vegs" that claimed to be as clean as they were convenient.

The macro- and micro-level relationships forged during and since the colonial period are crucial to understanding why French and British importers were able to secure such commitments from African export producers, albeit in quite different ways. Yet these relationships did not secure the producers themselves with any reciprocal recognition. Unlike France and Britain's own farmers, they commanded no place in the French or British national imagination; they were considered not part of the patrimony, nor stewards of the nation's rural nature. They just grew vegetables in places very far away from most consumers' lived experience, and places where, as later chapters will show, conceptions of racial difference still conditioned how Europeans did business in food.

In the decades surrounding the turn of the 20th century, the experience of rapid scientific, technological, and socioeconomic change fueled both ambition and anxiety in Europe's industrializing cities. Just as these responses to the space-collapsing effects of "speeded up capitalism" influenced artistic and literary production, intellectual inquiry, and geopolitical agendas (Kern 1983; Harvey 1989), so too did they inform the politics of food provisioning. In other words, ambitions to control the expanding spaces of food production and distribution, and anxieties about the risks these spaces posed both helped to motivate colonial conquest, the development of new regulatory institutions and technologies, and the consolidation of national foodways.

But these changes in the economic geography, regulation, and cultural content of food supply were also linked at a more fundamental level. All became imaginable and possible in times and places where certain kinds of *structural power* made them so. Anthropologist Eric Wolf used this term to describe the overarching political economic forces that structure the conditions of resource distribution and cultural production (Wolf 1999). In the realm of food supply, Sidney Mintz has used the notion of structural power (which he has called *outside meanings*) to understand why sugar became so extraordinarily central to the foodways of industrializing Britain. He showed how the power of the state to set trade and price policies, and the power of industrial capital to set wages and working hours, both framed the conditions under which different kinds of social actors—women and men, workers and bourgeoisie—consumed and valued sugar (Mintz 1986).

Similarly, the structural power of 19th century industrial capitalism enabled, in different ways, all the developments examined in this chapter. The states of Britain and France had the power to mobilize armies and military technologies for the conquest of Africa, thus securing markets and raw materials for mercantile and agro-industrial interests. State power to discipline domestic food markets through inspections and penalties helped to weed out the worst adulterators, while corporate food manufacturers and chain retailers had not only the power to secure purity from their suppliers but also, through advertising and other forms of marketing, to influence consumers' views about what purity looked like and why it mattered. Not least, the emerging consciousness of national foodways was due to the capacity of urban economic elites to support gastronomic culture, and to the capacity of the state to educate citizens and regulate markets in ways that promoted particular norms, practices, and commodities over others.

In France, this configuration of structural power promoted a claim of superior taste that all citizens (but especially women) had a responsibility to uphold—a responsibility that required them, among other things, to appreciate the aesthetics of fine food, whether or not they actually ate it. In Britain, the state and elite society prioritized other messages about food: about the virtues of thrift and plainness, and the drudgery of cooking. These messages were formed partly in opposition to the perceived decadence and "fussiness" of French foodways.

Clearly the state and elite economic interests did not by themselves determine how the modern institutions and meanings of food provisioning took shape. The moral voice of the anti-adulteration movement, the alternatives offered by consumer cooperatives, and the strikes waged by France's producers' associations all pushed the market and state to recognize norms of quality and fairness. These groups, like many other members of civil society, demanded protection from the risks posed by the ongoing commodification and geographic expansion of food supply. But what distinguished the food politics of the late 19th century era from those of earlier (and arguably later) periods was the power of the state and of corporate food capital to accommodate those demands while staying the course. The mass production, mass retailing, and international sourcing of the nation's food supply thus proceeded apace. More precisely, it proceeded into colonial regions where cheap labor and tropical lands offered new opportunities for feeding the mass market, provided these resources could be effectively exploited.

It is within these very broad historical conditions that networks of intermediaries carry out the trade in fresh vegetables between Africa and Europe. Whether they work out of Ouagadougou or Lusaka, Paris or London, their responsibilities and opportunities as intermediaries have been defined within broader transnational relationships, and informed by broader norms of goodness in food and trade. So far the discussion has focused on how such norms emerged in France and Britain, because they were central to the development of the different French and British structures of food retailing, as well as different contemporary anxieties vis-à-vis food globalization. To show how the transnational fresh vegetable commodity networks took on distinctive commercial cultures, the story now turns to Africa, where intermediaries worked within different conditions of structural power, and with sometimes quite different norms of goodness.

3

Burkina Faso

Rural Development and Patronage

From the air, the international airport in Ouagadougou, the capital of Burkina Faso, does not appear to be in the middle of anything except the desert. But every winter it becomes a center of intense activity and often high tension, as green beans from throughout the country pour into the airport packhouses. If all goes well, the beans are flown out the same day they are trucked in, and end up on dinner tables in France. In fact, things often do not go well, and so many green beans end up in soup pots closer to home. Indeed, the abundance of delicate green beans found in Burkina Faso's marketplaces during January and February testifies to the frequent failures of the country's export ambitions.

Green beans and other garden vegetables were brought to colonial Burkina Faso (then Upper Volta) in the early 20th century by French missionaries and colonial administrators who, apart from their personal interest in having these familiar foods available, saw the introduction of French vegetable gardening as part of their civilizing mission in Africa. They did not care much whether Africans ate *à la francais*, but they did hope that market gardening (or *maraichage*) would help feed growing colonial towns and, in the process, create a modern, industrious, prosperous and thus stable African peasantry.

Decades later in independent Upper Volta, remarkably similar goals fueled government and foreign development agency efforts to promote irrigated vegetable production for overseas markets. Especially when repeated droughts in the 1960s and 1970s raised concerns about long-term climate change, it appeared that peasants needed the income that irrigated, high-value export crops could provide in order to make up for possible shortfalls in rainy season staple grain production. So with generous foreign technical and financial assistance, the country's state-run peasant cooperatives became in the late 1960s some of sub-Saharan Africa's earliest exporters of airfreight fresh green beans. For many years, its export volume was second only to Kenya's.

By the late 1990s, Burkina Faso's green bean farmers missed the days when their crops were known as "green gold." Their country had dropped in the ranks of a growing number of African fresh produce exporters; no longer were the

Figure 3.1.
The green bean packhouse, Ouagadougou International Airport, Burkina Faso. Photo by author.

green beans served at holiday meals in France so likely to come from their fields. Their production costs had increased, yet prices had dropped. They worked harder than ever, it seemed, yet more of their beans were rejected. Privatization of the export sector was supposed to insure that they were paid more quickly and fairly for their labor, but instead compensation had become, at least for some of them, ever more unreliable.

How did this happen? Was Burkina Faso's faltering green bean export trade simply one of the many casualties of "techno-fix" development in the 1960s–70s, when Africa was flooded with donor money for irrigated export schemes that ultimately proved too costly to maintain? Certainly, poorly maintained machines and infrastructure made Burkinabé green bean growers' and exporters' work more difficult. But these seemed like straightforward problems compared to those posed by the overseas market, and by the network of social relationships that linked them to it.

Sahelian West Africa, it should be emphasized, did not just recently open up to the harsh world of international trade (Brooks 1993). Although Burkina Faso and its neighbors contribute little to world commodity markets, the region has been traversed for centuries by long-distance merchants, and its peoples are no more new to the challenges of cross-cultural commerce than they are to the risks of farming. But past long-distance trade dealt in durable high-value commodities (such as gold, salt, and kola nuts), and the perishable foods traded locally are not held to aesthetic or sanitary standards nearly as exacting as those governing the export trade. Quality, in other words, is not only defined differently in the export green bean business, but also achieved differently—through a set of technical practices and social relations quite distinct from those involved in the production and distribution of local foodstuffs.

In both the local and export trades, however, the delivery of quality ultimately depends on shared understandings of what constitutes fair and trustworthy conduct. Such understandings can be built across great distances, socioeconomic as well as geographic, but they can also fall apart. In the case of the francophone green bean commodity network, such understandings depended on the ambivalent intimacies of the postcolonial relationship. On one hand, colonial rule in Upper Volta, as elsewhere in Africa, was racist and abusive. It left behind stereotypes and resentments that still influence how French and Burkinabé actors perceive and relate to each other. On the other hand, colonialism left behind a shared national language, linked currencies, relatively direct transportation networks, aid and trade agreements, and expatriate communities in both countries. In short, colonialism provided Burkinabé exporters and French importers with many reasons to try to deal with each other rather than seek trade partners in less accessible and less familiar places.

These intermediaries work in a transnational cultural economy as paradoxical as the entire enterprise of producing green beans in the desert. It both recognizes and undermines the skills (or *métis*) of the peasant farmer. It values loyalty, but tolerates opportunism. It is organized around principles of egalitarianism, especially at the level of production, but is fundamentally sustained by entrenched, highly unequal patron-client relations. It attaches national identity—both French and Burkinabé—to the quality of the product, yet discourages investments in quality production. Finally, it promises "development" to poor farmers, yet acknowledges that if the farmers were less poor they would probably also be less suited for the arduous work of raising premium quality green beans.

Together these paradoxes make the francophone green bean network culturally distinctive. But as a case study, it illustrates two larger points about the many networks trading in food commodities from the global South. First, it shows how "development," as an imagined goal as well as a set of concrete institutions, fuels ambitions and forges affinities (individual, organizational, national) capable of producing and sustaining otherwise unviable commercial networks.[1] This chapter examines how development, both as imagined and as a set of institutions, has helped Burkinabé exporters pursue transnational commercial activities in the face of increasingly stiff odds. Second, the francophone intermediaries' strategies for meeting increasingly rigorous safety and quality standards illustrates how the "protection" of peasant agriculture serves to mask, now as during the colonial period, the reorganization of exploitation.

In the first two parts of this chapter, I examine colonial and early postcolonial efforts to feed Burkina Faso's cities and build a commodity export economy around peasant agriculture. I consider how these efforts were shaped by the broader objectives of French colonialism, by missionary activity, and by the entrepreneurial activities of the region's women traders. The last part focuses on the period from the late 1980s onward, when the Burkina Faso state, under pressure from the World Bank and other foreign donors, loosened its control over the fresh produce export industry. This era saw the emergence of private sector contract farming, an agricultural development strategy that, in principle, forges a "dynamic partnership" between smallholders and agribusiness capital. In reality, many of the contract relationships have suffered from mutual suspicion and deception, aggravated by uncertainties beyond the control of either party.

Colonial Upper Volta: Idealizing and Exploiting the Peasantry

French colonialism in West Africa was remarkable for the wide disparities between initial ideals and actual policies and practices. Three such contradictions defined the colonial experience in Burkina Faso. The first lay between the original vision of economic development, or *le mise en valeur,* for the entire French West African empire (l'Afrique Occidentale Francaise, or AOF) and the policies of uneven development that prevailed from the 1920s onward. These focused manpower and resources on "useful Africa," meaning those regions well located and richly endowed for export commodity production (Sarraut 1923; Conklin 1997).[2] The second contradiction lay between France's denunciation of slavery and barbarism and its own use of forced labor, recruited from the AOF's less "useful" colonies, namely Upper Volta and its Sahelian neighbors. The third contradiction lay between the populist ideals informing colonial development policies and the ways in which those policies often relied on and indeed reinforced the power of political and commercial elites. This latter contradiction continues to characterize many government and foreign donor rural development policies in postcolonial Burkina Faso.

Somewhat ironically, the very paucity of resources that the AOF devoted to Upper Volta helped to maintain the French ideal of a rural landscape populated and cultivated by peasants. In other words, the colonial government's miserly agricultural programs did little to encourage African rural enterprise based on large-scale farming. At most, ambitious and well-connected men and

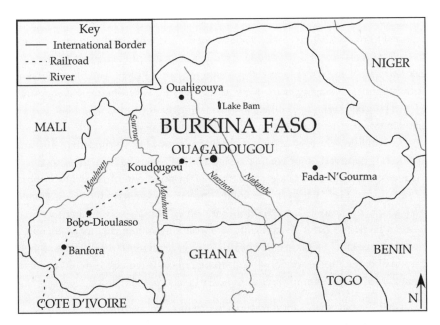

Figure 3.2.
Burkina Faso

women made commercial agriculture one part of diversified careers that also included trade and (at least for men) government employment. Market gardening fitted in well with these elites' strategies because it could be practiced seasonally and near the cities where they lived.

But simple neglect does not adequately describe colonial agricultural policy in Burkina Faso. As in other parts of Sahelian West Africa, colonial Upper Volta served as a terrain for experimentation, aimed at intensifying and improving peasant agriculture—that is, farming organized around the "family" unit, and aimed at both the market and home use.[3] The experiments were not simply technical but also social and political; they relied upon intra-village and intra-household power relations to mobilize the labor of women and youth, and the moral authority of local rulers to modernize as well as maintain social stability.[4]

The near total failure of these experiments has been well documented (Dumont 1978; Franke and Chasin 1980; Gervais 1987). Here I instead want to show how they were guided by the belief that peasant production was an efficient and socially desirable route to rural commercialization. Pro-peasant policies took as examples the groundnut and cocoa farmers of Senegal and the Gold Coast, who had responded enthusiastically to the international market both as producers and as consumers.[5] Although the social relations as well as ecological conditions of peasant production varied considerably between regions, French colonial thinkers such as Robert Delavaginette had high hopes for the productivity of African peasants in general. As he wrote in the preface to his 1931 novel *Les Paysans Noirs,* which was set in southern Upper Volta: "The black peasant is the central personality of the New African World. Far from being a character of cheap exotic literature, embellished and exaggerated, the peasant is a worker participating in the world economy" (Delavignette 1931).

Colonial advocates of "pro-peasant" policies also warned that Africans would be "deprived of judgment and morality" if removed from their "ancient" village way of life and made to work on European enterprises.[6] On a more positive note, they believed that family farmers were needed, both in France and Africa, not only to produce food and fiber, but also to protect the rural world against the city's destabilizing and polluting influences, moral as much as environmental.[7] Of course, for peasants to serve all these roles, much of their presumably traditional way of life had to be radically altered, as one document from the AOF's Economic Service enthusiastically recommended:

> Give the black peasant new tools, more modern instruments of work, make his field bigger, open new and more fertile land, give him the sense of prosperity, taste for savings and foresight, the desire for work which returns something . . . improve his village and his diet, attach him to the soil he lives on and which he knows as his nourishing Mother . . . bring him out of the era of hand cultivation to the age of plow cultivation, this is not an impossible enterprise; it is . . . to lead the black peasant to a new type of life.[8]

From the beginning, the imagined role of France benignly "leading" Upper Volta's peasantry toward productivity and prosperity clashed with the empire's need for a cheap and mobile labor force. In fact the landlocked, semi-arid Voltaic region appealed to the colonizers primarily because it was well-peopled, especially on the Mossi Plateau.[9] After a series of conquests, France took control of the region in the mid-1880s, and made it an official colony of the AOF in 1904 (Kambou-Ferrand 1993). For several years, colonial administrators recruited voluntary migrants to work on cocoa plantations in Ivory Coast and irrigated cotton schemes in the Niger River Valley. But when the harsh work and low wages attracted few workers, the first governor of Upper Volta, Frédéric Hesling, called on chiefs and other local authorities to provide men by the thousands.

Administrators justified the use of forced labor (a practice which clearly violated French civilization's enshrined commitment to *liberté*) on the grounds that it was in the "native's" best interest. According the lieutenant-governor of the AOF, Henry Carde, "obligatory" labor would be "strictly within the humanitarian defense of the native against his own [presumably lazy] nature . . . [it] will be justified [it] results in an increase in work which will result in an increase in money necessary to ameliorate his current standard of living."[10]

But even while Upper Volta exported vast quantities of labor, it was expected to be financially self-sufficient. In the early 1920s, Hesling launched a massive campaign to expand the cultivation of cotton as an export crop. This campaign distributed seeds to villages and required them to fill seasonal quotas. It did not, however, invest significantly in the reorganization or mechanization of production, on the assumption that family farms would simply absorb the additional workload. In fact, the combination of forced cash cropping and forced labor migration led to a dangerous decline in food supply; famine in the late 1920s led some colonial officials to warn of demographic collapse (Gervais 1987, 113).

At the time, Upper Volta budgeted so little for agriculture (4 percent of the colony's entire budget was devoted to an activity that supported 95 percent of the population) that major investments in technical improvements were impossible (Gervais, 1987). Still, the agricultural service did establish a small number of research stations in the mid-1920s. Their programs aimed to promote "modern" peasant agriculture instead of either the existing system of semi-communal production—in which lineage elders controlled the land as well as their kin's labor—or the wage-labor plantation system found in parts of Ivory Coast.

One of these research stations was located several kilometers north of Bobo-Dioulasso, an old market town in the southwest of the colony (now Burkina Faso's second largest city, with a population of approximately 500,000). Besides raising experimental cultures of cotton and other potential cash crops, the station aimed to teach young local Africans modern farming methods (such as plow cultivation) and then promote them locally. Once the local populace had learned *l'habitude du travail,* agricultural officials anticipated that "family farming"—meaning a man, wife (or wives), and children on a private plot—would spread naturally as the farmers themselves appreciated its obvious rationality and profitability.[11] In order to set examples, both the station's young graduates and respected local elders would receive all the resources, from seeds to bulls, needed to create model farms—"little centers of evolution" in both agricultural and social terms.[12]

In fact the "family farm" program produced what administrative records in 1932 described as "lamentable results": The cattle died, the station's graduates used their education to find non-farm jobs, and the elders used the agricultural service's handouts to reinforce their "feudal" control over agricultural labor[13] (Gervais, 1987, 119). But notwithstanding these failures, the administration still considered the Bobo Dioulasso region the colony's potential breadbasket, given its many small waterways, relatively rich soils and abundant rainfall (on average

1,100 mm (43 inches) annually, as opposed to less than 400 mm (16 inches) in the far north), and local populations who, even without "modern" farming methods, kept their granaries well-stocked with millet. For French administrators, the crops of interest included not only staple grains but also fresh fruits and vegetables commonly consumed in France. Administrators based in Bobo-Dioulasso initially experimented in gardens around their settlement; agricultural reports as early as 1903 record success with varieties ranging from green beans and potatoes to *petit pois* and strawberries.[14] Colonial hygiene experts did not consider these foods luxuries. As a Madagascar government journal explained,

> The cultivation of vegetables in hot countries is indispensable for the hygiene of Europeans who are called to live in them. If, in certain intertropical regions, the native is content to use the plants that he finds at his door . . . one of our biggest preoccupations when we move to the colonies, it is to introduce and grow at least some of the many and excellent vegetables that we possess in our temperate country.
>
> This responds to a true need. It is necessary, from the point of view of health in the hot countries, to give great priority to vegetables in the diet . . . (Bois 1924)

Colonial administrators in Bobo-Dioulasso were encouraged to note that the peasants already cultivated a variety of vegetables—peppers, greens, onions, tomatoes—in their own "kitchen gardens."[15] In order to expand the scale and diversity of production, the provincial agricultural ministry relied on a combination of modest technical improvements and, in keeping with its shoestring budget, force. In one riverside village five kilometers north of town, for example, the agricultural ministry dammed the river, dug irrigation canals, and established *le jardin publique,* a small vegetable plantation where men, women, children alike performed forced labor.[16] There, *l'habitude du travail* was instilled with the help of a whip, humiliation, and food deprivation.[17] In addition, the administration required the village's households to grow potatoes and vegetables on their own riverside plots, which they watered with hollowed-out gourds. Some years, Bobo-Dioulasso's potatoes fed colonial towns throughout the colony, including the capital Ouagadougou. During both World Wars, forced gardening helped feed the thousands of soldiers (both French and African) based in the Bobo-Dioulasso military camp.

Up through the end of World War II, the Upper Volta colonial administration restricted the marketing of foodstuffs. In Bobo-Dioulasso, however, gardeners sold their vegetables secretly, via local women traders, to the town's European expatriates. Some village men also found paid work in Europeans' private gardens. Even village children who attended mission schools learned to grow "European" vegetables, partly because this was considered a useful skill, but also because the school canteens needed cheap provisions. Missionaries introduced European-style gardening to other parts of the colony (notably the Lac Bam region, now a center for green bean export production) for similar reasons (Ouedraego 1995).

The end of World War II marked the beginning of a boom period in Bobo-Dioulasso and other colonial towns. With the abolition of forced labor and local trade restrictions in 1946, villager gardeners that had previously had their vegetables requisitioned could now sell them openly. Indeed the Bobo-Dioulasso agricultural ministry, faced with the challenge of feeding a rapidly growing town, encouraged them to do so: It offered gardeners seeds and technical aid, as well as the opportunity to win prizes for their produce at annual agricultural fairs. Another boost for the regional food economy came from Upper Volta's war veterans, many of who settled in or around Bobo-Dioulasso and invested their pensions in commercial agriculture, grain trading, and transport companies (Saul 1986). Like most of today's Burkinabé green bean exporters, the vets also brought to their business ventures the knowledge and authority acquired during their time in France or other overseas postings. And, along with missionary-educated Burkinabé civil servants, many veterans became consumers of the villagers' "European" vegetables.

The French government, meanwhile, stepped up its support for Upper Volta agriculture. Its newly established funding agency FIDES (Fonds d'Investissement pour le Developpement Economique et Social) paid for more than 3,000 hectares of irrigation, intended for rice and horticulture. Upper Volta's agricultural service opened several new training stations (nine of which specialized in horticulture) and launched nearly 500 pilot "family farms" equipped with plows and improved seeds. Although many proved no more successful than the previous generation of model family farms, they demonstrated the administration's continued commitment to the peasant model of rural development (Schwartz 1995).

Missionaries also promoted agricultural development (especially market gardening) during the post-war period, but for different reasons. By helping to create a prosperous Christian peasantry in the hinterland, they sought to demonstrate not just the Church's ongoing contribution to local economic development, but also the worldly virtues of Christian marriage and gender roles. In other words, the Church's financial and technical support for market gardening was part of a larger battle against polygamy and the religious beliefs, both Islamic and traditional, that sanctioned it (de Benoist 1987). As part of this campaign, the Bobo-Dioulasso mission equipped a group of "catechist-farmers" with seeds, tools, and horticultural training, and helped them set up their farms. Only married catechists were eligible for this assistance, however, because the wife as helpmate was considered a vital part of the example (de Montjoye 1980).

Women's labor was indeed critical to the post-war expansion of European-style gardening in Upper Volta, but the most influential players were urban-based woman wholesalers, who invested commercial capital in the expansion of their supply base. In the Bobo-Dioulasso region, such women typically came from families who had long traded grain, textiles, and other commodities, and thus had extensive connections in hinterland villages. These women encouraged village farmers to take up market gardening by offering them pre-season loans of cash and seeds, especially for high-demand crops like cabbages and tomatoes. The wholesalers then sold the harvests to retailers in Bobo-Dioulasso as well as to traders from cities as far away as Lomé and Abidjan.

Regional produce marketing has remained in women's hands, as it has throughout much of West Africa.[18] Just as retailers have promoted "exotic" produce in the Northern hemisphere, women traders have helped popularize "European" vegetables (and to a lesser extent fruit) in Burkina Faso. Like French food staples such as *café au lait* and baguettes, vegetables such as butter lettuce and green beans have become an appreciated if not always affordable part of Burkinabé foodways (Freidberg 2003). The growth of this domestic market has in turn mediated the risk of production for the export market because it provides gardeners with an alternative outlet for vegetables.

Postcolonial Green Bean Schemes

When Upper Volta gained independence in August 1960, its first president, Maurice Yaméogo, had been quoted a year earlier as saying that only "lunatics" would seek independence for a country that could not even produce its own matchboxes.[19] An exporter of cotton and migrant labor, Upper Volta continued to depend on France for much of its operating budget, and by the late 1960s Ouagadougou hosted a large community of international aid agencies. The country's food supply remained dangerously vulnerable to drought, which had begun to strike with increasing regularity, leading to famine in 1973–4.

Many agencies, then, primarily provided relief aid. But faced with the specter of long-term climate change, the Upper Volta government and its donors saw irrigation as the longer term solution to the problems underlying famine vulnerability: unreliable rains, shortages of arable land in the most densely populated regions, and rural poverty and unemployment. Irrigation would permit

Figure 3.3.
Women produce traders at the Grand Marché, Bobo-Dioulasso, Burkina Faso. Photo
by author.

not only rainy season rice production for domestic consumption (thus cutting
the need for imports), but also the production of export crops during the nine-
month dry season, when farming was otherwise unviable (Compaore et al.
1987). Horticultural crops such as green beans were particularly attractive because they generated more revenue and jobs per hectare than most other commercial crops—making them viable even on very small plots—and many people already knew how to grow them (LeMelle 1995).

Over the next two decades, the area of Upper Volta's irrigated and land
increased by several thousand hectares, mostly around large, centrally managed
pipe and canal irrigation schemes similar to those built elsewhere in sub-
Saharan Africa during the same era.[20] The main sites targeted for export horticulture included Lac Bam, north of Ouagadougou, the Vallée de Sourou, in the
country's far west, and the Vallée de Kou, near Bobo-Dioulasso. As during the
colonial era, the irrigation schemes (or *perimetres*) organized production
around small-scale growers. To obtain access to an irrigated plot, individuals
had to join a scheme's state-run cooperative, undergo training (*encadrement*)
and meet seasonal production quotas. The state-run marketing organization,
UCOVAM, controlled the distribution of inputs (seeds, fertilizer, pesticides) as
well as exporting produce to France, its sole market. The former colonial power
had not only the most direct airfreight connections, but also import-export companies accustomed to trade with francophone West Africa. In addition, of

Burkina Faso: Rural Development and Patronage

71

course, the French had a known appetite for fine-grade, hand-picked green beans, and they were willing to pay particularly good prices for them during the winter holiday season, which coincided with ideal growing conditions in the Sahel.

From the beginning, the country's green bean growers faced an assortment of socioeconomic and technical difficulties, some specific to the crop, and some common to large-scale agricultural projects across Africa. For example, their timing was often off. Growers often did not have land or labor available for green beans until after they harvested their grain. If those harvests came even a week late, growers had few beans ready to sell to France at Christmas, when the prices were best.

In addition, despite the horticultural schemes' stated objective of improving household food security, plots were rarely allocated to women, who often provide the bulk of their children's food. Plots did, however, end up in the hands of "weekend farmers"—that is, well-connected bureaucrats and businessmen who relied on hired labor to tend their beans. Poorer growers, meanwhile, often found themselves shorthanded, especially at harvest time. As in many other irrigation projects, male "household heads'" control over women's labor proved less assured than Western development planners anticipated.[21] Failure to keep up with production quotas not only meant less revenue, but potentially expulsion from the scheme. Poorer growers also could not easily endure the several months' delay between harvest and payment. The delays owed partly to UCOVAM's bureaucratic structure, but also its dependence on French importers for seasonal financing. This debt relationship gave UCOVAM little power to demand prompt payment, especially when exports fell short of projected volumes.

Another major (and enduring) problem was unreliable transportation both on the ground and in the air. Some of the largest sites, such as the Vallée de Sourou, were located more than five hours over bad roads from the Ouagadougou airport. If a lorry broke down en route—which was not uncommon given that many of the lorries were in bad shape—its fragile cargo might perish. It might also perish at the airport if flights were late, canceled, or full. Lack of cargo space was especially severe in 1984, the year after Thomas Sankara came to power and changed the country's name to Burkina Faso ("land of upright people"). In one now-legendary incident, typical of the young president's rash approach to problem-solving, Sankara disposed of tons of green beans stranded at the airport by making state employees take them in place of part of their salaries. The government described the forced distribution, unconvincingly, as part of its "Buy Burkinabé" campaign.

Unlike his predecessors (the country went through five coups d'etat between 1960 and 1983), Sankara openly criticized the "neocolonial" powers who encouraged his country to export luxury cash crops and import food aid. An avowed revolutionary, he described the Burkinabé bureaucrats and businesspeople who profited from these relations as "compradors" and "hucksters," and pledged to focus government resources on rural people's needs, such as clean water and clinics (Speirs 1991). But Sankara also recognized that tens of thousands of rural households bought food and paid for school fees with green bean income, and ongoing irrigation development could soon enable many more households to do the same (Sankara 1988). At the time, Burkina's winter beans had few competitors, so even when logistical difficulties resulted in uneven quality, they could still earn attractive prices. In light of these considerations, and in light of the possibility that climate change and desertification might make rainy season food production less and less viable,[22] it seemed only pragmatic to indulge the former colonizers' tastes. As it happened, climate change did not prove nearly as daunting as changes in the overseas market.

Entrepreneurial Developments

A series of events beginning in the late 1980s marked a period of upheaval in Burkina Faso's horticultural sector. First, as part of a broader economic liberalization program, the Sankara regime ended UCOBAM's (formerly UCOVAM) export monopoly. UCOBAM remained the country's single largest green bean exporter, but over the next few years more than twenty private companies—some just one-man operations—jumped into the business. Although some exporters had their own farms, they contracted out most production to smallholders. Many of these smallholders had previously supplied UCOBAM, but the exporters also sought new growers, including those in regions where there were no formal irrigation facilities but villagers had access to floodplain or riverside land.

Contract farming was not new to Burkina Faso or other African countries, but in the 1980s it was newly endorsed by development policymakers as preferable either to large corporate plantations or poorly managed state-run schemes (Little and Watts 1994). Contract farming appeared particularly suited to labor-intensive export crops like green beans because, in theory, it forges a "dynamic partnership" between agribusiness with its access to markets, capital, and technology, and small farmers with their presumed access to cheap yet disciplined family labor (Williams and Karen 1985; Jaffee 1995b). In practice, contract arrangements appeal to agribusiness in large part because they typically demand relatively little initial investment and no long-term commitment (Watts 1994).

Not long after Sankara began liberalizing the Burkinabé economy, he was assassinated in a coup d'etat in October 1987, and succeeded by Blaise Camp-aore, who moved quickly to mend relations with France and other Western powers (Englebert 1996). He also agreed to take on a World Bank structural adjustment program (SAP), beginning in 1991. The SAP provided millions of dollars of multilateral aid ($28 million over three years for the agricultural sector alone) but also required Burkina Faso to liberalize its trade and investment policies, and privatize most of its remaining state-owned industries. Along with the devaluation of the West Africa franc (CFA) in 1994, these measures had mixed consequences for the country's green bean growers and exporters. On one hand, they got rid of certain taxes and tariffs, and made exports from the CFA zone cheaper on the world market. On the other hand, they increased the costs of imported fuel, fertilizer, and seed, as well as the cost of basic services such as schooling and medical care.[23]

Once the state had pulled out of the green bean export business, it stepped back to "rationalize" the sector, at least at the top end.[24] "Rationalization" is often seen as a natural and necessary part of agricultural modernization, but in this case the immediate concern was not small and inefficient producers so much as the intermediaries to whom they sold their beans. Many of the private exporters had quickly run up huge debts with the national banks, while failing to meet their contracts with both suppliers and French importers. Concerned about the reputation of the Burkina Faso green bean industry, the state began limiting export licenses to operations with proper equipment (a refrigerator truck and storage facilities) and the proven capacity to export at least 100 tons of produce annually. By 1994 the number of active firms dropped from twenty-two to nine, including the now privately owned UCOBAM.[25]

Shortly afterward the French government's Agence Francaise de Devel-oppement (AFD) approved 18 million francs (approximately $2.75 million) in aid for the "restructuring" of Burkina Faso's horticultural export sector (which produced mangoes as well as green beans) (LeMelle 1995). The initial funds helped to create the Association of Professional Fruit and Vegetable Exporters (APEFEL), and to improve cold storage at the Ouagadougou airport. The aid package reenters the story later, but here it is significant for two reasons. First, it came at a time when Burkina Faso's green beans faced increasing compe-tition in the French market not only from Kenya but also former French col-onies, namely Morocco, Senegal, Mali, and Madagascar.[26] The intensified com-petition partly reflected the efforts of French importers, who had gone looking for a wider range of supply regions. But it also reflected the efforts of African countries to follow the advice of the World Bank and other donors and increase their production of high value agricultural export commodities. It just happened that many of these countries, as well as those in Latin America and Asia, gravitated towards the same commodities, among them green beans.[27]

Second, the AFD aid package provided resources mostly to businesspeople who, by national standards, were already well off. This focus corresponded with the Campaore regime's enthusiastic embrace of entrepreneur-led development—a vision laid out by the World Bank in its 1989 report *From Crisis to Sustainable Growth* (World Bank 1989). According to this report, Africa's indigenous entrepreneurs needed not only deregulation, but also training and financial assistance in order to better manage and expand their businesses. On one level, aid for established businesspeople like the green bean exporters marked a sharp departure from decades of state-planned development, and especially from Sankara's explicitly socialist agenda. On other levels, however, it very much echoed past programs. For one, it reaffirmed the colonial and postcolonial government policy of leaving commercial agriculture in the hands of smallholders. The program did not aim to restructure the horticultural export sector, but rather to make the exporters into more effective intermediaries between the international market and an estimated 30,000 peasant producers.

In addition, although the policy literature endorsing aid for African entrepreneurs portrays them as members of a dynamic new generation, many recipients of such aid (not only in Burkina Faso) owe their professional status to traditional development institutions, namely the state. They have worked for either the government itself, or foreign agencies providing aid to the government, or businesses providing services (such as transportation, construction, and rental property) to the agencies. Or, quite often, some combination of the above. They have attained elite status by building diversified careers and social networks that "straddle" the public and private sectors (Kitching 1980; Bayart 1993) and that have helped them adapt to changing conditions of resource access. In particular, they have been able to maintain access to resources provided in the name of development even though, in the wake of structural adjustment, they are no longer always funneled through the state (Gregoire and Labazée 1993; Fauré and Labazée 2000).

Burkina Faso's green bean exporters, in other words, belong to the latest generation of African elites to profit from their role as intermediaries between the forces of development—the state, the market, and the international aid community—and the peasantry. Over the course of the 20th century, such intermediaries have often been resented and typed as traitors and parasites. But they have also proven indispensable, insofar as they can communicate and command authority in diverse social realms.

In contemporary post-socialist Burkina Faso, the green bean exporters' intermediary role has acquired renewed legitimacy. But this role goes well beyond buying and selling. The exporters must also keep informed of the market's

Burkina Faso: Rural Development and Patronage

75

increasingly strict quality and safety standards, and communicate these standards to their growers; they must make sure that their buyers in France appreciate the difficult conditions of production; and they must maintain the loyalty and trust of both growers and buyers, even when things go wrong. This is a tall order, and comes atop the many family and community responsibilities expected of individuals of elite status. Not surprisingly, the exporters do not always succeed on all counts. But this makes it all the more worthwhile to examine in greater detail how they have constructed their careers and how they understand them.

Career Paths

Many of West Africa's regional and long-distance trades are dominated by particular ethnic groups. Within Burkina Faso, for example, Lebanese families are among the largest fish and textile wholesalers, Hausa merchants control much of the trade in kola nuts, and Dioula and Zara women dominate regional vegetable wholesaling between Burkina Faso and Ivory Coast. Clients, credit relations, and commercial lore are often passed from one generation to the next, helping to reproduce the exclusiveness of the trade as well as the group's mercantile identity.[28]

Burkina Faso's green bean exporters present a different profile. The approximately two dozen members of APEFEL, the exporters association, come from ethnic backgrounds as diverse as the country's national population (which is approximately 60 percent Mossi) and from families of farmers, civil servants, and professionals. Most, however, benefited from advanced education (several of them have studied abroad) and then employment that allowed them to save money and, above all, to accumulate useful skills and contacts.

For example, one exporter previously worked for an international aid agency that helped village cooperatives develop dry season commercial activities, including vegetable gardening. On the job, he became familiar both with the logistics of horticultural production and marketing and with the rural communities who later became his supply base. Another learned about horticultural exporting during his previous job at a failed state-run fruit-growing project. A third, an economist by training, has dabbled in a variety of export trades across Africa, but also spent two years at the United Nations in New York. Another worked his way up through a series of government posts, including ministerial positions in agriculture and finance. Yet another worked for a company that manufactures the cardboard boxes used for Burkina Faso's green bean exports. Besides sparking his interest in the trade, the job helped him identify both overseas buyers and their packaging concerns. He then worked for two years for other exporters, helping them find markets and financing, before going into business for himself.

Most of the exporters continue to have at least one, if not several, other sources of income besides green beans. Several deal in other commodities, such as fruit (mangoes, citrus, and bananas for both regional and export markets), regionally-traded vegetables (potatoes, tomatoes) and oilseed crops (sesame, shea nut). Some also draw income from real estate; renting urban villas to expatriate aid-agency employees is considered particularly lucrative. Others have parlayed their education and career experience into various forms of consulting such as in accounting, management, or computing. These are typically sideline activities, practiced when the occasion arises rather than actively pursued.

This diversification provides not only off-season income, but also security against uncertain harvests, transportation, and financing. It is as important to the risk management strategies of exporters as it is to peasant households. Indeed, unlike in Zambia, Zimbabwe, or Kenya—where many companies' sole enterprise is vegetable exporting—in Burkina Faso exporters cannot survive on green bean revenue alone. But while diversification is necessary, it can also be distracting.

Most exporters try to visit their growers frequently (at least once a week) during the peak season, primarily to deliver supplies and check on the progress of the crops, but also to demonstrate authority and commitment to their growers. Although the first activity can be delegated to a capable assistant, the second cannot, at least not convincingly. Some exporters, therefore, spend many hours each week traveling between their urban home and their growers' villages. But at least a couple who attempt to juggle multiple business are known for "disappearing" from the production sites for long stretches, leaving their growers not only without fertilizer and pesticides when they need them but also questioning the exporters' credibility. Such exporters end up with erratic and unreliable tonnage, which in turn undermines their credibility in the eyes of their peers and clients. Reputation, as I will discuss in more detail, is crucial in a trade that offers few other forms of insurance.

The career path of the exporter is not only diversified but also gendered. In 2000, only one member of APEFEL was a woman, the middle-aged widow of a wealthy man. Local and regional vegetable trading, as mentioned earlier, lies nearly entirely in the hands of women, and has made some of them quite wealthy (Bosch 1985). But they have not needed much, if any, formal education to get started, drawing instead on kin-based social networks for clients, credit, market-stall space, and training (Freidberg 1996b). They have also not needed to establish their credibility as female traders at the local or regional level; across much of West Africa, women's dominance of certain forms of commerce dates back centuries.[29]

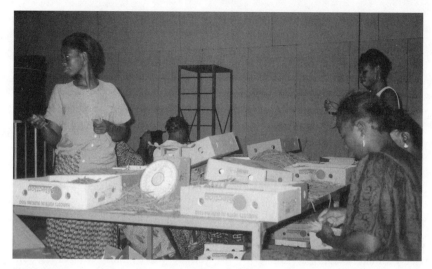

Figure 3.4.
Women packing green beans for export at the Ouagadougou airport packhouse. Although women dominate regional produce trading, most lack the capital and connections necessary for exporting. Photo by author.

In the export green bean business, however, not only intermediaries but also the heads of the growers' groups are predominantly male. The latter, according to the sole female exporter, do not like a woman telling them what to do: "The peasants, they say, 'woman, don't bother me.' " More concretely, relatively few Burkinabé women enjoy access to formal education beyond the primary level[30] or the resources required to start and maintain a green bean export business: thousands to tens of thousands of dollars for start-up costs (primarily for vehicles and cold storage facilities), up-to-date information about European market conditions and regulations, and, not least, time. "Exporting for a young married woman would be very hard," the widow-exporter explains, "you have to be there in the mornings. You have to be there in the evenings. And you have to go out late, to go to the airport, or if there's a truck broken down." Indeed, the exporters' hours are not only late but unpredictable. Green bean flights to Paris are nearly always scheduled to leave at night—in order to arrive in Rungis for the early morning market—but sometimes the planes arrive in Ouagadougou several hours late or not at all. In order to insure that their beans are properly cooled and handled, some of the exporters personally see off most, if not all, of their shipments, even if this means waiting at the airport until three in the morning. "If I were married, says the widow, "my husband would ask where I'd been . . . the men, they don't get asked."

French Beans and Food Scares
78

Figure 3.5.
Market gardener and his household labor supply. Photo by author.

Suppliers and Buyers

Trust is central to social life when neither traditional certainties nor modern probabilities hold. (Hart 1988, 191)

If you're in the green bean business, it's said, you cannot be honest.
—Mid-level employee in Burkinabe export firm

In theory, Burkina Faso's green beans reach the international market through a series of formal contract and commission relationships between growers, exporters, and buyers. In reality, they pass between actors possessing vastly different kinds and degrees of wealth and information. These differences make the legal basis of such relationships—especially at the upstream end, between growers and exporters—practically irrelevant. Participants in this trade thus place much more stock in an individual's reputation and past performance than in written agreements. Ideally, a buyer or supplier is not just a fellow party to a contract but a "friend," that is, someone who has proven both likable and trustworthy.

Research in other realms of West Africa commerce suggests that the idiom of friendship is central to exchange relations between people bound by neither kinship nor effective contract (La Fontaine 1975; Hart 1988). Unlike most of West Africa's local and regional trades, however, Burkina Faso's export green bean business is subject to increasingly strict safety and quality standards that are imposed from outside and are not subject to negotiation. These standards, set against a backdrop of an unpredictable climate, an unreliable infrastructure, and financial insecurity, make friendships in this trade all the more important but perhaps difficult to maintain.

How are the relationships between buyers and suppliers actually established? As mentioned above, some of the exporters had earlier jobs that brought them into contact with smallholders in irrigation zones. Others had kin in these zones. But some of the exporters had to go looking for growers in areas where they knew no one. In this early stage, an exporter would have to convince a group of smallholders (who might or might not be organized into an officially recognized cooperative or village *groupement*) that growing green beans for him would be more secure and lucrative than dealing with UCOBAM (which is still the largest single export firm) or growing some other dry season crop, such as vegetables for the local market. At the same time, an exporter had to assess these potential suppliers' ability to "work well"—in other words, to produce high-quality beans of the specified grade (nine mm maximum diameter for "fine" beans, six mm for "extra-fine") in the right quantity, and at the right time.

This work does not require particularly sophisticated equipment, but it demands very careful attention to detail and timing. Beginning with planting, growers should keep as close to the agreed-upon schedule as possible. Known as "le planning," the seasonal schedule specifies the first planting day—theoretically, shortly after the anticipated millet harvests in October or November—as well as harvest, delivery, and subsequent planting dates. In practice, weather, labor shortages, and technical mishaps make "le planning" as difficult (and effectively "false," as one director of a growers' cooperative put it) as it was in the early days of green bean exporting. But once the season does begin, fertilizer must be applied in adequate volume and at the correct stage of plant growth, or else yields will be too low. Pesticides, too, must be used before pests do damage, but not carelessly, and not so late in the growing cycle that residues might remain on the beans. The ground must be kept moist, but not flooded. For growers with access to land alongside functioning irrigation canals, watering is an easy task. But in some places growers rely on hoses or even just watering cans, which they may have to use twice a day during the hottest part of the season. The green bean vines must be tied up properly so that the beans themselves grow straight and unblemished; they must also be shielded from the harsh dusty Harmattan wind that blows down from the Sahara during most of the December-to-March growing season. Finally, when harvest time arrives, growers must have ample (and preferably experienced) hands available for quick and thorough picking, as well as for sorting and packing. Even a day's delay can upset the shipment schedule and allow the beans to grow too fat.

Because the green bean needs so much care, exporters obviously want growers who have enough household or hired labor to tend to their plots, whether they are one-tenth or two hectares in size.[31] But the simple number of people on hand does not always reflect the availability or quality of the labor supply. So exporters are even more concerned to find growers who, as individuals and as groups, are committed, disciplined, and in control of their workforce.

It is generally accepted in the green bean business that such growers are easier to find in the relatively dry and remote parts of the Mossi Plateau (in the center of the country), rather than in the more well-watered southwest or near urban markets. Some exporters, invoking a widely-held stereotype in Burkina Faso, claim that the Bobo and other historically "stateless" peoples of the southwest are "anarchic," and thus less suitable as green bean growers than the Mossi, whose village and regional chiefs still command considerable authority. But others argue that growers in the southwest and near cities are simply not desperate enough. As one exporter explained:

> Green bean work is very, very complicated and demands much labor . . . from the day you plant until the harvest, there's not a moment of rest. The Bobo peasants, in the West, they have other sources of revenue besides the green bean, and so ultimately they don't give a damn. They don't depend on it to live. It's paradoxical, but true. They have other products that take less work, like watermelons; they have less suffering.

The same logic discourages exporters from looking for suppliers around Ouagadougou, despite the advantages of proximity to the airport.

> Production in the urban area can be complicated. There they grow a lot of cabbage and peppers and tomatoes [for the urban market] and it's not easy to find people to work as diligently as the *haricot vert* requires. So I go a little farther out, in order to have quality.

When exporters seek growers in more marginal regions, however, they must be ready to bear extra costs, and not just for transportation. The narrower the growers' sources of livelihood, the more they depend on an exporter not just to provide seeds and other inputs and pay promptly, but also to loan (or give) them money for emergencies, on the farm or otherwise. Regardless of financial status, growers want an exporter who understands that they will put aside work on the green beans when they have to take a sick child to the clinic

Figure 3.6.
Young gardeners on the outskirts of Bobo-Dioulasso. They garden part-time, producing lettuce for the urban market. Photo by author.

or attend a village funeral. They want an exporter who is well connected—ideally to sources of donor aid—but who is also committed to getting *their* beans to market. Ultimately, the quality of growers' relationship with an exporter and the quality of the green beans they produce can depend greatly on how well this relationship helps them ease the chronic problems of scarce cash and an insecure food supply.

If an exporter "disappears" or proves stingy, his growers may sell the fertilizer intended for green beans or save it to use on their millet fields. Or they may sell the green beans themselves to another exporter; some exporters are known to buy up beans, covertly, that have been promised to (and financed by) someone else. These transactions sometimes take place in the middle of the night. Or the growers may sell the pesticides specified for vegetables and apply instead the much cheaper but more toxic chemicals used on cotton. This practice is potentially the most damaging not only to an individual exporter but to everyone involved in green bean exporting. If airport food safety inspectors in France detect residues of prohibited pesticides, the EU could indefinitely ban Burkina Faso's beans. Depending on the circumstances, the French importer purchasing the beans could also be held liable.[32]

Burkinabé exporters' views of growers' various cost- and risk-minimizing practices range from condescending to relatively sympathetic. Some say the peasants are ignorant and sly, and must be treated severely. This was the approach of one exporter who took me along, apparently as a prop, to a meeting with a group of prospective growers in a village outside Bobo-Dioulasso. He rented a Mercedes sedan for the occasion (rather than take his beat-up pickup) and spoke to the villagers in French, via a translator (though he apparently spoke Dioula, the local lingua franca). He told them that "the white man" now wanted better quality and fewer pesticides, and only Burkina Faso's peasants were to blame for the country's declining share of the overseas green bean market, because they did not use their farm chemicals correctly. He said that it was time to "get serious," and that the lazy should not even bother working with him.

Perhaps not surprisingly, this man's tough talk and fancy car fronted for a business that other exporters considered laughable, and that had already disappointed growers elsewhere. The more successful exporters, by contrast, expressed greater confidence in the peasants' skill and capacity to "produce quality," and said that they would work well once their relations with an exporter felt relatively fair and secure. Says one man: "Up until now the producer hasn't trusted the exporter. He's not motivated and therefore you can't lead him to do things correctly. The day when the peasant is sure that at the end of the season he'll be paid without problem, I assure you he won't put the [green bean] fertilizer on his millet."

Some exporters claim that to win this trust, the peasants must be paid for their work even if it means taking a temporary loss. Otherwise, they may refuse to grow beans for export the following year. This has happened in villages around Bobo-Dioulasso, where gardeners disillusioned with the export trade have switched to growing green beans and other vegetables for the local market. Similarly, individuals who control the allocation of irrigated plots say that it shows good faith to allow growers to plant a small portion of their plots with *les divers,* or vegetables that they can sell locally. Since sales of *les divers* provide regular cash flow (whereas green bean revenue only comes in at the end of the three-month growing season, or later) this small concession helps prevent work-disrupting budget crises.

However they encourage growers to work hard and honestly, exporters agree that they cannot compromise on the standards of the green beans ultimately shipped out under their names. Yet some of these standards are not easily enforced through at-a-distance contract relationships (nearly all the exporters live in urban areas). As of 2000, exporters' most common method of upholding EU pesticide residue standards was *sensibilisation*—that is, instructing growers what chemicals they could and could not use, and hoping they would do as told.[33] Traceability—an English term which, like "le planning," had entered the exporters' vocabulary relatively recently—was in the works, several of them said. But in most cases there was little evidence that green beans could be traced back to individual producers (or even production regions) once they were packaged for shipment.

Aesthetic standards, on the other hand, can be enforced during the post-harvest sorting, or *triage,* when all fat, bent, or otherwise flawed beans are supposed to be rejected. Growers sort and pack their own beans in 5 kg cartons, each marked with a number identifying the grower, but these are usually re-checked by packhouse workers in Ouagadougou. In the past few years most of the exporters have begun returning cartons to growers if they contain too many inferior quality beans. The point is not only not to pay them, but also to embarrass them. In the village communities where most growers live, shame acts as a powerful deterrent. Explains one exporter: "When we return the carton to the grower, we show it to everyone. That causes shame, and the next time the individual concerned works doubly hard . . . If it happens again, everyone knows who has done it, because there's a rumor that so-and-so has fat beans. In the village the people don't like to hear that."

Clearly, the "friendship" between an exporter and his or her growers is embedded in uneven but not entirely lopsided power relations: The exporter uses social status, market access, and control over certain resources to discipline growers, but this exploitative power is limited by the growers' ability to cheat or opt out entirely.[34] This option is more or less viable depending on the alternatives available to growers' households.[35]

The exporters' power is also mediated by their relationship to their own buyers, the French importers. Here the critical power imbalances are financial and spatial. Because green bean exporters can rarely get bank loans anymore (as a group they ran up too much debt in the late '80s and early '90s; the country's banks no longer want anything to do with green beans), most of them must rely on their French clients to finance the growing season. A pre-season contract specifies the amount invested, the tonnage expected each week, and, in some cases, the price. The exporters find this arrangement less than ideal partly because the financing, they claim, is often inadequate, meaning that they must struggle to provide growers with seeds and other supplies. In addition, the debt allows the importer to set the price—and then reset it if the quality of beans is poor or the market looks unpromising. One exporter compared this relationship to his vision of marriage: "When you are pre-financed by someone you become his wife." In other words, you do what he says.

The alternative, however, is not necessarily preferable. Some of the smaller exporters receive no financing from importers, and instead cobble together funds from family loans and their other enterprises. They sell on commission, which they claim gives them greater autonomy, but not necessarily a more secure price. One of exporters' most common complaints, in fact, is that they cannot know what happens to their beans once the plane takes off. If their French buyers say (as they often do) that the beans arrived in poor condition and had to be sold cheaply or thrown out, what can an exporter do? Digital photographs sent from the market back to source—a method already used in the tropical fruit trade—could resolve these doubts. But the French importers so far see no need to provide this information, nor do many of the Burkinabé exporters have the technology to receive it. At most, they can demand to see their importers' sales receipts, but this creates such tension that most exporters avoid it unless they believe they have been cheated out of significant sums. Perhaps not surprisingly, the commission relationships between exporters and importers are not only less familiar than contract relationships, but also often short-lived.

Both contract and commission relationships, then, leave the exporters vulnerable to exploitation and outright cheating. They all have stories about such incidents, and some are bitter. One exporter described the French importers as "the biggest bandits in the world." Another, however, emphasized that with time and experience the "wolves" posed less danger:

> After twenty years selling to Rungis there are things people do not do to you. They do them to the new guy. As they say in French, *les loups ne se mangent pas entre eux* (the wolves don't eat each other) . . . In other words, in the Mafia they respect each other. I'm an initiate now. At first, you do your baptism. You lose a lot of money. But then a brother protects you, and explains what you must do. Once you're known, it's done. You must always be vigilant, but I have fewer problems now.

Like other kinds of *métis,* in other words, the exporters acquire theirs by making and learning from mistakes (Scott 1998, 330). One thing they learn early on is the value of earning an importer's trust and loyalty—in other words, friendship. The importer who is also a friend is, by definition, an importer who will not cheat you (though he may expect favors) and who sympathizes when things go wrong—when a harvest fails or a truck breaks down. Such an importer also recognizes that friendship with an individual trade partner comes with a range of social (and potentially political) obligations and benefits. One exporter's description of his relationship with a particularly powerful French importer testifies to the value attached to such ties:

> When he comes to Burkina, he comes to the house, my family's house . . . and he comes to the chief's house, he knows his family. When we go to Paris, we visit him at home, because that's what

Burkina Faso: Rural Development and Patronage

85

friendship is . . . If (another import firm) calls and says "you produce quality green beans, we want to pay you X amount," I'll tell them I need to think about it, and then I'll call [my importer] and tell him . . . He will say *ooh la la,* and tell me I must not sell to them. That's friendship . . . [also] when he comes here, I have political friends, I introduce them. I take him to see ministers, and say, this is the man who buy the green beans. The ministers are content too. It makes a difference.

But not every exporter can hope to cultivate such a friendship. This is partly because only two or three French importers regularly pre-finance and purchase large quantities of green beans from Burkina Faso; the rest buy sporadically and only on commission. But it is also because not all the exporters have the authority and resources needed to earn these buyers' friendship. Some cannot repeatedly meet the quality and quantity specifications of their contracts because they do not exercise enough control over the production process. They cannot afford the temporary losses needed to win their growers' dedication, and they do not command the kind of social skills and status needed to win their buyers' respect. Put bluntly, the exporters who have enjoyed the most stable, generous relationships with their buyers are those who had the most going for them in the first place.

Meanings of Work

What we're doing is not just an intellectual and moral accomplishment.
Not at all. Economically, Madame, it's profitable! Provided, of course,
you've got the means.
—Exporter, Ouagadougou, April 1994

When the peasant wins, I win.
—Exporter, Bobo-Dioulasso, February 2000

In winter 2001, a French green bean importer sat at his office in Rungis and described Burkina Faso's latest season. It was *une situation dramatique,* he said, and ultimately a commercial bust. Increasingly unreliable airfreight connections were partly to blame (the Air France takeover of Air Afrique made things worse rather than better) but so were the Burkinabé exporters. He said they expected too much from the green beans, which faced an increasingly crowded European market, and that they could not, in any case, hope to export for more than four months a year. Inflated expectations led to careless spending, and ultimately the peasants were shortchanged. The exporters needed to accept that this market would buy only so many of Burkina Faso's green beans—probably not much more than 2,000 tons a year, he calculated, given surging exports from Senegal and Morocco, and the perennial dominance of Kenya. The market, moreover, would pay only so much for Burkina Faso's beans and, ultimately, support only so many of its exporters. Yet, he said with exasperation, even as demand for their beans shrank, the exporters' numbers increased—from fifteen to twenty-one between 2000 and 2001! There was simply not room for them all, he said; they were "condemned" to fail.

The French importer's assessment of the market was probably accurate, not least because he had spent most of his career building and supplying it. But his observation about the Burkinabé exporters' apparently irrational behavior raises an obvious question: why? Why did more and more people try to sell to a market that wanted fewer and fewer of them? The answer, I think, lies less in what the French importer called their "dreams" of miraculous improvement in the market itself than in the opportunities and status available to agro-exporters—especially those dealing in "non-traditional" commodities—in poor and predominantly agrarian countries such as Burkina Faso. These other meanings of agro-exporting work must, in turn, be understood in light of a vision of development that, since the early colonial era, has defined the incorporation of peasants into the world economy and agricultural modernity as a morally valid goal in itself, even if the peasants themselves benefit relatively little.

In colonial Upper Volta, this goal depended on the intermediary roles played by an assortment of local political authorities, elite merchants, and French colonial administrators. By the late 20th century, once Burkina Faso's postcolonial state had renounced active control over green bean exporting, responsibility for linking peasants to overseas markets fell to the private sector. At least some of the exporters are thoroughly versed in the era's neoliberal development discourse, and emphasize how, in contrast to the former state monopoly, they are *leger* (light, supple) and quality-conscious. They speak about how their entrepreneurial activity is generating wealth, and bringing the Burkinabé "brand" to the world market.

Aid agencies such as the World Bank, USAID, and Agence Francaise de Developpement (AFD) have, as mentioned earlier, all endorsed entrepreneur-led development, not least by aiding the entrepreneurs themselves.[36] France's AFD has provided the green bean exporters with the most direct support through its aforementioned program to "restructure" and "professionalize" the horticultural sector. By providing APEFEL with vehicles, an office in Ouaga-dougou (complete with secretaries, computers, telephones, and a fax machine) as well as funds for conferences and "learning tours" to Kenya, Zambia and Paris, the program has helped several APEFEL members pursue all their commercial activities, not just green bean exporting.

The young French expatriate administering the program out of AFD's Ouagadougou office acknowledged in 2000 that the funds had not yet accomplished their goal, and that some exporters were more professional than others. But he said that *on va faire le tri* ("we will sort them out," the same term used for green bean sorting) by denying aid to anyone found exporting substandard beans. In effect, AFD aimed to measure professionalism in terms of product quality—a proxy that would likely put more pressure on growers but would not necessarily lead to the consolidation of the export sector. Indeed, everyone in the business agreed that the quality of the green beans delivered to market depended more on exporters' relations with their growers than on the scale of their operations; with the right social skills, even the smallest exporters could therefore hope to forge relations that generated quality.

So to a certain extent, development aid makes exporting economically at-

Figure 3.7.
Green beans awaiting sale at the Rungis market, France. Burkinabé exporters seek to increase international appreciation of their country's "brand." Photo by Christophe Maître.

French Beans and Food Scares

tractive even if the market itself is not. But it would be wrong to conclude that aid alone, or the hope of attaining it, sustains otherwise marginally viable operations. The other important consideration here is the social and indeed moral status attached to the exporters' role. Many of them say that the best part of their work is "helping" peasants earn a decent living. The exporters talk about how much they enjoy the days when they pay their growers—"*c'est la fête*"—and about the improvements that green bean revenue has brought (or might eventually bring) to their communities. These range from the micro-trades women start with their personal earnings (selling dried fish or cooked foods) to village electrification. If nothing else, green beans give rural people a reason to stay put, rather than migrating to places where their livelihoods might prove even more precarious.[37] As one exporter says, "In doing this I feed many families. Many people earn from this work, and it pleases me to see this. People get by, doing this. It keeps the kids from leaving to go find work elsewhere, and that encourages me. The villagers are content where I work, because their children don't go to the city to become thieves. They have food, and they always have something to do."

In short, the exporters see their work as beneficent—as trade that aids. Even though their aid to the peasants may be unreliable and incommensurate with the peasants' own hard work, the exporters' claim still carries moral weight in urban educated Burkinabé society, where almost everyone lives with the burden of needy rural kin. And when things go relatively smoothly, the exporters' work does help rural people get by, which is not a small thing in a still predominantly rural and very poor country. But in the face of an increasingly competitive and demanding overseas market, the green bean exporters' own livelihoods have grown more uncertain. By the year 2000, they realized what they were up against; they knew that export horticulture was growing fastest and earning the highest prices in African countries where production took place on large, tightly monitored commercial farms. Some had even visited such farms in Kenya and Zambia as part of a World Bank-funded "learning tour," and marveled at their systematic quality control and white-glove hygiene. Yet they showed little interest in investing in their own version of the wage-labor plantation, even though Burkina Faso's land laws do not preclude this option. As most, a few exporters say that they would like to maintain their own farms in addition to contract relations with smallholders. "It's necessary to protect the producers," one of them said, referring to the country's peasantry, "and protecting them does not mean turning them into agricultural laborers."

Protecting peasant producers was also, of course, the stated social objective of colonial agricultural policies that opted for smallholder rather than plantation commodity production. It appealed to both colonial authorities and indigenous elites partly because it seemed less disruptive, but also because it did not interfere with the objective of extracting wealth from the countryside at minimal cost and risk. The colonial regime's use of harsh taxes and forced labor made blatant the contradictions of its peasant-based agricultural policies, and eventually made them unsustainable. In the postcolonial francophone green bean network, by contrast, the power to exploit rural land and labor is more dispersed, especially since the advent of neoliberal governance. The occupying forces are long gone; so too the strictures of state socialism. The downsized, deregulated state exercises little control over the day-to-day conduct of the network. Foreign aid organizations provide resources intended to encourage particular kinds of practices and relationships, but rarely oversee the widely scattered processes of negotiation, production, and exchange.

To an extent, this situation does protect Burkina Faso's green bean growers by giving them certain opportunities and options. They can appeal to exporters' moral obligations, and exploit their inability (or unwillingness) to spend much time in rural production sites. They can divert resources to more secure crops and markets or, depending on their circumstances, they can drop out of export production altogether. Thanks in part to the work of women traders, the domestic market for "European" vegetables is now no longer limited to European expatriates. Like foodstuffs from other parts of Africa and the world, vegetables such as green beans and salad greens have been incorporated into the region's historically pluralistic foodways—at least in the cities—and many people would eat more of them if their budgets allowed.[38]

But Burkina Faso's urban markets are already often glutted with fresh vegetables, and prices during the dry season especially are extremely low. For many vegetable growers in more remote regions, therefore, they do not offer a viable alternative to the overseas market. And while such growers enter into contract relations with exporters voluntarily, it is important to remember that such relations appeal to export firms, whether they are individuals with pickup trucks or corporations, only under certain political, economic, and social conditions.[39]

In the fresh vegetable trade between anglophone Africa and the United Kingdom, the conditions once conducive to smallholder contract farming changed as British supermarkets sought more "rational," consolidated supply chains. In Burkina Faso, smallholder green bean production remains feasible partly because of the French retail market's rather different priorities (as chapter 5 will discuss in greater detail), partly because of Burkinabé smallholders long-time experience, which gives intermediaries confidence that they can adapt to rising quality standards. Not least, persistent economic insecurity gives many smallholders little choice but to adapt to the market's standards, even though it means working harder for the same or declining returns. The conditions that compel smallholders to "self-exploit," as a scholar of Russian peasants once put it (Kautsky 1988), are clearly not unique to Burkina Faso. In some ways, they would look all too familiar to the contract farmers worldwide who produce commodities for globalized markets (Little and Watts 1994; Boyd and Watts 1997). That said, exactly how producers and intermediaries work within such conditions—how they negotiate and perceive the market's inequities, among other things—varies greatly even among commodity networks that deal in relatively similar goods. The next chapter illustrates this point by turning to Zambia, a country as poor as Burkina Faso, but one linked to the postcolonial fresh vegetable market through a very different set of cultural norms and social relationships.

4

Zambia

Settler Colonialism and Corporate Paternalism

For many years, urban planners' description of the Zambian capital Lusaka as a "garden city" seemed a cruel and even preposterous misnomer. Pot-holed and polluted, the city was more colloquially described as a pit. Indeed, parts of town rang with the sounds of a quarry, though the country's main mineral wealth lay several hours drive to the north. Lusaka's roadside rock-breakers, men and women who hammered limestone into gravel, epitomized to foreign journalists the disintegration of Zambia's once-booming economy.[1] But by the year 2000, the old planners' term for Lusaka had taken on an un-anticipated truth. The rock-breakers were still there, and probably not earning much more than the eight dollars a week they earned several years before. But now the roads they worked alongside led, in fact, to vast gardens—thousands of verdant acres producing the down-sized vegetables found in London's up-scale supermarkets: baby corn, baby carrots and baby patty pan squash; mini-ature chilies, *mangetout* peas, and, of course, fine-grade green beans. Lusaka had become a garden city on an industrial scale.

Agriculture on the margins of Lusaka was by no means new (Sanyal 1987), but now that it contributed to export earnings rather than simply the urban food supply, it fueled new hopes for economic recovery. Even though the horticul-tural sector (encompassing roses and fruits as well as vegetables) comprised only a small part of the national economy, it was by far the most dynamic part, growing at 20 percent a year.

Zambians had witnessed double-digit growth rates before, when postwar demand for the country's copper fueled what some observers saw as *the* African Industrial Revolution, a period of economic and social change "not seen in thousands of years" (Mitchell 1951, 21). The reversal of Copperbelt fortune from the mid-1970s onward gave cause for skepticism about any kind of boom, and the successes of the horticultural sector appeared particularly fragile. Apart from the intrinsic fragility of the commodities themselves, Zambia's vegetable export firms had to contend with supermarket clients who demanded much and brooked no slipups. More specifically, these supermarkets demanded that

Figure 4.1.
Factory attire at a vegetable packhouse outside Lusaka, Zambia. Photo by author.

their African fresh vegetable suppliers comply with stringent codes of standards covering everything from packhouse hygiene and packaging quality to environmental sustainability and social welfare. In addition—and in sharp contrast to their French counterparts—the U.K. supermarkets expected their suppliers to submit to ongoing tests of compliance, both on-site and at a distance. Suppliers who failed to keep "up to code" could be summarily "delisted," and possibly shut out of the U.K. market altogether.

To a certain extent, the U.K. supermarkets' strict standards reflected British consumers' concerns about how their food was made—concerns shaped by a recent history of food scares, as well as by a national press that made the most of corporate scandals, especially those related to food. But standards also served the interests of retailers seeking to increase their market share and assuage public worries about their already powerful control over the national food supply.

As of 2000, Zambia's vegetable export industry was even more concentrated than the United Kingdom food retail market. It consisted of two companies, both financed by foreign capital and run by European expatriates. Both expanded and upgraded rapidly in the 1990s. The larger of the two companies supplemented production on its own land with produce from other large-scale, white-owned farms. Both companies had taken modest steps to increase opportunities for black Zambians in vegetable exporting, as well as to reinvigorate an ailing, but more "Zambianized" rose export business. But these efforts took place within the confines of an unforgiving export market, an impoverished economy, and a society where race and class relations have been shaped by a history of white settler and mining company colonialism.

This history is crucial to the story of Zambia's entry into the "baby veg" market, and must be linked to and distinguished from the broader history of white settlers in British Africa. As the colony of Northern Rhodesia, it attracted only a fraction of the number of whites who settled in the more temperate Southern Rhodesia (now Zimbabwe) and Kenya. Although Northern Rhodesia's white farmers enjoyed market protection and privileged access to the fertile land along the rail line, they never gained the political clout of their counterparts in the other two colonies. Nor did their presence provoke the kind of violent liberation struggles the latter experienced.

In 2000, Zambians both black and white dismissed the possibility of white farming becoming the source of a Zimbabwean-style political crisis; the land is too abundant, they said, and the whites too few. Yet during the colonial era, Northern Rhodesia's white settlers emphasized their common community with their Southern Rhodesian counterparts, and chafed under the authority of Britain's Colonial Office. To them, government statements about the "paramountcy of native interests" smacked of the effete and easy moralizing of London-based bureaucrats and politicians who, they believed, could not possibly appreciate the challenges of "pioneering" civilization in Central Africa (Gann 1964, 241–3).

In postcolonial Zambia, the white farmers growing vegetables for export faced a terrific irony. Not only had the British government stopped trying to regulate their affairs but so, too, had the Zambian government. Indeed, rapid liberalization in the 1980s and 1990s left Zambian agriculture more open not only to foreign investment, but also to competition from agro-export powers ranging from South Africa to the United States. White farmers complained that, because of such competition, they could no longer make a living just producing grain, beef, and milk for the domestic market. So they took up growing baby vegetables—crops that Zambia's climate and cheap labor could produce nearly year-round. Yet in venturing into this frontier of high-value export agriculture, Zambia's commercial farmers fell under a new version of British rule. As suppliers of a market that is both highly concentrated and acutely anxious about the "goodness" of its food in every sense, the farmers found themselves more subject to the economic dictates and moral politics of its former ruler than ever before.

This chapter examines how the overlapping histories of colonialism and corporate paternalism have shaped the cultural economy of vegetable exporting in postcolonial Zambia. These histories gave rise to material conditions, social relations, and conventions of quality assurance dramatically different than those characterizing vegetable exporting in Burkina Faso. Together they make for a commodity network than in some ways runs much more smoothly than the francophone green bean trade, and that appears more socially progressive and technologically advanced. As in the many other South-North commodity networks where suppliers must help to boost the brand image and the profit margins of corporate retailers, however, managerial talk of "partnerships" and "social responsibility" jars with the retailers' determination to obtain maximum quality at minimum cost.

From Frontier to Company State

For more than two centuries after the establishment of a small Dutch colony on the Cape of Good Hope in the mid-17th century, European merchant companies viewed southern Africa primarily as a landmass to be circumnavigated en route to Asia. But the discovery of first diamonds in Kimberley in 1867 and then gold in the Transvaal in 1886 dramatically changed the region's relationship to an industrializing Europe. The promise of vast wealth fueled the European scramble for the continent's territory and gave rise to a particular form of colonialism in southern Africa. Speculators large and small arrived first, and in many cases settled. Then came the need for capital to build mines and railroads. So Britain, the region's dominant imperial power, reverted to the mercantile practice of granting royal charters to well-financed companies. The charters gave the companies rights to develop and administer vast concessions of land, with relatively little supervision from the homeland government. The companies' presence in turn shaped not merely the economic infrastructure of the region but the entire colonial culture, well beyond the reaches of the mining towns they built.

This culture drew on Britain's own vision of a "civilizing mission." France's *mission civilatrice* in West Africa, as described in the previous chapter, aspired

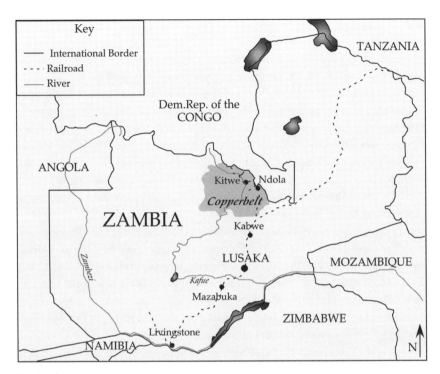

Figure 4.2.
Zambia

to create an empire modeled after its own countryside, where the economy was enriched by science and technology, but grounded in peasant communities and values. Britain's civilizing mission in southern Africa, as understood by the civil servants sent to carry it out, did not really focus on the countryside, though agriculture officials saw good political and economic reasons to support the emergence of a "progressive" African peasant class. Rather, industrial work was to be the "great civilizer." The experience of wage labor was supposed to teach African workers an appreciation for money and what it could buy; for punctuality and order; for the Protestant work ethic, and indeed for Christianity itself. Urban living would also give Africans an opportunity to witness and emulate European civilization (Trollope 1973, 368; Schreuder 1976, 300–3).

The area now known as Zambia did not initially appear an attractive place to bring this civilization. It was landlocked and malarial, and lacked fertile highlands. Unlike much of West Africa, it also lacked the political and commercial infrastructure needed to mobilize peasant-based export agriculture. When the missionary David Livingstone first traveled through the region in the early 1850s, he found local populations preoccupied with defending themselves against gun and slave traders from the coast and cattle raiders from the south (Livingstone 1858).

For Livingstone, disease and insecurity signaled the need for British colonialism and settlement. By bringing in modern medicine and enforcing the abolition of slave trading, he believed, the British imperial presence could open up the region to "commerce and Christianity." Although the British government initially opposed formal occupation, Livingstone's vision appealed to Cecil J. Rhodes, the British-born South African entrepreneur who made his fortune in diamonds and then gold. Explorers' accounts had convinced Rhodes that more fortune lay in the Zambezi river region (Zambezia), and in 1889 he received a Royal Charter for his British South Africa Company (BSAC) in order to claim it.

Charter (or "concessionary") company colonialism enabled Europe's imperial powers to open up regions for resource extraction and trade at minimal risk and cost (at least in theory) to their own governments (Coquery-Vidrovitch 1972). In Zambezia, BSAC agreed that in return for rights to any mineral wealth discovered, it would build a railroad, maintain law and order, protect British territorial claims, and all the while respect the laws and property of the African populations in its domain (Gann 1964; Slinn 1971).

Over the next several years, Rhodes relied on both private troops and British civil servants to establish BSAC authority over first Southern and then Northern Rhodesia. Where the local chiefs resisted treaties, the company used force. From an early date, then, corporate capital wielded formidable clout in Zambia. Together the two Rhodesias made up, in essence, a company state, but one that depended on the British government for diplomatic and military support as well as administrative personnel. Even after the administration of Northern Rhodesia was taken over by Britain's Colonial Office in 1923, the BSAC retained significant landholdings as well as mineral rights. The investments and decisions it made on behalf of its shareholders had an enduring effect on Zambia's economic geography (Galbraith 1974).

From the beginning company rule also brought uneven development. Although Northern Rhodesia would eventually yield far greater mineral wealth than its southern neighbor, it was first and foremost expected to yield labor for Southern Rhodesia's mines and settler farms. With this priority in mind, the company invested in the transportation and administrative structures needed to assure the flow of labor—a railroad, a system of African taxation, and labor recruitment. But it neglected and indeed discouraged African education, which was considered a waste of shareholders' money, as well as a potential threat to the docility of the labor force (Kuster 1999, 238).

The company also did not encourage settlement in Northern Rhodesia, partly because it did not want settler farms to divert labor migration to the south.

Apart from missionaries, then, most of the early whites in the north were transient traders, prospectors and hunters (Brelsford 1965). By the turn of the century, however, rising land values in Southern Rhodesia sent poorer white farmers to squat on land further north, where they were known to steal crops and cattle from African homesteads (Palmer 1983, 92). The British high commissioner for South Africa, Lord Selborne, warned that if the company allowed many white settlers into Northern Rhodesia,

> they will live to be sorry for it. Those settlers will not, as a rule, succeed. They will consequently be discontented; they will try to live on the natives, in itself a great evil, and they will vent their discontent on the British South Africa Company . . . They will expect the Administration to coddle them, and the railway to carry their goods for nothing. They will begin to look to politics as a remedy for economic success. (Palmer 1983, 92)

The BSAC ultimately developed a policy of "selective" land sales in the hopes of limiting the settler population to a small number of "stable, substantial," preferably Anglo-Saxon farmers. But Northern Rhodesia's reputation as a wild, vast frontier of "cheap land and cheap cattle" attracted a more motley collection of prospective buyers: Afrikaners who had lost their land in the Anglo-Boer war, traders of suspect ethnicity (described as "Peruvian types"), and British nobility who had no intention of actually living there (Vickery 1986, 75).

The preferred settlement areas were along the still-advancing rail line, and especially on the fertile, well-watered Tonga Plateau (which has since become one of the centers of export vegetable production). The incoming settlers applied to buy large tracts of land—on average 4,000 acres per tract—which were in many cases used by Africans for farming, cattle grazing, or wood-gathering. Although the BSAC had pledged not to interfere with any of these activities, it nonetheless sold the land, though requesting that the new owners not disturb African livelihoods. Not surprisingly, this ambiguous compromise led to conflicts between settlers and Africans, especially as both populations expanded during the first three decades of the twentieth century. By 1915 officials in Northern Rhodesia had agreed that the "permanent solution" to such conflicts was to create Native Reserves, similar to those in Britain's other settler colonies (Vickery 1986, 89).

Putting Africans on reserves obviously contradicted previous pledges to respect their property rights. But this policy ultimately won support even from the officials and missionaries most sympathetic to African interests, who reasoned that white settlement was inevitable and irreversible, and that reserves would protect Africans against further property disputes and the presumed dangers of overly rapid socioeconomic change. This vision of benign, "protective" segregation accepted that Africans on reserves would not have direct access to the rail line, because their "simple wants and way of life" did not depend on markets as much as whites (Vickery 1986, 88). But it also assumed that the reserves would allow Africans plenty of room to practice their traditional extensive agriculture and cattle grazing. The settlers, however, wanted reserve landholdings restricted to "bare subsistence" levels, to force Africans to come work on their farms (Gann 1964, 217).

The Native Reserves marked the first of a series of concessions won by settlers despite their relatively small numbers and the ongoing doubts (and at times outright criticism) expressed by some members of the Colonial Office (Wetherell 1979). Another important measure was the Maize Control Act of 1935–6, which assured white farmers a better price than African farmers. Proponents of the Maize Act argued that it would "protect" African farmers against shady private traders. But, as one Colonial Office official pointed out, the Act would also created a maize market "rigged so as to keep in production a body of white farmers who if exposed to the full blast of native competition would disappear."[2] One Colonial Office member said that the need for such rigging demonstrated that Northern Rhodesia "should never have been allowed" to become a white settler colony, to which another could only reply, "We have got the European farmer . . . and we cannot kill him or even avoid keeping him alive" (Palmer 1983, 101).

Despite such attitudes in the higher reaches of the colonial administration, white farmers secured government protection at least in part because they enjoyed much more political clout than even the most important African chiefs. In the early colonial period, they exercised this clout largely through the informal channels of settler social life. Memoirs and other historical accounts of this period portray a predominantly male white community whose members lived on large isolated farms, but met at social clubs, bars and sporting events in the railroad towns.[3] By the mid-teens, white farmers had founded a cooperative society as well as the Northern Rhodesian Farmers Association. In 1923, the colony passed franchise laws that gave only literate, male, and propertied British citizens the right to vote. But elections represented only a small part of settler political activity; the cocktail parties known as "sundowners" could prove more important political occasions than formal meetings (Gann 1964, 239).

Yet all these privileges failed to help Northern Rhodesia's white farmers with one of their perennial problems: lack of labor. In certain regions, notably the Tonga Plateau, Africans became commercial farmers in their own right. But many more migrated seasonally rather than work on settler farms. Mine work in Southern Rhodesia or later Northern Rhodesia's own Copperbelt was perhaps more dangerous than farm work, but it paid much better. Indeed, even farmers in Southern Rhodesia paid three times the wages of those in the North (Vickery 1986, 101). But wages were not the only issue; especially during the early colonial period, farm work was associated with beatings, inadequate food, and bosses who treated their workers like slaves (and many of the white farmers had, in fact, migrated from South Africa, a former slave society). Tellingly, when Africans arrested for non-payment of taxes were given a choice between three months of farm labor and going to prison, they chose prison (Vickery 1986, 101).

During periods of extreme economic hardship (such as the years of the Great Depression), African laborers tolerated work on Northern Rhodesian settler farms. Otherwise, farmers who mistreated their workers often quickly lost them. In centers of white settlement like the Tonga Plateau, Africans spread the word about cruel and unfair employers, who were subsequently subjected to unofficial boycotts. But white farm households who cultivated a reputation for decency might enjoy a relatively stable labor supply. A good "boss," for example, took care of workers' pecuniary emergencies, while his wife provided nursing care (Gann 1964, 199).

The farm labor scarcity was compounded by the fact that for many years, farms, like other employers, neither sought nor were encouraged to hire women. The reasons provided for this bias were varied and to a certain extent contradictory. On one hand, white farmers claimed that women were "lazy" and, insofar as they needed training and distracted male workers, "more trouble than they were worth." On the other hand, members of the colonial administration recognized that female farming fed the male labor force; they feared that hiring women would jeopardize the colony's food supply (Hansen 1989, 124). Only after World War II, when the booming Copperbelt intensified the scarcity of male farm labor, did some farmers turn to women for certain tasks, such as grading tobacco.

By 2000, Zambia's white farmers generally did not lack for labor, except for certain skilled positions. Yet they remained conscious of their reputation as employers, especially as Zimbabwe's President Robert Mugabe stepped up threats to expropriate his country's white owned farmland. In particular, Zambia's white farmers remained conscious of the standards of employment and employer paternalism established during the reign of "King Copper."

Industrialization, "Detribalization," and Settler Anxiety

The development of copper mining brought about the second stage of company-controlled economic development in Northern Rhodesia. Although the BSAC initially granted concessions to several mining companies, control of the industry quickly fell two corporations: Ernest Oppenheimer's Anglo-American Corporation and the American-owned Roan Selection Trust (Sklar 1975, 30–32). Such concentration made possible the industry's rapid growth; it also gave the companies nearly total control over the construction and governance of the Copperbelt (Gann 1964, 206–7). Certainly the Northern Rhodesia government could not have afforded to do as much. Because the companies paid most of their taxes in the United Kingdom, the government had no budget either to complement corporate-driven development in the Copperbelt or match it in any of the colony's other provinces, where services and infrastructure remained poor (Roberts 1976, 192–3).

The companies quickly took on the region's historic repute as "the white man's grave." After bringing tropical disease experts to provide advice on malaria eradication, they built hospitals, drained swamps, and instituted worker feeding programs, all helping to make the Copperbelt "as healthy as any place in Africa."[4] The two corporations then built a series of company towns next to their respective mines. They planned the neighborhoods and allocated the housing; they built roads and sewer systems, sports fields and cinemas. Company-built housing was segregated by race as well as employment level, but even the simplest dwellings were sturdy and well-ventilated, and considered superior to worker housing elsewhere in southern Africa (Gann 1964, 211). In the tin mining town of Broken Hill, the company provided five-acre plots for workers to build family-size compounds and keep gardens. In short, Northern Rhodesia company towns outdid their models in the United States. Within their boundaries, the relationship between employer and employee became "not a simple exchange of money for work, but of money plus house, land, rations, local government and social services for work" (Wilson 1941, 22–23).

The company's provision of all these goods and services did not, however, prevent mine workers from organizing to push for better pay and living conditions. A strike at Roan Antelope in 1935 set the precedent for a series of actions in the 1940s. Outside the mines, meanwhile, associations of African teachers and clerks lobbied the companies and the government for reforms, and domestic servants (at that time nearly all male) staged strikes (Roberts 1976, 203–4; Hansen 1989, 166–9). Yet farm laborers, historically the most transient and geographically dispersed workforce, remained unorganized (Datta 1988).

For observers of Northern Rhodesia's rapid industrialization, the workers' actions demonstrated that town life was driving "detribalization," a process with monumental consequences. As the director of the Rhodes-Livingstone Institute, Godfrey Wilson, described it: "Over the heart of a poor and primitive continent civilization has laid a finger of steel; it has stirred a hundred tribes together; it has brought them new wealth, new ambitions, new knowledge, new interests, new faiths and new problems." (Wilson 1941, 9).

One of the central problems, according to Wilson, was that change was occurring not just rapidly but unevenly. Remote rural areas had benefited little from the colony's new wealth, while in urban areas conditions varied from the relatively well-serviced company towns to the "thoroughly unhygienic" housing found in government-designated Native Locations (Gray 1960, 258). In the face of such disparities, Wilson claimed, "men and women alike find themselves morally and intellectually unsuited for the new conditions" (Wilson 1941, 14). Many Europeans, however, worried not that Africans were unprepared for modern urban life, but rather that they liked it all too well. In Lusaka, the capital city, Europeans looked disapprovingly upon their servants' taste for ballroom dancing, fancy clothing, and gambling (Hansen 1989, 191).

The colony's Europeans also looked to their own media for evidence that the "European style of life" remained, in the face of apparent African "detribalization," different and superior. Newspapers with predominantly white readerships featured reports on white society events in Lusaka and fashion shows in London, recipes for fish and chips and fruit tarts, and critiques of improper and unhygienic behavior (Kallman 1999). A regular column in the *Northern News,* "The Man in the North," discussed the challenges of finding clean restaurant food in a land where "savages" ate with their hands.[5] Advice columnists and advertisements promoted cleaning products that would help women keep house "like in London" (Hansen 1989, 57).[6]

While identifying culturally with Europe (and especially the United Kingdom), most settlers increasingly resented the British government's role in colonial affairs (Kallman 1999). By the late 1940s, they openly criticized Britain's taxation of the copper industry and its unwillingness to support the colony's consumer goods industries (which meant that many creature comforts had to be imported), and above all the Colonial Office's support for African land rights. Seeing themselves as the target of Britain's postwar "civilizational guilt complex," (Gann 1964, 416) the colony's white settlers called for an end to British rule and the creation of a federation of the two Rhodesias and Nyasaland (now Malawi).

Closer ties with the white supremacist regime of Southern Rhodesia, in particular, appeared the best way to protect settler interests (Gray 1960). But the Central African Federation, formed in 1953, only fueled the region's African nationalist movement. Independence for Northern Rhodesia appeared inevitable by the end of the 1950s; with the election of Kenneth Kaunda as the first president of Zambia in 1964, it became official. Over the next several years, an estimated 50 percent of Zambia's white farmers left (Dodge 1977, 66). They had never been the target of anti-colonial hostilities (in contrast to Kenya and later Southern Rhodesia) and they were not threatened with expropriation. Still, some were no doubt put off by Kaunda's diplomatic break with Southern Rhodesia in favor of closer political and economic ties with socialist states such as Tanzania (Roberts 1976, 225). If nothing else, it was clear that the white farmers, despite their wealth, would no longer enjoy as much political clout as they once did. Even among Zambia's Europeans they were a small minority (than less than 10 percent) and did not necessarily share the concerns of whites working in Lusaka or the Copperbelt.

It was well known, however, that the few hundred white farms left in Zambia produced the bulk of the country's maize supply, as well as important quantities of minor crops such as fruits and vegetables. Despite a few localized postwar government programs aimed at improving peasant agriculture, colonial economic development policies did little to make commercial farming a feasible and attractive livelihood for black Africans, and nothing to staunch the exodus of young men and women to the cities (Palmer 1983, 108). The relatively prosperous African farming communities, such as those in Tonga Plateau's Mazabuka District, owed less to government help than to particularly favorable ecological conditions and good market access (Vickery 1986).

Independence did not radically alter the government's neglect of African agriculture. Kaunda's political philosophy of Humanism—advocating "man-centered" development over the pursuit of wealth—invoked the ideals of a supposedly classless, non-materialistic pre-industrial Africa (Kaunda 1971). But in fact most of his constituents lived directly or indirectly off industrial wages, and they wanted their government to provide jobs, schooling, and good urban services. For the first decade of independence, these development priorities prevailed. The mining industry was nationalized, and its highest management positions "Zambianized" (Burawoy 1972). By 1971, Zambia's mineworkers earned an average of 1,000 pounds annually, on par with wages in Europe, and at least five times more than Zambian farm laborers. Meanwhile, Zambian food imports doubled in value between 1964 and 1974, even as much of the country's arable land remained uncultivated (Roberts 1976, 232–6). At the time, this trend provoked little concern; copper prices were strong, the conditions of international lending easy, and theories of Third World modernization had, after all, predicted a "take-off" like Zambia's (Rostow 1960; Ferguson 1999).

The 1975 collapse of world copper prices exposed the precariously narrow, heavily indebted foundations of Zambian prosperity. But even then neither the government nor international donors made serious efforts to diversify the national economy, which drew 90 percent of its export earnings from copper (Ferguson 1999). Instead the government undertook a series of liberalization measures, recommended by the International Monetary Fund and the World Bank. These failed to reduce the national debt but succeeded in driving down just about every other measure of national economic and social well-being.

Between 1970 and 1983, real per capita earnings fell by one-fifth. Infant mortality rates rose to pre-independence levels, while child malnutrition rates climbed from 6 percent in 1980 to 23 percent in 1991 (White 1997, 59).

Liberalization was supposed to redress the "urban bias" of the government's market interventions, and thus benefit producers of food and export crops (Sano 1988). In reality, rising production costs, the deterioration of the country's infrastructure, and the depressed domestic market turned the 1980s into a difficult decade for Zambian farmers, both black and white. Mounting political unrest and government flip-flopping did not help matters any. After anti-austerity riots in the Copperbelt in 1986, the Kaunda administration first abandoned its economic reform plan and then, three years later, undertook a new, equally unpopular one (White 1997, 60). The government that had Zambianized its foreign-owned industries now scrambled to lure foreign capital back into the country. But there would be no quick fixes. By the time Kaunda's party was voted out of power in 1991, the "African industrial revolution" was a fading memory; Zambia had become one of the poorest countries on earth.

From Mineral to Vegetable: Corporate Horticulture

If you want to be a player on the world stage, you've got to be at
standard. It's a sad economic fact. And number one is management.
Number two is having the right infrastructure.
—Upper level manager, Zambian horticultural export company

Although late-1980s liberalization proved politically fatal for the Kaunda regime, it generated a fresh crop of agro-export initiatives. Relaxed foreign exchange controls gave producers of export goods easier access to hard currency, which commercial farmers needed in order to buy spare parts and agricultural chemicals from abroad. They needed it so badly, in fact, that initially it did not matter if their export sales were profitable, as long as they earned enough from sales on the domestic market to keep their farms operating.

The first fruit and vegetable exporters in the late 1980s were predominantly white farm households with enough land and capital to cultivate a few exportable crops alongside the maize and livestock. These households typically also had contacts in the United Kingdom, and some idea about how to locate wholesale buyers there. Initially they experimented with crops that, for whatever reason, they thought might sell well. Based on what they knew about trends in London restaurant hors d'oeuvre menus, for example, some farmers grew melons and avocado. Others exported white asparagus, and even sweet corn.

They managed to find buyers for these products because the United Kingdom food retail market in the late 1980s and early 1990s was not nearly as concentrated, demanding, or abundantly supplied as it would soon become. In sub-Saharan Africa, only Kenya sold much horticultural produce to Britain. So for a few years, it was possible for several of Zambia's commercial farms to export directly, despite their lack of experience and specialized facilities. By the mid-1990s, however, a series of changes on both continents shrunk both the field of exporters and the size of their commodities.

First, the Zambian economy continued to relax currency controls, so that farmers (like everyone else) could buy dollars or pounds at the bank; they did not need to export melons. Second, access to the British retail market became much more difficult, as the largest supermarkets "rationalized" their supply base and imposed stricter safety and quality standards on those who remained. Lastly, Zambia's 1991 elections made it newly attractive to foreign investment. Well before foreign multinationals moved back into the country's decrepit Copperbelt at the end of the 1990s, two emerging market investment firms had put millions of dollars into upgrading horticultural production and processing facilities.

The first of these investors, the Commonwealth Development Corporation (CDC), was at the time an arm of the British government, though soon to be partially privatized.[7] It bought a private farm on the outskirts of Lusaka in the early 1990s. The University of Zambia also took a minor stake in this venture. The farm had previously supplied vegetables to the Lusaka market, and already had some packing and cold storage facilities in place. The CDC brought in expatriate managers for what became York Farms, built additional facilities, and expanded and diversified the farm's production. For a number of years York was the largest and then the only vegetable exporter in Zambia, with several hundred hectares under cultivation. It also produced roses for export, as well as maize and soybeans for the local market.

In 1995, a new company, Agriflora, began exporting fresh vegetables from Zambia. The company's founder and general manager, a young British entrepreneur who spent his childhood in Kenya and studied water management in the United Kingdom, came to Zambia in 1991 with an initial interest in export floriculture. The country's improved image in the eyes of foreign investors made it possible, he said, "for people like myself" to access long-term finance. Greenhouse-grown roses, in particular, require substantial up-front financing— about a half million dollars per acre. In the early 1990s, dozens of Zambians received foreign donor-supported loans for rose farming, but most failed relatively quickly, often because they did not keep pace with the rising standards of the European flower market.[8] Agriflora, however, started on a larger scale and kept growing.

In 1997, the investment firm TransZambezi Industries (TZI) bought a majority share in Agriflora. Incorporated in the British Virgin Islands, TZI had previously invested mostly in Zimbabwean industries and services. But Zambia, according to Agriflora's founder, "had started to get a reputation as a peaceful country with a good future," and British food retailers as well as investors were taking an interest in its horticultural potential.

Initially Agriflora had no farms of its own; all its production came from twenty-five to thirty outgrowers, medium-sized commercial farm households who, in several cases, had previously exported vegetables directly. Most of these farms (like the white farming community in general) were clustered around Lusaka or the town of Mazabuka, one-and-a-half hour's drive to the south. As before, they needed hard currency as well as liquidity; *mangetout* peas brought in much more regular income than maize. Now, however, they also needed an intermediary to package their produce and make sure it met the U.K. market's increasingly rigorous and complex standards. Agriflora became this intermediary. But like York Farms, it needed to work through a British import firm in order to do business with the country's top supermarkets. The export company managers depended on their respective "agents" at these firms not only to arrange purchases but also to help them understand and implement supermarket standards, and to demonstrate the kind of innovative and committed spirit that the retailers expected of their suppliers. Especially because the two Zambian export firms were competing against large and well-established produce exporters in Kenya and Zimbabwe, they needed to carve out high-value niches.

In the late 1990s, Agriflora began purchasing farmland on the outskirts of Lusaka. This move into production departed from the common wisdom of the horticultural industry in the 1980s, when large companies typically relied on contract farming (Jaffee 1994). It responded, however, to the supermarkets' concerns about control and reliability. As Agriflora's owner explained, "the markets are forever saying 'well, how do you know the outgrowers are going to produce it tomorrow? What if they wake up and decide, well, we don't want to do it'?" By buying first hundreds and then thousands of acres of land, Agriflora became a more credible supplier.

By the end of the 1990s, Zambia still had only two vegetable export companies, but both had established themselves as year-round horticultural exporters, each boasting state-of-the-art packing and cold storage facilities. Compared to Burkina Faso's green bean export business, the Zambian industry's product range was impressively diverse. York and Agriflora exported not just green beans (referred to as French beans, and always trimmed in advance), but also runner beans, *mangetout* peas, sweet peas, baby corn, baby patty squash, baby leeks, baby chilies, and roses. They packed most of their vegetables in

Figure 4.3.
Ready to be wrapped. Combinations of pre-trimmed, pre-packed vegetables offer Zambian horticultural exporters higher value than single-vegetable packages. Photo by author.

125- to 500-gram plastic "punets," some in colorful three-vegetable arrangements. Agriflora also assembled "high care" products—chopped vegetable combinations, suitable for stir-frying.

Together, the two companies made export horticulture the most dynamic part of the Zambian economy. In a country where poverty had only worsened for years on end (by 1998, 73 percent of the total population lived below the poverty line[9]), the horticultural companies' rapid growth generated support, but also expectations.

The support came from a government and a foreign aid community eager to promote private sector success stories, especially ones that created jobs in and around Lusaka. Horticulture is much more labor intensive than other kinds of commercial agriculture in Zambia, and employs a much higher proportion of women. In 2000, Agriflora employed 3,500 workers, approximately 60 percent female (not counting workers on its outgrowers' farms) and York Farms 2,500, approximately 80 percent female.[10] Compared to what mineworkers earned two decades earlier, most horticultural industry workers were hardly well-paid. At least 60 percent were classified as seasonal or casual labor, and in 2000 most, whether as packhouse workers or piece-rate field pickers, earned little above the country's minimum wage of approximately one U.S. dollar per day. But for the government and foreign donors, the standard for comparison was not the prosperous past, but rather the current conditions of widespread unemployment and irregularly paid work in the informal economy. By these standards, a dollar a day looked good.

In order to encourage further job creation, German, Norwegian, and EU aid monies helped the two companies, as the dominant members of the Zambia Export Growers Association (ZEGA), open a private horticultural school in 1998. Christened the ZEGA Training Trust, the school offered on-farm technical training for certain company employees (such as crop sprayers and field managers) as well as a two-year degree program that would produce graduates capable of filling technical and management positions previously staffed by expatriates.

The companies' interests in the training program were both economic and political. First, they needed more skilled labor for technical and middle-managerial positions than Zambia, with no history of horticulture, offered. As one Agriflora manager put it, "The expertise wasn't exactly sitting on the shelf." They also needed more of these skilled employees than they could afford to import from abroad.[11] In addition, the two companies' top managers wanted to show that export horticulture offered black Africans opportunities for advancement.

For its part, the Zambian government allowed the Training Trust to use a public agricultural college as its campus, and exempted ZEGA from certain taxes and duties. Altogether, the corporations running Zambia's vegetable export industry have benefited not just from foreign investment capital and from the government's eagerness to attract more of the same, but also, especially in the case of Agriflora, from "trickle down" development aid. The latter reflects in part the donor agencies' enthusiasm for private enterprise development in general, and private sector "non-traditional" export agriculture more specifically (Little and Dolan 2000). But it also reflects the companies' successful performance of a familiar role in Zambia. By demonstrating how they were bringing the country not merely jobs and foreign exchange but also advanced skills and technologies, they raised hopes that they were capable of, as one Agriflora manager put it, "revolutionizing Africa."

The mining industry, of course, claimed this role first. And while Zambia's two vegetable export companies, as of 2000, hardly compared in scale to the companies that built the Copperbelt, their managers recognized the expectations created by a history of corporate paternalism in Zambia.[12] Unlike the Copperbelt mining companies, Agriflora and York Farms did not have to compete with other employers by offering high wages. But their managers still saw good reason for, as one of them put it, "looking after your people." For one, they needed workers motivated for tasks such as picking, grading, and trimming baby vegetables—tasks that, although classified as "unskilled," nonetheless require considerable attentiveness and precision. A York Farms manager, referring to the company's practice of distributing daily a high-protein energy drink to all its workers, explained, "Let's be fairly hard about it. If our people are not healthy and happy, we're not going to get the work from them." Agriflora's cafeteria served the traditional meal of maize porridge and beans, but added meat on weekends—"to encourage them," according to a packhouse manager. For a company to offer workers free or subsidized food and drink is not, of course, unusual, but it takes on particular significance in countries where many workers may get barely enough to eat. Agriflora also provided workers' buses to and from Lusaka, and on-site sports fields.

The managers also had to consider how their employees talked about and represented their companies. They worried, not unlike their U.K. corporate customers, about press coverage, especially by scandal-hunting journalists. One York Farms manager, for example, noted how the company paid special attention to the appearance of the crops and the workers in the one field visible from the main road. More generally, both companies maintain much tighter access to their facilities than do the export companies in Burkina Faso, and their managers referred repeatedly to the media's unfair portrayal of African horticulture. Consumers in the United Kingdom, said one Agriflora manager, assume people like himself are "those guys in Africa who are whipping the people in the fields, making them work instead of going to school, they work them until they're dead and then don't give them an aspirin when they've got a headache; that's the perception, because only the negative side has ever been painted."

But the managers also wanted to foster good relations with the "local community" of Lusaka, rather than having everyone "looking over the fence." Such considerations became especially important in light of the Zimbabwean government's mounting hostility towards white landholders. The Zambian company managers stressed, however, that their situation was entirely different, not only because of the relative abundance of land, but also because of the industry's image. "We're not really classified as 'big white farmer'" said one Agriflora manager. "It's more corporate, investing big money, creating lots of jobs . . . and therefore I think that it's seen as a very positive development."

In fact, both companies' top managers were all white, and Agriflora, for most of its history, had depended on white farmers for much of its produce. But the distinction between "corporate" and "white farmer" enterprise does make sense in Zambia—and indeed, throughout southern Africa—and it is understandable why the horticultural industry wanted to be identified with the former rather than the latter. Foreign corporations in the Copperbelt had brought jobs and infrastructure, and had eventually conceded to labor's demands for better employment conditions. Their investments brought Zambians, or at least some of them, a taste of prosperity and a sense of progress (Ferguson

1999). White farmers, by contrast, were historically viewed as some of the most abusive and lowest-paying employers, and as the political opponents of modernization. Although they produced much of the country's food, they were not seen as contributing to its economic development in any broader sense.

The Outgrowers

In its basic geography, Zambian horticultural production developed directly out of "traditional" white settler agriculture. As of 2000, it occupied only a small fraction of the country's arable land, but it was some of the most fertile, irrigable land, and within a 90-minute drive (on generally good roads) of Lusaka and its airport. The farms, although small compared to their Zimbabwean counterparts, are much larger than those of most black Zambians.

In other ways, however, horticulture is as non-traditional in Zambia as the crops it produces. While farm management and labor in Zambia has historically been primarily male, most of the horticultural outgrowers in 2000, like most of their workers, were women. It should be noted, however, that the number of outgrowers fluctuated and had dropped considerably from a few years before, for reasons discussed below. Agriflora at one point had twenty-five to thirty outgrowers; by 2000 it had only six or seven.

The remaining growers were white women whose husbands or male relatives managed their farms' production of maize and beef. The women had taken responsibility for the vegetables in part because (like "farm wives" elsewhere in the world [Sachs 1996]) their time was considered more flexible. But at least a few of them had also been attracted by the challenge and even, as they described it, the "fun" of growing novel crops. The outgrowers living around the town of Mazabuka, for example, belonged to a community of white farm households who had known each other for years. Members of this community kept in touch via radio phones (as regular phone lines were often down) and socialized at the town's polo and golf clubs. A number of the women had taken up horticulture around the same time, and they consulted each other frequently about their crops.

From the beginning, Zambia's outgrowers hired women to pick their crops, just as the company packhouses hired mostly women to sort, trim, and pack produce. It is taken for granted in the industry that picking is woman's work because, as one York Farms manager put it, "The chaps are just not dexterous enough for it." Picking work requires not only "dexterity,"[13] but also a tolerance for long and often irregular hours (especially during peak harvest times), much stooping, and an ability to work quickly—picking pays piece-rate—yet attentively. One outgrower said that her average pickers earned the equivalent of 50

Figure 4.4.
Field workers on a Zambian farm. The vast majority of vegetable pickers are women, who are considered more "dexterous" than men. Photo by author.

pounds a month, but the fastest earned twice that much, even when they did not work every day.

Indeed, women's domestic responsibilities made missed days inevitable, and were among the reasons why few were promoted to higher-paying, more permanent positions as crop scouts, field managers, or sprayers.[14] In addition, some of these jobs required more education than most rural Zambian women have, and pesticide spraying, in particular, was off-limits for women due to the possible risks to unborn children. Despite these constraints, the outgrowers emphasized that one of the reasons they liked their work was that it enabled them to create many jobs for women (the number ranged from 60 to 500 workers, depending on farm size) who, they said, would spend their earnings responsibly, unlike many men.

The outgrowers did not start off with much expertise. One woman noted that in the beginning, "What I knew about gardening was dangerous." Although some women had previously grown vegetables for their own families, the varieties they produced for export were foreign to the typical meat-centered diet of most Anglo and Afrikaner farm households. The aesthetic quality standards were also much stricter than those for the local market. The outgrowers received some counsel from Agriflora agronomists, but they saw many of their crops fail. As one said, "Five years ago when we started, we had fun, we did all sorts of silly things . . . Anne[15] and I were guinea pigs, basically. We tried pots of spring onions; we tried melons. Because this was all new—all these new ideas coming in—nobody had a clue how to grow anything. The baby aubergines weren't babies. We had a lot of good laughs over these sorts of things."

The outgrowers also enjoyed having a first-name relationship with Agriflora's top manager, and those who still produced for him described a sense of loyalty. "He has me wrapped around his little finger," said one. But this friendly relationship was complicated by the company's prerogative to reject a large proportion the outgrowers' produce. In principle, Agriflora buys "all export-quality product," as defined by standards of size and aesthetic quality. In practice, according to most of the outgrowers, the company's rejection rate seemed to depend more on market demand than on how their crop looked. Consequently, many found they earned less, and less predictably, than they expected, according to the projected budgets provided for them by the company. In addition, they found that these projections assumed "an ideal crop" fifty-two weeks a year, when in fact they often lost weeks' worth of harvests to disease, pests, or inclement weather.

Agriflora's top management downplayed the risks posed by these natural hazards, as evident in the following exchange between a manager and me:

> At the end of the day, our outgrowers don't have any risk at all because we've provided all the inputs and we buy their product at a pre-agreed price, and we guarantee to take the whole crop.
> *Guaranteed?*
> Yeah.
> *But what if the quality is substandard?*
> Well, obviously we'll only guarantee to buy what is export standard. And because we give them free technical advice, there's no reason why they can't produce good quality export standard . . . as long as, you know, we give them the right type of seed that produces the right kind of product, they've got nothing to complain about as long as they put the fertilizer in and put the chemical over there. There's nothing complicated about this stuff; you plant it, and six weeks later you pick it.

If a grower still ended up with substandard crops, he said, "99.9 percent of the time it's [the grower's] management problem. Every grower gets a manual . . . all they have to do is follow A,B,C."

Outgrowers typically did not share this faith in the power of managerial expertise to overcome the vagaries of nature. And most of them had dropped out of export horticulture by the year 2000. "It's not profitable," concluded one former grower, "it was never profitable." This was due partly to the high rejection rates and crop losses, but partly also to the costs of conforming to the food safety, environmental, and social welfare standards of the U.K. supermarkets. These standards became increasingly elaborate during the late 1990s, and the money required for new on-farm infrastructure and equipment, as well as additional personnel, came from the farmers' own pockets. At the same time, the prices they received for their crops remained flat. If anything, the supermarkets were competing to keep their fresh produce prices down, especially after Wal-Mart entered the U.K. food retail market in the late 1990s.

In addition, the standards became the source of new kinds of tedium and stress, which were only indirectly related to the physical labor demands and natural hazards of agricultural production (especially since the outgrowers' workers did most of the hard labor). Even though the outgrowers had spent many years (and in some cases most of their lives) on commercial farms, they now found they were doing very different work than the kinds they knew. The pace, for one, was fast and unrelenting. As one outgrower said, "The vegetables don't wait for anybody . . . it's seven days a week, fifty-two weeks a year . . . It's one of those businesses where you have to be really on the ball." But the outgrowers had to be "on the ball" for more than just their crops. Like the Agriflora and York Farms managers, the outgrowers were expected to deliver to the U.K. market not just a physical product, but also a *performance,* demonstrating their adherence to the market's standards of sanitary, sustainable, and ethical farming. As in the many realms of professional life now subject to "rituals of verification," the methods used to assess the quality of work ended up transforming it altogether (Power 1997).[16]

The Standards

As the Zambian vegetable export industry grew, so too did the number of standards that the industry had to meet. These standards were delineated in codes of practice developed either by individual British retailers or import firms, by trade associations (such as the British Retail Consortium and the Euro-Retailer Working Group [EUREP]), or by multi-stakeholder initiatives, such as COLEACP, Social Accountability International, and the Ethical Trading Initiative (ETI).[17] The ETI "base code," the least technical of the codes but also one that explicitly addresses the British public's concerns about working conditions on Third World export farms, is discussed in greater detail in chapter 6 (Orton and Madden 1996). Some of these codes overlap; some, like the EUREPGAP protocol, are also quite lengthy. All the same, in 2000 ZEGA published its own horticultural code of conduct, which applied to its rose exporters as well as the vegetable exporters. The ZEGA code was in accordance with the external codes as well as Zambia's own agricultural labor laws. As a national-level industry code it carried no legal weight and did not directly affect exporters' relations with their buyers. More than anything, it served to promote the "image" of the country's produce—to demonstrate, according to one York Farms manager, that country's entire horticultural export sector "came to standard." Describing how the Colombian flower industry's labor practices had been the subject of a "major scandal" a few years prior, he boasted that the same could not happen in Zambia:

> That's where we were able to say as an industry, hey, Zambia's
> clean. Can't touch us . . . our social ethics are good . . . we're teach-
> ing people how to handle things and do things right—not perfect,
> show me one that is in the West, in the States and in the U.K. surely,
> you know, the perfect place. And we've probably got to be better
> than them because we're Africa. We're obviously Third World, we're
> obviously developing, we're obviously big and nasty so we actually
> have to be holier than thou.

The ZEGA code, which was developed by top managers from Agriflora and York Farms in conjunction with a British horticultural consultant, does indeed emphasize the growers' need to accommodate the concerns and perceptions of the overseas market, as seen in the section on worker welfare:

> Worker Welfare in third world countries is currently attracting atten-
> tion in the European market place. The buying public is being ap-
> praised of "undesirable" practices and pressure is being put on pro-
> ducers to evaluate and improve conditions for workers . . .

And especially in the section on food safety and food spoilage.

> Food safety is of paramount concern to consumers in Europe: Sev-
> eral food scares, e.g., salmonella in eggs and BSE in cattle, have sen-
> sitized the public. . . . Extensive legislation is in place to protect con-
> sumers and any breach of the regulations is heavily and publicly
> punished. . . . In a market place that is very competitive, financial
> penalties and bad publicity have a large effect on sales so buyers are
> understandably concerned about the facilities and procedures used
> by suppliers.
>   There is also a problem of 'Identity' whereby customers associ-
> ate fine beans with Africa not with a specific farm or even with Zam-
> bia. Thus any problem that is identified will affect the market for all
> other producers in the sector and the region and it becomes impor-
> tant that all the producers comply with the basic standards . . .

Together, the external codes and ZEGA's own code outline standards covering everything from packhouse hygiene and pesticide storage to labor rights to farmers' responsibility to preserve the "natural beauty" of their surroundings. In the eyes of the supermarkets, however, not all standards are weighted equal. In terms of wildlife protection, for example, the EUREPGAP protocol "encourages" growers to develop a plan to conserve biodiversity and to "take action to avoid damage and deterioration of habitat" (EUREPGAP 2000, 14). But traceability and certain food safety measures are critical perquisites for doing business with the U.K. supermarkets. This is partly for legal reasons; if a potentially unsafe product made it onto a store shelf (for example, a punet of vegetables with detectable pesticide residues), the supermarket could avoid liability by demonstrating due diligence—in other words, that it had done everything reasonably possible to protect its customers from such a product.[18]

As part of their performance of due diligence, the supermarkets conducted periodic audits of their Zambian suppliers. Sometimes this involved no more than a faxed request for the records tracing a particular item, such as 250-gram punet of green beans. A technical manager then had to provide information about how that punet was produced: what plot the beans came from, when they were planted, what chemical treatments they received, when, and by whom; when they were harvested, and by whom, and how long they spent in the packhouse. The supermarkets expected fast turnaround—not always easy, especially if the beans came one of Agriflora's outgrower farms in Mazabuka, where the phones often did not work. The outgrowers had to have their books in order so they could respond immediately to a request for production data.

York Farms, which kept all its production and accounting centralized, had an advantage over Agriflora when it came to responding to unannounced audits. The company's technical manager boasted about his fast turnaround time—"My record's about an hour and a half"—as well as about the quality of his bookkeeping: "Anybody can come on to this farm any time without notice and they can see our records and I'll guarantee you they'll be as damn near 100 percent as they'll ever be, and they won't be fixed, they won't be pretty, you know, they'll be accurate. We have to be."

Occasionally, the supermarkets conducted on-site audits, carried out either by their own employees or by their importer. These site visits were not simply inspections; in keeping with the supermarkets' stated policy of "partnership" with their fresh produce suppliers, the visits were also intended to allow buyer and supplier to discuss their respective concerns and future plans, and ideally to solidify both sides' sense of commitment and trust. Whether this in fact occurred depended on who came. The top managers of Agriflora and York Farms had gotten to know their importers quite well by 2000, and so their visits were relatively informal. When supermarket buyers or managers came, however, the export firms and outgrowers had to prepare for a full-scale "presentation." This meant making sure all the traceability records were in order, and all the fields and facilities were visibly in compliance with the supermarkets' standards.

The hygiene standards resembled those in most food industries; they required workers to wear headscarves and, in the packhouse, coveralls, and to wash their hands with an anti-bacterial soap. In addition, the ZEGA code of conduct recommended that "only people who appear to be clean and healthy should be recruited" to work in the industry. One company's packhouses took the extra precaution of posting a guard in the washroom. He was supposed to monitor not just hand-washing but also visits to the toilet—the assumption being that frequent visits signaled illness, and that a sick worker, as the ZEGA code of conduct notes, could contaminate the product. Although the code requires workers to stay away from work if they are sick, one packhouse manager said that most workers did not want to report illness because they would not be paid. Therefore, surveillance was necessary. "We're dealing with people who aren't very used to sanitation," explained an expatriate packhouse manager,

Figure 4.5.
Hygiene on the line. The white coats of Zambian packhouse employees contrasts with the casual attire of their Burkinabé counterparts. Photo by author.

"you have to treat them like children." Hygiene is somewhat less tightly monitored in the fields, but outgrowers must still provide a certain number of toilet and washing facilities, depending on the size of their farms.

A few outgrowers expressed scorn for their customers' fear of microbes. Said one former grower, "they (the British people) have no antibodies in their system at all." He added that Africans living in poor neighborhoods "thrive" despite the germs, but in the "civilized world" people are so used to eating "sterile food" that "they get the least little bug and keel over." On the other hand, the outgrowers generally praised the industry's efforts to cut back on pesticide use, though they pointed out that the market still expected perfectly unblemished produce.

In addition to checking on the basic technical and sanitary conditions of production, the supermarkets came to see evidence of compliance with social welfare standards. These became increasingly important in the late 1990s as British non-governmental organizations pressured the supermarkets to demonstrate their commitment to ethical trade (Orton and Madden 1996). Although specific expectations varied between supermarkets, they generally wanted to see medical facilities and health workers on-site, housing or a housing allowance for permanent workers, proper protection for workers handling pesticides, compliance with national minimum wage and other labor laws, day nurseries, and no child labor (defined as under fifteen years old).

For outgrowers, the social welfare standards had become a sore point, and not simply because it cost money to build and staff clinics and day nurseries. At least some of them had, in fact, built housing and schools for their workers long ago and resented the Europeans who, as one outgrower said, "think we don't care for our staff."

Moreover, the outgrowers argued that certain supermarket standards of "ethical trade," especially those related to the care and employment of children, did not actually conform to local social norms and economic conditions. As one grower said, "You've got to have a crèche [nursery] for the women who come to work and have got babies or small kids. Now it's not in these people's culture to employ somebody to look after them. They don't do that sort of thing. They either bring the baby with them or leave with an older child, or a sister. They just won't do it. And it's awfully wrong, because these people, they work all the time with their baby on their back."

Another outgrower said that her family had built a day nursery, but did not insist or even expect the women workers to leave their babies there. A third said she simply refused to build one, because it made no sense.

The outgrowers also criticized the supermarkets' ban on child labor because it did not even allow for children to help their mothers after school. A number of them pointed out that they had grown up working on farms, that children still picked potatoes and delivered newspapers in the United Kingdom, and that this kind of employment was no more harmful—and in fact much more economically vital—in Zambia. As one outgrower noted,

A couple of years ago I planted gooseberries. The women hated picking them. Wouldn't pick 'em. So when the kids came home from school, I said, all right, you can pick them; you can eat as many as you want, but you just pick them. And they loved it! Absolutely loved it. It gave them a little bit of pocket money. I'm not talking about the little ones, but the twelve, thirteen-year-olds. And it was great. All right, I didn't make a penny on it. It didn't make a difference.

Her husband added,

You've got to understand. In a Third World country like this, there are some heads of families who are only fifteen or sixteen. We've got an AIDS epidemic here. Whole families get wiped out. All the parents. You're left with one or two kids to take care of the rest. How are they supposed to do that? There are no social services here.

What social services existed were provided by missions, non-governmental organizations or, up to a point, by the commercial farmers themselves. Especially as AIDS took an increasingly heavy toll (the country has among the world's highest HIV infection rates), the farmers found that customary forms of aid to workers—driving sick family members to a hospital, helping pay funeral expenses (this is required by Zambian labor law)[19]—became increasingly burdensome. Not surprisingly, the supermarkets' unwillingness to share in such costs, despite their touting of "ethical trade," did not go over well. As one outgrower's husband said,

With guys from [Supermarket X] coming here, we have to build them a clinic, a shop, a school. In our case, we built the school, I don't know, twenty years ago, so that doesn't affect us. But the shop and the clinic and everything else, I said, well, pay for it! Oh no, oh no. "You're going to pay for it." That's part of them signing a contract with you. Er, they don't sign contracts; that's part of their program in buying from you. You have to meet all this criteria.

The export company managers also expressed ambivalence about the supermarkets' power to impose their standards, and the accompanying costs, on their African suppliers. On one hand, they were proud that the horticultural industry could claim the best environmental and labor record of any agro-industry in Zambia, and they recognized that their own companies' growth had depended on the U.K. supermarkets' demand—unparalleled elsewhere in Europe—for both high volume and high quality. On the other hand, they worried that neither consumers nor the supermarkets themselves appreciated how much their industry spent on producing quality, as well as good working conditions. One manager wished that the supermarkets would do more to inform their customers about the "social impact" of African horticulture, because then "people would have the feel-good factor when they buy these products—I think that's important for anybody." Even more importantly, he said,

> If anything I think the supermarkets should start—well, you know, they're the ones asking "have you got a clinic on every farm?"—well, yeah, ok, we're doing that, but if you really want to do it then pay us one p [pence] a packet more. Put it on your packet that the one p is going back to Africa to build a clinic. Send us the money, we'll contract someone and build the clinic . . . The Europeans want these developments. We also want them. They all cost money and someone's got to do it . . . I feel that's really time that the markets start to participate in what they're preaching . . . actually what they're doing by trying to drive prices down and trying to be more competitive—they're making life tougher down here. Well, maybe they don't care . . .

Indeed, this was perhaps the greatest concern shared by managers and outgrowers alike—that the supermarkets did not ultimately care how much their African suppliers had invested in meeting their demands.

Everyone realized that consumer demand, especially for foods such as "ethnic" and "baby" vegetables, was not necessarily stable. As one Agriflora manager noted, "If U.K. consumers woke up tomorrow and decided not to eat snowpeas, we'd have a problem." It would not take such an eventuality, however, for Zambia to lose its market.

In mid-2000, its snow peas enjoyed strong demand, due largely to reduced exports from drought-stricken Kenya and conflict-ridden Zimbabwe. But already in those countries (Kenya especially), many export companies had been weeded out of the supermarkets' "rationalized" supply base, and competition would likely become only stiffer. One export company manager noted that this made it difficult to pressure their supermarket buyers on any front, saying, "Here they are buying your product, so how far can you push them? How can you upset them? Because at the stroke of a pen you could be not supplying them."

Such remarks contrasted sharply with the confidence expressed elsewhere in the export company managers' accounts. They were confident, in other words, that with proper technology, infrastructure, and management, high-value horticulture in Africa could become a viable mass production industry, characterized by economies of scale and highly standardized products. They also believed it was best to achieve this transformation through corporate enterprise rather than state planning or development project aid (even if the corporations did, in fact, rely on such aid), because not only did it create jobs and disseminate skills, but it also exposed Zambians to the rigors and virtues of the market. And, of course, for those managers who were also shareholders, it made them a profit.

The export company managers' confidence has been nurtured by both rapid success and by Zambia's openness to concentrated corporate capital. This openness, I believe, goes beyond simply liberal trade and investment laws; it also describes the enduring acceptance, at least among the urban working and professional classes, of a development discourse constructed during the decades when investment by foreign mining corporations helped make Zambia one of sub-Saharan Africa's most prosperous nations (Ferguson 1999). That is not to say this discourse, which portrays foreign corporate investment as a modernizing, progressive force, goes unquestioned. In 2000—a year when Zambians saw their country's copper mines sold for a song to foreign interests—it was not difficult to find people who, if asked, said that they believed the country's most dynamic sector should be more open to black Zambian farmers, rather than entirely controlled by two white-run companies. Some of these people either already worked in the industry as middle managers or rose growers, or were interested in producing vegetables for export—but not if they had to sell through one of these companies. These sorts of opinions, however, were muted compared to the support that the companies enjoyed from Zambia's powers-that-be, and compared especially to the hostilities leveled at white agro-enterprise by the government in neighboring Zimbabwe.

In their confidence in the power of management and technology, as in their professional experience, the export company managers had much in common with their U.K. clients. These two parties enjoyed relationships in which, unlike in the francophone trade between African exporters and French importers, relatively little needed explaining. As one British produce importer commented, it was "no coincidence that all successful fresh produce sources in sub-Saharan Africa have a white face to front the business—supermarket buyers and technologists want people on the ground who speak their language and think like them."

Yet, just as the friendly relations between Agriflora's outgrowers and managers were complicated by commercial imperatives, so, too, did the company managers recognize the precarious nature of their "partnerships" with the U.K. supermarkets, even if they did think alike. As one of them put it,

The big supermarkets won't give you written contracts. So it's all on trust, you know, but then, tomorrow they could drop you like that.

Zambia: Settler Colonialism and Corporate Paternalism

121

And one hopes that they have some sort of moral undertaking . . . you know, if they dropped us like that basically it would put thousands of people's livelihoods at risk, just with [our company] alone. One would hope, one hopes to get that message across more and more to the supermarkets.

The Smallholder Turn?

As white farm households dropped out of export horticulture at the end of the 1990s, Agriflora faced a potential supply crisis. In order to keep up with the U.K. supermarkets' high-volume orders, the company not only purchased more land for its own production but also launched a "smallholder" program. The program would help Zambian landholders on the outskirts of Lusaka organize growers' cooperatives, through which they would be eligible for loans to finance up to four hectares of drip irrigation equipment on their properties. The company would also provide cold storage containers, seeds and agricultural chemicals, and extension agents.

Figure 4.6.
Two members of a smallholder horticultural export cooperative. Like many participants in Agriflora's smallholder scheme, they live and grow green beans in a relatively affluent suburb just outside Lusaka. Photo by author.

French Beans and Food Scares

On one level this program demonstrated great savvy. By incorporating more black Zambians as producers rather than simply employees, it responded to those who, "looking over the fence," might resent the company's prosperity. The program also made the company eligible for aid from donors seeking to promote smallholder commercial agriculture. USAID, for example, provided funds for the irrigation equipment loans, while the Japanese government financed cold storage construction.

On another level, however, Agriflora's management made some questionable assumptions about both its own capacity to incorporate smallholders into a commodity network that prioritized control and consistency, and about the smallholders themselves. First, it assumed that Agriflora could maintain traceability and rigorous quality control on well over 100 scattered farms, whose owners had little or no experience with export production or cooperative membership. Indeed, the head of one cooperative admitted that most of its members knew nothing about farming, period. "We find ourselves incapacitated by lack of knowledge," he said. In mid-2000, the first year of smallholder production, Agriflora was training a pesticide "spray team" to treat all the cooperatives' crops, having promised its supermarket clients that the smallholders themselves would not keep agricultural chemicals on their farms. But the smallholders complained that the company's extension services were inadequate, and some said that they had lost crops due to insufficient spraying.

Second, Agriflora's smallholder program assumed that the market would tolerate an experiment that might result in irregularities in the quantity and quality of the company's produce. Yet the accounts of importers and supermarket produce managers in the United Kingdoms (discussed in chapter 6) suggested that they had little patience for any experiment that might jeopardize their commitment to consumers' safety and eating enjoyment. One importer said that only if Agriflora maintained tight "command and control" over its smallholders would the supermarkets sanction the program. In other words, it would have to adhere to what has become known in the industry as the "benign dictator" model of outsourcing. For Agriflora, this condition posed a challenge that was as much political as logistical.

Last, the program assumed that smallholders would accept prices and conditions that white commercial farmers had rejected. In particular, it assumed that the smallholders had lower overhead costs because they employed "free" family labor and that, unlike the white commercial farmers, they did not have (as one Agriflora expatriate manager put it) "lifestyles to maintain." In fact, most Zambians owning land on the outskirts of Lusaka were fairly affluent. The people who joined Agriflora's "smallholder" cooperatives in 2000 included retired civil servants, aeronautic engineers laid off from the downsized Zambian Airways, bank managers, and high-ranking military officials. They used hired labor (even family members have to be paid, they noted) and had "lifestyles" (as well as many family members) to support. It was far from clear whether horticulture would prove either profitable or worthwhile for these individuals—even though, as the head of one cooperative noted, their previous professional experience helped them understand the priorities and value of high-value export production. A former middle manager in a large Zambian company, he said he and his neighbors were not "peasants":

> [P]easant farmers have limited ambition. . . . In economics they call it
> the "hierarchy of need." Our friends right at the bottom [Zambian
> "peasants" in more remote rural areas], they're quite happy. . . . So if
> you're starting an outgrower scheme you're not going to go to the
> real bottom. You will go somewhere in between the second and
> third layer where you do not have to do too much persuading,
> where you do not have to explain what's foreign exchange, what the
> advantage of this and that are, etc. You go to a group like our group,
> people who have worked but are in semi-retirement, you explain
> things to them and they'll pick it up.

He went on to say that he and the others in his group would be patient with Agriflora, partly because they understood that profits do not always come immediately, and partly because they felt "loyalty" to a company that had "done something good for them." "They've given us a semblance of supervision and a market," he said of Agriflora, and the cooperative members appreciated this even if, perhaps, white commercial farmers took it for granted. Yet ultimately he expected, and would know how to recognize, a fair price. If you are a "middle class Zambian" like him, he said, "you know what you want and you can do your sums."

Another cooperative member, a former engineer, expressed similarly mixed feelings towards Agriflora's smallholder initiative. It was a good program, he said, but,

> You know how it is working for a big capitalist company. They take
> everything. They leave you just enough, just enough to send your
> lady to the salon and have a couple of dinners and that's it, full stop!

In 2001, Agriflora reported a 620 percent sales growth and a 1,100 percent increase in operating profits according to its partial owner, TransZambezi Industries.[20] York Farms' exports increased by a much more modest 20 percent, but the company also expanded its production of organic baby vegetables—already a huge growth area in the U.K. retail market. In a region of Africa where the news about agriculture, whether for export or local consumption, was more often bad than good, Zambia's horticultural export firms entered the 21st century with great promise. Certainly their prospects appeared much brighter than those facing Burkina's green bean business. Yet their success generated a formidable range of expectations about how they would perform as corporate intermediaries and employers.

Shareholders expected continued high returns, while their smallholders expected, eventually, a share of these returns. Members of the predominantly casual workforce had few opportunities to express their expectations, but the companies' top managers clearly recognized that, to appear to be "looking after their people," they had to provide more than dollar-a-day wages.[21] They needed to perform this paternalistic role because it accorded with the expectations of not only local Zambian society but also (and arguably more importantly) those of the U.K. supermarkets. More broadly, these distant clients expected all the actors involved in Zambian fresh vegetable export production—managers, outgrowers, workers, and indeed the vegetable commodities themselves—to pass ongoing and increasingly rigorous tests, all designed to give consumers confidence in the quality of their high-value purchases. Whether or not baby vegetables eventually brought postcolonial, liberalized Zambia the kind of "revolutionary" socioeconomic changes seen in the colonial-era Copperbelt, they had already brought a new, albeit largely unseen form of overrule.

5

France

Expertise and Friendship

We exist because we try . . . to make our connaissance *valuable.*
—Exotic fresh produce wholesaler, Rungis market

Q*ue voulons-nous manger?*—What do we want to eat? The French government posed this question in 2000 as part of a Ministry of Agriculture project on l'Etats Generaux de l'Alimentation (EGA), or the "General State of Food." It also recruited thousands of citizens to respond in surveys, discussion groups, and a national colloquium, which were all duly recorded, analyzed, and interpreted by market researchers. Described as an effort to promote debate and dialogue around the French public's "true" food concerns, the EGA seemed an extraordinary overture from a government not known for soliciting public opinion on policy matters (Marris 1999). But then, it was an extraordinary time. In the previous five years, mad cows, dioxin chickens, and listeria had found their way into the French food supply; opposition to genetically modified organisms (GMOs) had mushroomed into a major political crisis; a millennial shipwreck off the Brittany coast had dumped huge quantities of potential carcinogens into some of the country's richest fishing waters. Media coverage of these affairs had played up the roles of government officials who were either corrupt, incompetent, disingenuous, or simply unable or unwilling to address questions about possible food risks (Jaillette 2000; Mamère and Narbonne 2001). The government badly needed to show that it was listening, and that it could protect the public's health. Yet the EGA findings, while inconclusive in many respects, did show that alleviating public anxieties about the food supply would take more than stricter safety measures (Joly and Marris 2001). For the French were concerned not only about mad cow disease and listeria, but also the loss of their culinary patrimony. In particular, they feared that globalization would force upon them the travesties of "Anglo-Saxon" food culture, from Big Macs to biotech maize.

Figure 5.1.
Sunday at the market. By the turn of the 21st century, many French citizens feared for the future of their country's culinary patrimony. Photo by author.

France's fresh produce importers would probably find the EGA's findings old but ironic news. After all, the importers had helped to globalize one prominent part of the French diet, namely fresh produce. For much of the past century France, unlike Britain, had produced much of its own fruit and vegetable supply. But its greengrocers, markets and restaurant menus had also long featured fresh produce from much further away, especially during the winter. Once this produce came only by sea, and commanded prices that only holiday feasts or high levels of disposable income could justify. By the late 20th century, however, even the most fragile and perishable of exotic products, such as extra-fine wintertime green beans from Africa, had become widely available and relatively affordable—such that they were no longer considered exotic at all.

For the importers, finding suppliers of these products in Africa had not seemed such an exotic enterprise either. It simply took them farther down a path trodden by generations of intermediaries like themselves: traders based in metropolitan markets who took advantage of extending transportation networks to seek out fresh produce in regions with earlier springs and milder winters and varieties found nowhere else. Certainly, they had to deal with new technologies (airfreight refrigeration), unfamiliar climates and national regulatory codes, and, not least, different local norms of commercial exchange. But people in their profession—trading short-lived products over long distances—coped with newness and difference on a daily basis. Unpredictability and imperfect translations animated their markets and placed a premium on the friendships forged with suppliers, buyers, and even competitors. In any case, overseas supply countries such as Burkina Faso were not so foreign. Not yet a decade removed from French colonial rule when it first flew green beans to Paris, the country's language, currency, laws, and even its market gardens looked more than a little familiar. So too did the French-funded rural development programs that aimed to modernize and commercialize the ex-colony's peasant agriculture.

The cultural economy of French food retailing offered, by today's standards, relatively favorable conditions for produce importers venturing into airfreight trade with Africa. In particular, the predominance of small retailers who cared more about the trustworthiness of their suppliers than the packaging of their products assured a tolerant market for rough and irregular shipments. These small retailers in turn advised their customers and selected produce for them and thereby encouraged them to purchase new and otherwise unadvertised products. Not least, the customers themselves (most of them women) expected to spend more than a third of their household income on food. Compared to their British counterparts, they also spent a relatively large proportion of their day cooking and eating.

During the last three decades of the twentieth century, the entire system of French food provisioning changed more dramatically than during any comparable time span in modern history. The food scares and controversies of the late 1990s drew attention to certain aspects of this transformation: the industrialization of food production; the loss of national sovereignty over regulation concerning, say, raw milk cheese; the invasion of "McDo" and fast food more generally. They also raised concerns about the future of the rural environment and livelihoods, consumers' health and gustatory pleasure, and indeed the core of French cultural identity.[1]

For French fresh produce importers, the headline controversies mattered little compared to the quiet but steady changes in French food retailing and consumption patterns. Like produce wholesalers, they faced a retail market increasingly less appreciative of the goods and services they had traditionally provided, and less understanding of the risks they took on a daily basis. Despite government regulations aimed at protecting le petit commerce, supermarkets and hypermarkets (defined as stores of more than 2,500 square meters) were gaining a greater share of fresh produce retailing, and they cared above all about price, volume, and prompt delivery. Consumers, meanwhile, were gravitating toward the big stores and the convenient foods they offered because their own lives and priorities were changing. Women had less time for cooking and shopping, and youth had more mobility. Though long lunches and trips to the open-air market were still considered defining parts of French food culture, these activities became increasingly relegated to weekends and holidays.

Most of France's Parisian-based produce importers viewed these changes from the strange vantage point of Rungis, the wholesale market that replaced the historic *Halles Centrales* in 1968. Located just outside the capital's peripheral highway, Rungis boasts of its status as the world's largest fresh food market, with an annual turnover of 2.45 billion euros in fruit and vegetables alone (2000 figures). But its vast docks have seen many companies close down and much business shift to the supermarkets' centralized distribution centers. Shifts in the local geography of the market thus reflect the larger transformations in French food provisioning, and the way they have marginalized independent fresh produce importers and wholesalers.

These intermediaries nonetheless remain central to the story of how African green beans found their way on to French greengrocers' shelves, and why late 20th century food scares played out quite differently in the francophone commodity network than in the anglophone one. This chapter addresses two sets of questions. First, building on chapters 2 and 3, I want to consider how agrarian history has informed French norms of food nature, broadly understood, and how in turn these norms have shaped intermediaries' understandings of food risk and quality, and the expertise required to handle both. Clearly different kinds of expertise are valued in different settings and *métiers*. As chapter 2 discussed, France's gastronomic tradition has produced highly codified knowledge—tomes of ostensibly universal laws of *haute cuisine,* nonetheless taught and practiced in gendered and class-stratified settings—while assuming and depending on the experiential knowledge, or *mētis,* of chefs and farmers.[2] What *mētis* does the importers' *métier* demand?[3] More specifically, what must they know, and demonstrate that they know, about food's nature? This question is important for understanding not just the workings of the Burkina Faso-France green bean trade during the "anxious age," but also the longer history of how France's fresh foodways have become increasingly globalized.

The second set of questions, also building on previous chapters, considers the role of trust and friendship in the francophone commodity network. Granovetter's (1985) assertion that commerce and other economic activities are "embedded" in networks of personal relations now seems obvious, if not understated.[4] Still, the French produce traders' work offer insights into how such relations can generate, as Granovetter put it, "both enormous trust and enormous malfeasance" (1985, 492). In particular, how do relations of trust (and malfeasance) forged within the networks of a spatially bounded marketplace—where people interact face to face and on a variety of levels, not just as buyers and sellers[5]—both influence and draw influence from those relations forged within the long-distance commodity networks supplying that market? How do these different networks draw boundaries between insiders and outsiders, between those who might be trusted and those who can be cheated? These questions must of course be framed historically: in this case, with an eye toward how the colonial encounter provided opportunities for both colonizers and colonized to define themselves against the other—and to continue doing so in postcolonial encounters, commercial and otherwise.[6] The answers, in this case, can shed some light on the seemingly unlikely survival of the Burkina Faso-France green bean trade. How, in a market that one Burkinabé exporter likened to a wolves' den, do Burkina Faso's green beans still find a place?

Nature in the Peasant Nation

"The peasant, whose silence does not signify absence of thought, who ranks as the greatest of French philosophers . . . might be described as our silent master."
—Edouard Herriot, 1934 (cited in Wright 1964, 13)

When asked about the differences between French and English foodways, French produce traders do not hesitate to invoke familiar national stereotypes. These stereotypes not only naturalize the superiority of French taste (as something inborn, genetic); they also invoke broader French norms about nature, in food and on the farm. These norms form part of France's self-identity as a peasant nation.

Most industrialized nations hold tenaciously to romanticized myths of their country's peasant agriculture, even if their peasants largely disappeared centuries before, as in the United Kingdom (Wiener 1981), or never really existed, as in the United States (Page and Walker 1991). France is unique in this regard in that peasant agriculture did not simply persist but indeed provided livelihoods—often miserable, but livelihoods nonetheless—for a large proportion of the country's population until the mid-20th century.[7] Certainly, the pro-peasant rhetoric circulating in Parisian political and intellectual circles has often shown little appreciation for the hardships facing the country's smallholders, just as many Parisians have had little sympathy for peasant organizations' more reactionary political demands. Even so, as historian Gordon Wright observed in the early 1960s, "Nowhere else do so many city-dwellers regard their peasant ancestry as a mark of distinction" (Wright 1964, 1). At the least, nowhere else in Western Europe can so many city dwellers claim such recent peasant ancestry, making it possible to relate "idealized images of peasants' happiness" to real childhood memories spent on the ancestral farm (Paxton 1997, 180).

The survival of the French peasantry into the 20th century has influenced not only the country's food trade policies (which have remained more overtly protectionist than those of most European countries) but also its domestic fresh produce market. This market is quite different from Britain's, even though large-scale retailers now dominate both. In turn, these retail markets demand different kinds of products, services, and expertise from French and British importers. Although the importers, like the public, take these differences in French and British food culture for granted, it is worth briefly exploring their historical origins and their transnational reach.

Three provisos are necessary here. First, as French sociologists have shown, French perceptions of food quality and purity are clearly not homogeneous, much less unchanging.[8] In the last part of the 20th century, generalizations about what "the French" like to eat were undermined not only by the increasing influences of immigrant foodways but also by supermarkets and fast food franchises, which succeeded in selling French consumers on all kinds of value-added foodstuffs that previous generations would likely have found unappetizing. Second, France's relatively late urban transition is not the only historical explanation for the differences between French and British norms of food "goodness" in all its forms. Stephen Mennell's *All Manners of Food,* for example, roots French food culture's lesser emphasis on time and money-saving shortcuts (frozen and canned food) in the courtly traditions that established elaborate cuisine and leisurely dining as markers of distinction and, ideally, sources of pleasure (Mennell 1996). I do not argue for or against this interpretation but simply mention it to signal the many possible historical influences on contemporary food norms. Lastly, one cannot assume in France or anywhere else that consumers' opinions about food, as expressed in surveys, focus groups, and other settings, say much about how they actually consume it.[9] The point here is not that France's peasant past necessarily "explains" contemporary food shopping and eating habits, but rather that it provides ideas and ideals that, in turn, help sellers of fresh produce make sense of their market.

Most broadly, France's agrarian history has given rise to an ideal of rural nature quite distinct from the Anglo-Saxon ideal of pristine wilderness (Williams 1975). As Paxton observes, in France it is not the empty lands that are most sacred (as in the United States and, arguably, Britain) but those "where the human community is most intact" and actively cultivating (Paxton 1997). This version of the Arcadian myth has long justified agricultural support programs aimed at keeping vulnerable farm households on the land; more recently, it put a particularly French spin on the debate over GMOs. French public opinion was largely indifferent about the issue until 1997 when, in response to the government licensing of a particular genetically modified maize variety, it turned overwhelming negative (Marris 2001). One of the forces behind this shift was the anti-GMO campaign launched by Confederation Paysanne (CP), the farmers' movement also known for its opposition to "McDonaldization" (Bové, Dufour, et al. 2001). Significantly, CP's claims focused less on food safety than on cultural survival. They emphasized how GMOs threatened the French ideal of a "worked nature"—an ideal on which CP members, as peasants, could claim to be the ultimate authorities because they inhabited and maintained it (Heller 2002). The confederation appealed, in other words, to the French belief in (or perhaps the need to believe in) the peasant's practical, situated expertise, or *mētis*.

Although this belief has historically assumed that peasant expertise does not extend far beyond the farm, it has helped to limit French anxieties and mystification about what happens on the farm. This does not mean that many Parisians understand in any depth the technical and biological processes of agricultural production, only that it is perhaps easier for them than for the average Londoner to envision these processes in a concrete but also positive light. In turn, these different agrarian visions may help explain why the food scares that hit the meat, poultry, and dairy industries in the late 1990s had relatively limited consequences for other parts of the French food supply. For whereas in Britain the mad cow crisis unleashed events and movements that affected all kinds of food suppliers and intermediaries, French fresh produce importers interviewed in mid-1999 saw questions about the effects of the BSE scare as odd and characteristically "Anglo-Saxon." They pointed out the obvious: cows and green beans are very different things. As one importer put it:

> Excuse me, Miss, for what I'm going to say: the Anglo-Saxon culture is very finicky, and afraid of every little bug. We are much less cautious about these things and I think that we live as long as the Anglo-Saxons, so in my opinion it's a question of culture. I know, from when I sold Cameroon's *haricots verts* to the United States' great French restaurants, that the regulations, from the hygienic point of view, were strict, and in my view a bit exaggerated. And it is out of politeness that I say "a bit exaggerated"! With fruits and vegetables you don't risk getting sick—or in any case they don't present the same risks as products like *charcuterie,* like meat, like fish. It's totally different. So one shouldn't apply hygienic standards to products that aren't exposed to these problems.

Or, as the director of a French importers' trade association put it, "You can't have big problems [with fruits and vegetables], not like with meat. You might feel a little sick, but you're not going to die."[10]

Similarly, a 1999 study of French consumers' attitudes toward the health and environmental sustainability of the food supply found that, despite largely negative views of grain and livestock farming, most consumers viewed fruit and vegetable production as relatively "natural" and benign, especially when practiced on a small scale (Moreau-Rio 1999). In fact they viewed *small* more favorably than *organic,* which many considered either a costly gimmick or a retrograde method that, again, did not appreciate the farmers' skillful use of modern agricultural technologies. By 2002, views (and sales) of organic food had improved, but the French public still trusted farmers as a whole to protect the food supply much more than they trusted supermarkets or the government.[11]

French consumers' trusting views of fruit and vegetable farming, at least compared to British views, meant that retailers and importers felt little domestic pressure to implement traceability in their fresh produce supply chains. Not until the European Union mandated traceability by January 2005 did the fruit and vegetable sector began taking more concerted action. For fresh produce importers, this meant that the very term "traceability" did not even enter their workaday vocabulary until several years after it had become standard procedure in U.K. fresh produce supply chains. Indeed, when asked about it, some French importers purposely pronounced the word with an exaggerated English accent, to emphasize its foreign origins.

The differences between French and English norms concerning the handling of food are also apparent in its packaging. English tourists to the continent have long remarked on the French habit of perching bare baguettes on the table or, worse, carrying them under the armpit. One has also traditionally found relatively little packaging of fresh produce in France—even in the supermarkets. This is partly because the French supermarkets have always concentrated more on discount pricing (as opposed to value-added brand name goods) than have their U.K. counterparts. But for the fresh produce traders it also reflects French consumers' longstanding (albeit perhaps fading) preference for fresh produce they can either choose themselves or have a knowledgeable *commercant* or farmer select for them.

This preference, and the converse suspicion of certain kinds of processed and packaged foods, has long challenged certain food industries, especially those aimed at a mass market. In the late 19th century, for example, working class urban households commonly went into the countryside to buy their meat directly from farmers, even when the equivalent products cost less, in terms of time and money, at the butcher shops. Canned meat proved an even harder sell, partly because of its association with botulism, but also because it looked and tasted unnatural. With help from government-sponsored educational campaigns, consumers gradually came to appreciate the convenience of canned goods (Bruegel 2002). But they remain suspicious of fresh, packaged produce, which in a 1999 survey was viewed unfavorably by 60 percent of the population

(Moreau-Rio 1999). French fresh produce traders, not surprisingly, explain such views as yet another sign of French consumers' superior taste. As one importer put it,

> French consumers have a notion of quality, they recognize the quality of products, and the English don't . . . The French consumer generally knows how to choose his product, and he very much likes to choose it. Which is not the case in England. There, all the products these days are pre-packed. They're products the consumers don't know, so they have the quality controlled for them, so that they can eat without worry.

The fact that French consumers care little for pre-packed produce means that the suppliers have not needed to bother with the additional hygiene measures required for such products. As another importer explained:

> At the level of sanitary regulations, France is behind Britain, and that can be explained by our old-fashioned style of consumption, old-fashioned and not necessarily stupid. That is to say, the French consumer needs to touch and see the products. He doesn't yet want the plastic box like you find in Britain or the United States. It doesn't in-

Figure 5.2.
Tasting the produce at a Parisian market. Photo by author.

France: Expertise and Friendship

terest him; for now he likes to do his shopping, to buy his kilo of leeks, his kilo of tomatoes, and to see that in a plastic box doesn't inspire much confidence.

As the next section describes, French supermarkets and some of their largest fresh produce suppliers (for example, Dole) have succeeded in overcoming such attitudes for fresh vegetables deemed particularly tedious to wash and prepare, such as salad greens.[12] But smaller-scale importers expressed skepticism about the French consumer's willingness to accept other kinds of prepackaged produce:

> The Frenchman isn't in the habit of buying cherries in plastic. It's necessary to touch and to taste a cherry. More than that, he needs to be able to taste it right there in the store. It's free, anyway! That makes him content, and then if the cherry is good he may buy some. That's one of the differences between the Latin and the Anglo-Saxon. Cherries under plastic were tried, but it didn't work. [The hypermarket chains] Carrefour and Leclerc told us, "Yes, it will work," but it didn't! And I don't think that's going to change much in the years to come. You won't see any revolutionary changes at this level.

Employees at Dole France, by contrast, did anticipate such "revolutionary changes," once the French housewife appreciated not just the convenience of packaged produce but also its superior hygiene. The latter has arguably become a greater concern because supermarkets, unlike greengrocers and market vendors, cannot easily prevent consumers from squeezing and sampling the produce. One importer suggested that the answer to this problem lay not in packaging, but rather in a return to traditional methods of retailing:

> The self-service method of selling fruits and vegetables runs contrary to the concerns of the consumer, who wants products that not everyone else has picked through. . . . In my opinion, a return to the sale of fruits and vegetables by a salesman or woman would make it possible to sell better quality and riper products, would bring more satisfaction to the consumer, would reinvigorate the market for fruits and vegetables, and would employ more people! I think it's a good socioeconomic compromise.

This compromise, he later admitted, was less likely than the slow advance of packaging. But as of 2003, the market for pre-packed *haricot vert* remained very small, and supplied almost entirely by Kenya. Unlike the British market for such products, France's has provided little incentive for the development of pre-packing facilities in other cheap labor countries such as Burkina Faso.

It should be noted that France's preference for "natural" as opposed to packaged green beans does not translate into a greater tolerance for natural variations in the vegetable's size, shape, and overall appearance. On the contrary, the French bean aesthetic is as exacting as French garden design and, unlike in the United Kingdom and other Northern European countries, the market seeks only the "fine" and "extra fine" grades. This preference for the slenderest beans has historically given the exporting countries of francophone Africa, with their history of growing garden crops for French colonials, one of their few comparative advantages; according to the major French importers, farmers in former British colonies (with the important exception of Kenya) tend to produce beans that are "too fat."

Yet by the end of the 20th century, simply producing slender beans was not enough (nor, for that matter, simple). For whereas different kinds of French retailers still had somewhat different quality standards—greengrocers and restaurateurs with affluent customers expected and paid more for finer and more consistently flawless beans than the hypermarkets—overall, these standards had grown stricter over time. Even the cheaper retail chains, according to veteran produce traders, had become increasingly uncompromising in their demand for uniform and unblemished products. French expectations of a beautiful and carefully worked nature thus posed challenges to importers and their African suppliers that were if anything, more formidable than official hygiene standards.

French Food Provisioning 1960–2000

The young woman would have liked to grab hold of everything . . .
Round her, people were frantically piling objects into the metal trolleys
. . . Women reached out towards the stands of food. They rummaged in
the refrigerated bins, taking pots, cubes, packets. They took dozens of soft
cheeses, cartons of milk, tubes of creamy spreads, packets of gelatine . . .
Even the children excavated in the shelves at their level, piling the
foodstuffs into little toy trolleys . . . None of the people knew what they
were doing. How could they have known? . . . Food was no longer
anything but shapes and colours.
—The Giants (Le Clézio 1973)

In 1999, France, home to some of the world's most vaunted food boutiques, also became home to the world's second largest "hypermarket" chain, after Wal-Mart. Carrefour, which opened France's first hypermarket in 1963, bought out Promodes, another French chain with a broad international as well as national presence. The deal won approval for warding off an anticipated foreign takeover, either by the Dutch retailer Ahold or Wal-Mart itself; it also gave Carrefour control over 25 percent of the country's retail food market. Clearly, French consumers had already become habitués of *la grande distribution,* and not for just their staple groceries but also, increasingly, the fresh foods they had long bought at markets and specialty shops.[13] These tendencies were less apparent in Paris, where zoning laws limited store size and many outdoor markets still attracted a largely pedestrian clientele. But in suburban and even some rural areas, the big stores had carved out a large swath of the food retail landscape. By 1998, in fact, 83 percent of French households frequented a hypermarket or supermarket at least once a week, and bought nearly 70 percent of their food there (Eymard 1999).

The shift in French food shopping patterns occurred very quickly; thirty years before, supermarkets accounted for only a little over 10 percent of the country's retail food purchases. Fresh produce, in particular, consumers tended

Figure 5.3.
At your service. France's food specialty shops face formidable competition from hypermarkets and downtown "superettes." Photo by Christophe Maître.

to buy either at outdoor markets (22.7 percent), greengrocers (9.8 percent), or small general food shops (*alimentation generale*) (38.2 percent). Nearly half of all households (44.5 percent) in the late 1960s also kept their own vegetable gardens or fruit trees. Food provisioning habits in the 1960s, in other words, differed relatively little from those of previous generations.

But in fact the conditions for a rapid change in these habits were already in place. French households' real buying power had doubled since 1950, allowing them to purchase not just previously unaffordable foods but also durable goods like cars and freezers, which changed how they shopped for food. In addition, the DeGaulle government's commitment to the modernization of French commerce and urban planning had created a favorable legislative landscape for hypermarket expansion. The dramatic changes in consumption and retailing were mutually reinforcing, and both were part of the broader socio-economic transformation of France during the postwar period known as the *Trentes Glorieuses* (roughly 1950–1980). Certain aspects of this transformation would eventually have significant consequences for the fresh produce trade.

First, during the early part of this period, France became, finally, a thoroughly urban nation. Between 1946 and 1968, the urban population increased from barely half to two-thirds of the national total. Immigration and population growth contributed to the high urbanization rates, but so did a massive rural exodus (McMillan 1992). To accommodate the new urban dwellers, government legislation encouraged the construction of suburban bedroom communities and, in their midst, new commercial centers that would include traditional shops, recreational facilities, and, not least, *les grands surfaces*—in other words, large stores like those already found in the United States and Britain (Gatti, Green, et al. 1997). The opening of Carrefour's first hypermarket in 1963 thus responded to an explicit government planning objective.

The hypermarkets' discount prices also responded to the government's concerns about inflation, which at the time trumped the objections of small retailers. By the early 1970s, second thoughts about the benefits of the hypermarkets' gigantism led to the passage of stricter store-size laws, but these only kept the most massive stores out of city centers. As the large chains opened new stores of all sizes and independents closed down or sold out, *la grande distribution* continued to consolidate its control over the French food market (Gatti, Green, et al. 1997).

This consolidation occurred despite big chains offering, until quite recently, little in the way of expert service or product quality, both supposedly core features of French food culture (Baret, Janet-Catrice, et al. 1999). Their fresh produce sections, in particular, typically offered only a limited range of common, often tired-looking fruits and vegetables, piled in vast bins. But market research surveys suggested that French hypermarket shoppers did not care much about presentation as long as things were cheap. A 1991 European study, for example, found that 64 percent of French consumers chose their *grande surface* according to price, as opposed to 44 percent of Germans, 35 percent of Dutch, and 27 percent of British (Ducrocq, 1996, 16). These figures could reflect that the French, unlike the British, had plenty of alternatives to hypermarkets, if and when they wanted better service and better quality produce. And in fact through the early 1990s, most kinds of specialty shops (with the exception of *boulangeries*) withstood competition from the big stores much better than did small independent groceries. Outdoor markets, as well, still accounted for approximately one-third of fresh produce sales (Ducrocq 1996).

Yet even if markets and small specialty stores still figure importantly in French ideals of quality food shopping, the changing priorities and rhythms of daily life in the late 20th century led more and more households to opt for the perceived practicality of hypermarket shopping. Women's growing role in the paid workforce was perhaps the single most important cause of change. Between 1962 and 1990, the percentage of women in paid employment nearly doubled, from around 40 percent to around 80 percent, depending on the age group.[14] As elsewhere, this shift made the late hours of the hypermarket attractive, if not absolutely necessary, for the growing proportion of households with no one at home during the day. The hypermarkets' wide-aisle design, product lines, massive shopping carts, and easy parking also encouraged bulk purchases. By the end of the century the only groups who were not shopping much at hypermarkets and supermarkets were the elderly, who tended to be less mobile and more inclined to patronize local shops for social reasons, and in certain areas, well-off professionals who sought the service and status offered by specialty shops (Larmet 1999).

New time constraints also favored purchases of food requiring little or no preparation (Pynson 1987). Although a typical French hypermarket offers a more limited selection of "ready-meals" than Britain's Marks and Spencer, processed foods account for an increasingly important part of the typical shopping basket (See table 5.1). Frozen vegetable sales, for example, increased 7.8 percent annually between 1960 and 1975, and since have increased steadily, albeit more slowly, while fresh vegetables sales have been nearly flat.[15] Demand for most fresh fruit (except for certain exotic varieties) has grown slowly, as yogurt and other dairy desserts have replaced the traditional fruit course (Monceau et al. 2002).

As discussed in chapter 6, increasing consumer demand for convenience foods cannot be separated from large retailers' increasing control over the food supply as a whole. Through advertising, promotions, stocking patterns and, not least, their role in driving down the overall cost of food, large retailers have encouraged consumers to try buy the kinds of value-added processed

Table 5.1
Percentage of certain foodstuffs (by volume) in the French diet.

	1960	1980	2001
Traditional staples[1]	23.1	12.6	9.5
Red meat	11.2	11.2	6.6
Poultry/fish	14.0	14.0	14.4
Prepared meats	5.9	8.3	11.7
Fresh vegetables	8.5	5.7	5.4
Fresh fruits	7.3	6.1	5.8
Cheese	4.1	6.8	7.3
Yogurt/dairy desserts	0.3	1.2	2.8

Source: Monceau, Blanche-Barbat, et al. 2002.

[1]potatoes, dry beans, eggs, flour, rice, bread, pasta

products that suit their own centralized distribution systems and offer higher profit margins than traditional staples (Grignon and Grignon 1986, 163; Wrigley 1998).

At the same time, however, the large retailers have come to dominate the market for fresh produce, despite its inherent risks and technical challenges, and despite many French consumers' attachment to the service and ambiance offered by outdoor markets and greengrocers. In fact, as part of their bid to win over such consumers, some French hypermarkets and supermarkets "boutiqued" their interiors by designing the different sections of their stores in the same style and colors as traditional *boulangeries* and market halls, and training their employees to act as salespeople rather than merely shelf-stockers (Raffoul 2000). They also broadened their selection of fresh fruits and vegetables, and hired *animateurs* to advise shoppers on how to choose and prepare them. In short, the large retailers aimed to offer all the services of the *petit commerçant,* but on a mass scale and at a discount price.

In the eyes of some critics, the hypermarkets' growing control of the food supply is just one of several trends threatening a core feature of French cultural identity, or what the director of the National Council of Culinary Arts called *l'exception culinaire française* (Lazareff 1998). His book by the same name warns that if the French do not resist the "temptation of easiness"—as offered by one-stop shopping and fast, solitary meals, and by the easy tastes and textures of Big Macs and frozen dinners—they will lose the capacity to appreciate the gustatory and social pleasures of fine food (Lazareff 1998, 168). The "general state of food" forums indicated that many French citizens felt the same sense of loss even while succumbing to an increasing array of tempting, easy meal options. Fresh produce traders shared these concerns but for somewhat different reasons. For them, the late 20th century changes in French food provisioning altered not simply the market's demand, but also the very social character and skill requirements of their *métier*. The place to begin exploring this *métier* and how it has changed is *les Halles Centrales,* Paris's former wholesale market.

The Belly of Paris

At the crossway in the Rue des Halles cabbages were piled up in mountains; there were white ones, hard and compact as metal balls, curly savoys, whose great leaves made them look like basins of green bronze, and red cabbages, which the dawn seemed to transform into superb masses of bloom . . . splotched dark purple and carmine. At the other end of the markets, at the crossway near Saint Eustache, the end of the Rue Rambuteau was blocked by a barricade of orange-hued pumpkins, sprawling with swelling bellies in two superposed rows. And here and there gleamed the glistening ruddy brown of a hamper of onions, the blood-red crimson of a heap of tomatoes, the quiet yellow of a display of marrows, and the somber violet fruit of the eggplant; while numerous fat black radishes still left patches of gloom amidst the quivering brilliance of the general awakening . . . Florent was suffering keenly. He fancied that all this was some supernatural temptation . . .
—Emile Zola, *The Belly of Paris,* 1873

Writing in the 1870s, Zola described a marketplace that had operated, with only occasional brief interruptions, for nearly seven centuries. He was not the only observer to see *les Halles*'s vast size and central location as emblematic of Paris' devotion to its stomach; nor was the main character of his novel, the famished Florent, the only one perturbed by the sheer volume of food hauled daily to and from the city center. Throughout the 19th century, Paris's leaders looked to moralize and modernize a market that had long ago outgrown its medieval-era physical and legal infrastructure. Baltard's majestic pavilions, constructed in the middle of the century, brought traders much-needed shelter, Hausmann's urban planning made way for new rail lines, and regulatory changes opened up the market to an increasingly internationalized food supply (Thompson 1997). Although several decades later the market was finally relocated altogether, the commercial practices, relationships, and regulations established at *les Halles* gave lasting meaning to the produce importer's work.

Trade at *les Halles* was long subject to the decrees and interventions of the monarchy, whose political legitimacy depended above all on the adequate provisioning of Paris (Kaplan 1984). Only a limited number of authorized merchants were permitted to sell each of the major food commodities, assuring them a near monopoly. After the Revolution, the city took control of the market and began progressively opening it up to free trade, partly for ideological reasons but also to meet the food supply needs of a rapidly growing city. Liberalization proved far from straightforward, however. Produce did pour into Paris, brought by expanding trade networks from as far away as French-occupied North Africa and the Spanish Canary Islands (Husson 1875). But with fewer checks on merchants and greater distances between them and their suppliers came greater possibilities for commercial deception and irresponsibility. By the 1890s, nonpayment and other abuses ran rampant at *les Halles,* leading to widespread calls for stricter regulation (Prudhomme 1927). The city responded, creating in 1896 the professional category of the *mandataire,* one of the predecessors of the contemporary fresh produce importer.

According to the 1896 law, *mandataire* candidates had to be French nationals with clean police records and financially secure enough to pay at least 5,000 francs deposit for their floor space. They had to pass three exams: one on commercial law, one on the market's own regulations, and one specific to their food specialty, such as cheese, fruits, or poultry. Once granted a post, *mandataires* were permitted to sell only their clients' goods, and only on a specified commission; late or unduly low payments were grounds for punishment, including possible eviction. They were assisted in their transactions by *les forts,* official "strongmen" appointed by the police prefecture not simply to haul heavy loads, but also to insure that they were delivered to their rightful owners. *Mandataires* could not sublet their spaces nor pass them on to anyone other than accredited *mandataires,* who in turn were obliged to inherit their predecessors' suppliers. In short, such regulations clearly restricted the *mandataires'* commercial liberties, but they also conferred a professional identity and, indeed, an elite privilege, as only they were permitted to sell inside the covered wholesale pavilions (Prudhomme, 1927).

Outside, however, a wide range of sellers operated—some officially recognized, and thus subject to the same rules of "honorable" trade as the *mandataires,* some not (Du Camp 1873, chapter 8). The outdoor sellers included the market gardeners from the city's outskirts, middlemen who sold for them, vast numbers of small-scale retail vendors (most of them female), and independent wholesale and import houses, including those run by immigrant Spanish, Italian, and North African merchants selling produce from their homelands. These latter traders, along with the *mandataires* who specialized in early-season products, helped make *les Halles* a true *marché modiale* by the early 20th century (Poher 1912; les Halles, 1925).

But this market was also a neighborhood quite literally embedded in the social life of central Paris.[16] This first *arrondissement* neighborhood was characterized by a thorough mixing of classes and occupations; bosses and laborers, prostitutes and drunks frequented the same bars, and many merchants lived nearby, often on the same streets or even the same houses as their workers and apprentices. It was also a neighborhood of round-the-clock activity, as the market operated at night, freeing the streets for through-traffic by day (Chemla 1994, 182; Thompson 1997). Although the wholesale commerce at *les Halles* was not open to the public, its bistros attracted Parisian late-night revelers.

For the merchants and other people who worked at *les Halles,* the nocturnal operating hours made it difficult to have much social life outside the market. This no doubt contributed to its now legendary conviviality, as celebrated in several published memoirs and remembered vividly by those who grew up there (Jullian and Meyer 1983; Lageat 1993; Colin 1998). According to one trader's son,

> A child could traverse the market at night, and nothing would happen to him. It was like a village. And when someone was unhappy, everyone supported that person; there was huge solidarity. There was a lot of alcoholism as well, because the bistros were right next to one's work . . . but it was like a family. I was born in *les Halles;* it was a fantastic neighborhood, lively all the time. You knew everybody there . . .

In addition, older traders and traders' sons remember how the relatively small scale of commerce and limited technologies (minimal refrigeration, no mechanized transport within the market)[17] made for a more sociable atmosphere than they later found at Rungis, simply because so much more human labor was needed, and so much more face-to-face buying and selling. As two traders remember:

> Supermarkets didn't exist yet, so my clients were all small—*épiciers,* greengrocers . . . there was a great deal of activity, but all very atomized, small-scale trade. There weren't any big clients buying pallets, in any case there weren't any pallets . . . At the time in Paris everything was manual; the trucks arrived, and one unloaded the cartons one by one, put them on the ground one by one, passed them on one by one . . . It was physically draining. But from the point of view of human relations, it was very agreeable. There was an ambiance, a sort of *promiscuité* [openness]; at night it was *la fête*. It was physically hard but very agreeable.

> It was crazy, the hustle and bustle inside, the human contact every day. You saw everybody. You saw the restauranteur come at two in

Figure 5.4.
Mechanization has greatly reduced the need for manual labor at Rungis, the market that replaced *les Halles* in 1968. Photo by Christophe Maître.

the morning, in a hurry because he wanted to go sleep, or the restauranteur, having slept, rushing through at eight in the morning, and then all the market vendors . . . I had friends everywhere. . . .

With such bustling commerce came not only many friendships but also the satisfaction of rapid, regular turnover—a high priority for all merchants, but especially those selling perishable produce. As one importer said,

From the human point of view, we'll always miss the old *Halles*. There was conviviality, friendship, fraternity. People knew each other, they saw each other all the time. It was a world where there was nothing but small-scale commerce; where everything was finished off every day, everything began again the next day; where everything was new, every day.

Of course, sometimes it was easier for traders to "finish off" their stock than other times. Because most could not store their produce for long periods, they

needed to cultivate a sense of timing for price cutting—no sooner than necessary, but not after their produce deteriorated—as well as a regular clientele, so
they would not often have to resort to price cutting. One former *mandataire*
of luxury fruits remembered,

> To get rid of a batch that was a little bit tired was better than to risk
> losing it altogether, because as soon as it's blemished it's worth noth-
> ing . . . That happened to me sometimes, like everybody else . . .
> Sometimes the buyers would take the lots to pick through them . . . I
> would tell those guys, look, you've done good business with me,
> you're going to help me, you take that, do what you can with it . . .
> But happily, I didn't only have business like that . . . In the end we
> had good clients and good sales and we sold steadily . . .

Traders also valued good relations with their competitors. Especially
among the immigrant importers, recalls one Italian man, the relatively small
scale of most enterprises encouraged collaboration; traders were necessarily
"competitors and friends at the same time:"

> If one could take another's customer, one would. Still, things were
> done correctly. If, for example, I knew you worked with a particular
> supplier, I wouldn't go looking for him, because one couldn't do
> that . . . The Italian "colony," which I knew well—my brother, my
> uncle, all them—had a heap of friends like themselves, importers,
> and everyone got along well. There was competition but everyone
> was fair and true to their word. That was the essential thing. If you
> lost the trust of your colleagues and clients, you were done for . . .
> because in the end, colleagues, competitors, they have to help each
> other. For example if you had a license to import small quantities,
> two or three tons, you couldn't order a [train] wagon to deliver just
> two tons; that would be too expensive. So you got together with
> others to make a group purchase. It was necessary, if you will, to
> have correct and friendly relations to do business . . . My father, he
> had a neighbor from Naples, a huge competitor, they were always at
> war! Still, they sometimes made their purchases together . . .

The cost and delays of long-distance communication also favored several
relations with one's suppliers; importers could not check up on them regularly,
and thus had to trust them to produce and ship what was needed.

> I knew the wives of my suppliers, the children, everybody. We im-
> ported from Sicily—lots of lemons, some oranges. We knew inti-

mately the people we did business with, and they knew us. They were ties of friendship, really. But we had to communicate rapidly; there wasn't time to write letters, contracts; business goes faster than that. Even the telephone, calling abroad you might have to wait four, five, six hours to get a line . . . Often we called in the middle of the night, because it was faster and cheaper! But everything was done like that; there was much more trust than today . . .

If nostalgia has made many traders' recollections of *les Halles* rosier than the reality, it is clear that the sociability of the marketplace made the otherwise difficult conditions of their work more enjoyable and, in some ways, more secure. At the least, traders counted on norms of friendship to reinforce commercial obligations of their buyers and suppliers, and to temper competition among sellers of like products.

Traders also counted on the market to trust and value the commercial know-how that, like other kinds of *mētis,* they typically acquired (and still do) through apprenticeship rather than formal education. As the above quotes suggest, traders had to know how to react quickly to unpredictable market conditions, especially since they dealt in highly perishable goods. Part of this knowledge was social; they had to know who could help them get their goods to market and get them sold. It was equally important, however, for traders to have intimate knowledge of their products. As the same Italian importer put it,

At Rungis today, the wholesalers sell a little of everything, so they can't know their products well. At *les Halles,* they were much more specialized; everyone sold only a few products . . . From the point of view of *connaissance,* they were much more professional than today. My father, my uncle; they taught me a great deal. . . . My father, if you gave him a lemon, he could tell you what country it came from, if it had seeds, if it had a fine skin, what variety it was; he only had to look at it. He knew his product well.

Many contemporary traders still take pride in "knowing their product," but this no longer means the same thing. With the standardization of fresh produce, traders' appreciation for subtle differences in taste and texture has become less relevant than precise information about where to get particular grades of particular products at different times of the year. In any case, older traders say, they have relatively few opportunities to demonstrate their more qualitative knowledge. Many of their clients, especially the supermarkets buyers, do not care, or at least do not actually come to the market, instead placing their orders by fax or hurried phone calls. So older traders miss the face-to-face contact of the old market not merely for social reasons but also because their selling tactics relied on the performance of expertise. As one man explained, standardized size and quality categories are neither as meaningful nor as effective:

> Take, for example, tomatoes of category 1.57–67. Theoretically, if this were an industrial product, they'd all be identical. But when it comes to fruits and vegetables, these products, from the visual and gustatory aspect, can be totally different. So if you cannot explain over-the telephone to a potential buyer that your product is like this or like that, he's going to rely on a standard that means absolutely nothing. So it's a bit frustrating to not be able to defend one's product.

It should be said that not all older traders missed the old days at *les Halles;* some had more vivid memories of the cold nights and filth and heavy toil. Yet they did all miss the basic supply and demand conditions of the old days, at least in the 1950s and '60s. The main challenge during this period, older traders remember, was not selling, but rather finding enough supply. Said one importer,

> During the last years of the old *Halles,* we were coming out of a postwar food situation; people had suffered, they hadn't eaten well; production had fallen and wasn't nearly at the levels it is today, and there was hardly any importing. All this meant that products were sold at prices that allowed everyone to make a living. There was enough to pay the producer, pay for transport; the wholesaler earned his living and everyone was content. . . . But now there's so much competition that there are times when the prices are such that you don't make any money, or you lose it. So now everyone has to pay close attention to their accounts. Before we were like the Bur-kinabé, we didn't keep track, and yet at the end of the year we had always earned something!

Ironically, the very conditions that traders remember so fondly of the post-war period—the crowds of customers eager to buy their goods, the dependence on in-person selling techniques, the prices that kept even small enterprises afloat—government officials viewed as evidence of the market's obsolescence. By the early 1950s it was clear that *les Halles* generated far too much traffic than its city-center location could support. Indeed, the nightly gridlock had begun to hurt certain areas of the market itself because buyers increasingly made their purchases on the periphery, rather than trying to reach the pavilions. In addition, the market's hygiene facilities were decades behind the times.

Once it became clear that the market had to be relocated, the main questions for government planners became not just where to move it but also (and of greater concern to most Parisians) what to put in its place in the First Arrondissement (a subterranean shopping mall, it turned out). For many wholesalers, however, the big question became whether even to make the move to the new suburban location of Rungis. There they were promised fewer trade restrictions (the *mandataire* system would be abolished), modern cold storage facilities, proximity to Orly airport and regional rail lines, plenty of parking—but also considerably higher overhead costs, and potentially the loss of the many clients who did business with them primarily out of habit or because they were nearby. Perhaps not surprisingly, hundreds decided against the move in favor of retirement or a new line of work. Of the 918 fruit and vegetable wholesale firms in operation during the last years of *les Halles,* only 393 reopened at Rungis (Chemla 1994, 168). Also gone were many of *les forts,* whose physical strength had been rendered obsolete by freight elevators and forklifts.

Rungis: Wholesale Changes

The Rungis market stretches across 230 hectares, encompassing 40 cavernous warehouses, 25,000 parking spaces, and an assortment of office buildings, shops, and restaurants. Eleven of the warehouses are devoted to fruits and vegetables; trade takes place on the ground floor, and traders' low-ceiling of-

Figure 5.5.
Rungis, the market "in search of a soul." Photo by Alice Hartley.

fices line the mezzanine. Described by its boosters as the world's biggest fresh food market, Rungis' very vastness makes it a lonely place to traverse by foot. The actual market now runs from early morning until around 11 A.M., but merchants conduct much of their business over the telephone (and increasingly by e-mail) during regular business hours. At lunch they drive to one of the market's several bistros; after work they navigate the *peripherique* with the rest of the Parisian area commuters.

Early on, Rungis became known as a market "in search of a soul." Journalists' comparisons of *les anciennes Halles* and the new market emphasized the latter's "functional" and "sterile" design, and the lack of the smells, sounds, and colors described by Zola. The market's planners tried to combat this ambiance problem by building other attractions. As a 1970 newspaper article noted, Rungis was trying to invent "a new folklore":[18]

> Drugstores, football clubs, a "cinema drive-in" (automobilists, like in the USA, will be able to watch a movie from inside their car) with hostesses in phosphorescent outfits, circulating on phosphorescent mopeds. All this should . . . incite Parisians to come visit the world's biggest food market. At least that's what its merchants and restaurateurs hope . . .

Whether or not Rungis succeeded in attracting Parisian fun-seekers (it did not), what the merchants really hoped for, of course, was to do enough business to cover their increased operating expenses and still turn a profit. Within a few years it became clear that many enterprises in the fruit and vegetable sector were not achieving this goal, despite an initial jump in the volume and value of commerce for the market as a whole. In fact, a 1979 survey revealed that more than 60 percent of the fruit and vegetables enterprises at Rungis were in financial trouble (Chemla 1994, 168); around two dozen had already gone under and more than a hundred would eventually follow.

Neither scholars nor the French public paid much attention to the troubles of the Rungis fruit and vegetable wholesalers; the one semi-detailed study largely blamed the merchants themselves for failing to adapt to the demands of modern food distribution. Unlike the other wholesalers at Rungis (in the meat sector especially), they did not specialize, but instead diversified—in some cases offering more than 300 kinds of fruits and vegetables (Chemla 1994, 218, cf. 311). They also maintained their varied packaging and selling methods (some sold on commission, others were resellers) and resisted a proposed system for disseminating price information electronically within and beyond the marketplace (Chemla 1994, 167–68). In short, most fruit and vegetable wholesalers did little to accommodate the large retailers, who consequently sought to circumvent them entirely.

Yet it is not difficult to understand why many wholesalers, especially the smaller ones, opposed a system that would have encouraged customers to shop only according to prices posted on video screens. It is also easy to see why they did not want to deal in only one or two products. Both kinds of "rational" adaptation to the demands of modern food retailing would have devalued their existing expertise and, to the extent that they reduced wholesalers' jobs to the delivery of large quantities of uniformly graded produce, would have also moved them one step closer to obsolescence. Wholesalers who later began supplying large retailers describe such transactions as necessary but not enjoyable. As one importer-wholesaler described it, in the age of hypermarkets, the product had become little more than an "economic vector," and the wholesaler the agent responsible for pushing it towards the realization of its cash value.

In any case, the rise of the hypermarkets was just one of several changes in French food provisioning—alongside the massive increase in the supply and a shift toward convenience-oriented consumption—that wholesalers by themselves could not do much about, and which created altogether less favorable market conditions. In turn, changes in shopping and consumption habits, as described earlier in the chapter, were closely related to yet-broader changes in the French economy and thus employment patterns—changes that provided

Figure 5.6.
Rungis before dawn. Like other large-scale retailers, the French hypermarkets demand uniform produce and packaging. Photo by Christophe Maître.

younger generations many alternatives to the trades practiced by their parents. At Rungis, as in the small independent grocery sector (and for that matter, farming), this meant that many enterprises shut down because one generation retired and the next did not take over. The decline of the *petit commercant,* in other words, reflected changes as much social as economic.

The more interesting question therefore is not why the Rungis fresh produce traders' numbers declined, but rather how their profession survived. Although they pursued diverse strategies, one of the most common was to join, initiate, or extend transnational commodity networks, and especially networks that stretched into the southern hemisphere. The globalization the French greengrocer's shelf, in this sense, reflected not merely the incursions of multinational agribusiness, but rather the collective action of a wide range of intermediaries dealing in fresh but foreign fruits and vegetables.

The Import Empires

The largest companies in the Rungis fruit and vegetable market were in some ways a breed apart. They were less threatened by the rise of large-scale retailing in France than smaller wholesalers, not simply because of their size but also because most of them were already importing and in some cases producing overseas by the mid-20th century. These companies, among them Ponoma, Agrisol, Compagnie Fruitiere, SIIM and Azoulay, typically dealt in bananas plus a range of other ocean-freighted tropical and counter-season fruit; many of their products came from the Americas as well as Africa. They were engaged in transnational commercial relationships, transportation, and processing operations (for example, banana ripening) that the large French retailers could not easily circumvent. Although the retailers' expanding market share in the last part of the 20th century enabled them to push these large companies on certain fronts such as hygiene and packaging standards, they continued to depend on them for an expanding range of goods and services (Codron 1996).

In particular, these companies expanded the range of tropical and counter-season fruits available to the mass market to include not just bananas or citrus but also mangoes and wintertime peaches. By supplying supermarkets across France with these products, such companies helped to make the French food supply less seasonal and regionally diverse, and the exotic more banal. The people engaged in this work at a day-to-day-level, however, emphasized its variety and unpredictability. A management-level employee for one of the largest companies insisted that, mass scale and modern distribution technologies aside, the globalized fresh produce business was "not an industry:"

Industry, it's different . . . after you sign a contract, it lasts a year and nothing changes. Whereas we in the fruit and vegetable *métier,* we work in products that are perishable, dangerous, which are perpetually competitive, because we work with nature, too. So if a country has no more of a product, we find some in another country. As the saying goes, *la nature a horreur du vide,* so if there are no more avocados in Mexico, we'll find some in South Africa. If there are no more in South Africa, we find some in Israel . . . there's always all that. All that makes it a *métier* in which you're always questioning, you're always wondering. No, it's true! If someone says to me, "No, I know, it's like this or that," he's wrong, there is no "truth". There is no one truth; there are truths, many truths. The truth about Chilean apples is different than the truth about South African apples is different than the truth about New Zealand apples for example . . . So all that makes for a *belle soupe!* But that's what impassions. It's a *métier* you cannot do halfway.

It is worth noting that multinational fresh produce firms expected their suppliers, whether in South Africa or Chile, to adhere to the "one truth" of aesthetic quality, as defined by grades and standards for each commodity (Tanaka and Busch 2003). Still, this man's description of his work—while not necessarily representative of the views of French managers in these firms, especially younger ones[19]—differs strikingly from the accounts of intermediaries working for corporate importers and retailers in the United Kingdom. The latter more often boasted about how they could, in fact, manage their products as if they were industrial commodities.

Although the largest and oldest French produce importers shipped much of their fruit by sea, a number of them also dealt in airfreight counter-season vegetables, including green beans from Africa. They all considered it a minor, even trivial commodity relative to their overall trade—relegated, in the case of Dole France, to its "other vegetables" division. They did not produce green beans on their own land, but rather on contract with African exporters. The employees in charge of these transactions clearly took pride in their ability to understand and accommodate the cultural norms of their African suppliers, and to tolerate the risks that their business poses. In some cases, they suggested that it was a particularly French competence, or at least one that Anglo-Saxons lacked. It should be noted that in describing their own cultural sensitivity, these individuals did not hesitate to make sweeping (and often patronizing) generalizations about *les Africains.* As one man explained his company's decades-old trade relations with West Africa:

We're still there because we've tried to adapt. If you go there with an American spirit or a German spirit, then you'll probably fail, because when you say to these [African] guys, you've written that, you've signed a contract, now you've got to do it. They can say we can't because that's that; then you go into *les palabres* [negotiations]. . . . We're interested in the arts and the culture, and we like the people. We want to do business with them. You've got to accept the fact that they don't think the same. They don't behave the same. What they're interested in is not the same . . . You have to adapt. You have to accept that they fail. You have to accept that you are probably going to lose money, and you have to accept to send money . . . and this is where it hurts, because when you send a million francs to Africa, basically you're sure that you won't see them again.

So under those conditions, how do you decide who can be trusted?
We often fail. We try to understand the failures.

How long will you give somebody?
A season, couple of seasons. Fifteen days. The first thing an African guy will tell you is OK, I understand, I'll do it, I'll comply with it, I'll sign the paper. Now I need 500,000 francs. This is where I think the Germans would walk away; a Germans would not send the money like that . . . a supermarket chain, Carrefour, would [also] have trouble with this money. You have to explain to our financial people that yes, it's OK to send a million francs to "this guy." And you've got no addresses in [for example] the Ivory Coast, so the only address that you get is a postal box. And so he's got this postal box. Here we send it to his personal account, but that's normal. When is he going to send the fruit? Well, eventually in 14 months . . .

These large companies' capacity to send their African suppliers large advances helped assure the companies get what they want. As another man said,

It's necessary to adapt to their system. They must adapt to our needs, and so we must also understand their problems. Their problem, effectively, is cash. When the market prices are good and they have cash, they'll also have lot of product. [This company] has the means to pay, so we do it, and it helps them a lot.

As discussed earlier, French retailers showed much less interest than their U.K. counterparts in the conditions of production in their overseas supply regions. French importers interviewed in 1999 said repeatedly that the big retail chains wanted cheap prices, prompt deliveries, and uniform quality, not detailed information about, for example, on-farm chemical use. This attitude gave importers considerable autonomy. As one employee for a large import firm said of the French supermarkets:

> They put their trust in us. One mustn't do wrong by them. That's to say that just because they don't demand traceability doesn't give us permission to do no matter what . . . They want, finally, a product that conforms to regulations, so there's no pesticide residues . . . that we check on ourselves, we're very careful about that. Now to know who planted, who seeded, where a lot came from, who packaged it . . . no, I don't think they want that . . . It's not the precision that the English supermarkets demand of their producers in Kenya. In Kenya it's fantastic, but is it useful? Either a product conforms or it doesn't.

By 2001, importers acknowledged that French supermarkets, in reaction to the 2000 BSE scare in France as well as a new wave of EU food safety regulation, had become more demanding. Although they did not expect their importers to implement traceability systems immediately, they did demand that their products conform to increasingly comprehensive *cahiers de charges*—that is, lists of standards concerning the hygienic, environmental, and even social conditions of production. Representatives of Dole France, a company much more concerned about protecting a brand image than any of the other French import firms, emphasized that it had its own environmental and social standards and had not waited for the supermarkets to impose them. Individuals at other firms, however, expressed doubt about whether such standards could or even should be enforced. One importer described the paperwork he filled out for the supermarkets as *ouverture de la parapluie,* or the "opening of the umbrella:"

> We need to sign loads of papers for the supermarket chains saying "I know there is no child working on our plantation. We don't use this [chemical] product." Etc., etc. As long as they've got papers from us, they're happy. Nobody's checking. . . . We signed the papers. Like everybody, like Nike signing paper.
>
> *Saying no child labor.*
>
> Yeah . . . who's convinced that there's no child working in Nike factories?
>
> *Well, apparently Sainsbury's goes to Africa. They send people there, you know, once or twice a year. So apparently they do go look, but—*
>
> Well, where are they going to look? I mean, if you go to Africa, they can go and see [company X], the biggest plantation. So they find no child working there . . . there are some abuses, but you've got to be

careful not to go too far. We try to monitor for that. But there's no way to control it entirely . . . there are loads of small-scale farmers, little farmers, normally the family works there, and the family needs that desperately . . . The child is working somewhere . . . that's normal, and if you tell the [African] guy "don't do that," he will be offended.

Many of the people working for U.K. import firms and supermarkets, as discussed in chapter 6, expressed similar doubts about the appropriateness of prohibiting child labor on African farms, but they were much more concerned about the measures taken to insure that child labor is never found on any of their African suppliers' farms. The British intermediaries, in other words, did not feel that paperwork alone provides sufficient "bulletproofing" (Strathern 1999) in a commodity network subject to regular auditing and intense media scrutiny.[20] French importers' greater nonchalance reflected their confidence that neither French supermarkets nor anyone else (that is, the French media) intended to check up on them. They preferred, for the time, just the *parapluie*.

Compared to their U.K. counterparts, the large French import companies had much more say in decisions about where and with whom to do business. And unlike most smaller French wholesale firms, they could tolerate the risks involved in sending money into regions where such advances are necessary and expected. They could afford, in other words, to engage in patron-client relations on a transnational scale, and thereby secure supplies from places that would otherwise lack the means to produce for export. These patronage relations in turn helped large companies obtain year-round supply and competitive prices—both especially important priorities if they sold primarily to the big retail chains.

Tolerance for risk, however, did not always translate into patience with perceived cultural difference, especially as alternatives became easier to find. At least four of the big firms that had historically imported green beans from Burkina Faso had stopped by 2001. Instead, they were doing business in African countries where settler colonialism (both British and French) had made it possible for them to find more "professional" suppliers. Presumably, given the demands of the contemporary French market, "professional" suppliers could more reliably make the large volume, uniform quality deliveries that these firms' supermarket clients demanded; they may also have been suppliers with their own sources of pre-season financing. Yet this was not always clear from the explanations provided by these firms' representatives, which fell back on generalizations about race and "African culture." As the director of one large firm said of its former trade with Burkina Faso, "We stopped because it was too compli-

cated, a bore, and we never found the people there necessary for this work."
In general, he said,

> When we work in Africa, most of our suppliers are whites . . . We
> have a few black suppliers, with whom we can't act in the same
> manner. Obviously culture plays a preponderant role in commerce,
> and the African culture, the habits of African life, make things very
> complicated.

Surviving Small

*The little ones, we're the little mice, and [the supermarkets] need the little
mice so that they don't get eaten by the [other] big guys . . . That's our
role. One must be always awake, to think a lot and to react vit vit vit so
as to get ahead of the group and to alert Carrefour or the others . . . We
have specialties, and it's through specialties that we manage to stand
out. Why? We know our subject by heart . . . We generally get
information very fast, before everybody else.*
—Director of small import firm, Rungis

Big companies like Dole dominated French fresh produce importing by the
end of the 20th century, but conducted most of their business in corporate
offices and distribution centers separate from the Rungis wholesale docks.
There, dozens of much smaller companies, most of them employing fewer than
twenty employees (and in a few cases only two or three) handled much of the
trade in exotic and counter-season produce. They fell into three categories. The
"couriers" were the least visible; they arranged shipments for other merchants,
renting only office cold storage and space. The more numerous importer-
wholesalers sold their own produce on the main floor and made their overseas
phone calls from upstairs offices. Last, several wholesalers occasionally bought
imported produce on commission but more often just bought it at Rungis and
resold it to a range of retail clients.

Most of these companies were family-run, insofar as the owners—nearly
all men[21]—had at least one or two relatives working for them. Many of the
newer companies were started by men (often themselves relatively young, mid-
30s rather than 50s) who left other companies, typically taking a few loyal
suppliers and customers with them. Appearances revealed little about the scale
and health of their enterprises. Some of the most prosperous and internationalized kept the shabbiest offices, and only a handful maintained Web sites. They
typically kept long hours; it was not unusual to find someone who came to

work at five in the morning to check on a shipment still in his office making phone calls at five in the evening. All felt the pressures of a market increasingly controlled by large retailers and transnational trade firms, but had varied strategies for coping with them.

Couriers and the newer importers most commonly specialized in the niche markets that larger importers had not yet captured. These firms' directors explored and experimented; they went abroad looking for the best producers of star fruit; they commissioned small batches of baby vegetables to see how they would sell. Many of their products would never prove popular, and those that did would likely attract the attention of the big firms. Still, the specialty importers said they preferred niche markets. The director of one well-established exotic produce firm explained why he would never trade in bananas:

> I can't fight against Dole or Chiquita. Plus there's a lot of competition in [mass] products . . . There are perhaps 100 companies selling oranges. So the supermarkets have a lot of choice, and they want to

Figure 5.7.
Pre-packaged "baby" vegetables are still considered niche products in France, unlike in Britain. Photo by Christophe Maître.

discuss the price a lot. By contrast, not many people import products like the Australian huckleberry. That's why we stick with products like that.

Small importers also said that their size allowed them to maintain better relations with their suppliers. The same man continued:

Many suppliers complain about how they are treated by big [import] companies because it's much more impersonal, whether they call or actually come to visit. The person isn't there, they pass you on to someone else. The supplier, when he calls, he likes to have an immediate response, he wants to speak to the boss right away and then decide. So that's maybe one advantage we have over the big firms.

Small wholesalers, meanwhile, sought to compete on the level of the services offered to clients. For example, one middle-aged third-generation trader, having concluded by the mid-1990s that traditional produce wholesaling was doomed, refashioned his business to make it more attractive to large Parisian-area retailers. Recognizing that even the best organized hypermarket buyers sometimes found themselves short of a particular product, he made sure that

Figure 5.8.
Smaller wholesalers rely on their customers' need for personal service and last-minute orders. Photo by Christophe Maître.

France: Expertise and Friendship

159

individual buyers knew they could call on him to rapidly procure and even deliver whatever fruit or vegetable they needed. He also began hiring out his own employees as *animateurs* to help supermarkets set up displays and promote exotic and other specialty products. This service, he said, responded not only to a need of consumers—who knew less and less about how to choose and prepare fresh produce—but also to a fundamental problem of the hypermarkets.

> Our future as wholesalers is to try to reintroduce into the big stores the conviviality of the marketplace . . . They have as few employees as possible, and they pay them as little as possible. And thus they face a contradiction: They want to sell so many different products, but they have so few employees proposing them that people don't know what to buy anymore. Why buy one product rather than another? . . . And if there's nobody in the store to advise you, it's not easy. So I think the work for professionals like us is to bring to the store the kind of professionalism and personnel you used to find at the corner store. We need to bring them our products, of course, but also our savoir-faire.

Unlike Dole and the other larger import firms, the smaller ones rarely advanced money to their suppliers, and generally preferred to work on commission if they were not entirely sure how well products would sell. Like the big firms, however, they emphasize that a good *commissionaire* treats his supplier well:

> Selling on commission doesn't mean you can sell at whatever price and take your cut and liquidate the merchandise in any old way. You have to take account of the price that [the supplier] hopes for, you have to know to make an effort, you have to keep him well informed, to send the him records of the daily sales by fax, in short to act correctly. Otherwise you lose your supplier very fast and after that your image and reputation. Everything depends on whether you're working for the short or long term. Given that I have two children to feed . . . it's better that I work for the future.

Importers' descriptions of their supplier relationships abounded with these sorts of righteous statements. Everyone at Rungis knew, however, that importers did not always "act correctly" towards suppliers. Particularly vulnerable were the small and relatively inexperienced overseas exporters who, not unlike the peasants who supplied Paris from southern France in the late 19th century, could neither know what happened to their products after they shipped them[22]—whether they arrived in good condition, whether and how much they sold for—nor hope to prosecute dishonest buyers. Their vulnerability was perhaps compounded by the importers' reliance on stereotypes to rationalize unscrupulous actions. No one, of course, would admit to such actions outright, but the jokes and rumors that circulated among Rungis traders suggested that the perceived unreliability of African suppliers—or at least some of them—provided support for a cheat-or-be-cheated mentality. As one importer put it:

> In the black countries it's very difficult to find competent people because the blacks don't think the same way as us and don't understand our needs . . . When I say 'the blacks' I mean above all the blacks of West Africa, because in South Africa it's the whites who run everything and in East Africa people are more refined. The Kenyans have a much more realistic approach to commerce; they understand the needs of Europeans much better than West Africans. In every country there are people who work badly and people who work well, but in the West [of Africa] they work more badly than well. Those who work well are practically white in their head. It's not a story of racism, it's a story of reality.

Colonial regimes also typed different African populations as more or less "refined" (or "evolved") and hardworking in order to decide which colonial subjects would be educated, which would be hired as soldiers, and which as domestic servants. Then as now, it was easier, politically, to "let culture do much of the work of race" (Stoler and Cooper 1997, 35). Culture could be invoked as the "reality" explaining why certain colonized populations should be treated differently than others, and why all of them (even those "practically white in their head") should be treated differently than Europeans. In Rungis, such characterizations allowed for a looser code of conduct, and thus a broader range of acceptable business practices. Taking advantage of someone who might fail you anyway could seem, if not exactly right, then at least not too wrong, especially if your competitors were doing the same. The comments of two small import firm owners during a late Friday afternoon beer-drinking session revealed more about this moral logic than most of the statements Rungis traders made in more formal interview settings. After describing what they called *le probleme Africain*—African exporters always wanting cash advances, then sending poorly packaged, poorly labeled products—the conversation shifted back to Rungis. Speaking of a competitor who was hiring the staff and buying the technologies needed for full traceability (which in 1999 put him well ahead of most exotics importers) they said that he must have financed this upgrade by "stealing from the Africans." By contrast, they said half-jokingly, "We only steal from them a little."

The Green Bean King

In between the largest, oldest import-export firms and the niche marketers, a few medium-size companies at Rungis pursued strategies that, on the surface, appeared unviable in the face of Dole-scale competition. They imported mostly commonplace tropical and counter-season products, among them African green beans, and sold them to diverse customers; some bought pallets, others bought truckloads. They had no widely recognized brand image; neither did they offer any particularly innovative services. Perhaps most curious, they continued to finance horticultural production in African countries that other Rungis traders dismissed as too risky.

Among these medium-sized firms, the story of one in particular sheds light on how transnational traders can parlay cultural *connaissance* into economic power. The company Selection, founded in 1970, was by the end of the century the largest green bean importer in Europe and the world. It was also the single most important green bean buyer in Burkina Faso and other exporting countries in francophone West Africa. Much of this story is about Selection's founder Yves Gallot—often described by others in the business as *le roi d'haricot vert* (the green bean king)—and his friendships with African exporters. In Burkina Faso, he forged most of these friendships during a period of expansion and optimism in the green bean trade, and maintained them through years when, he claimed, they cost him sizable sums of money. As discussed in chapter 3, however, the economic worth of friendship among West African traders cannot always be measured in terms of season-to-season profits and losses.

Gallot founded Selection at Rungis after working as a wholesaler's assistant at *les Halles*. He originally went looking for business in Africa, he explained, because farmers in Spain and southern France already had regular buyers in Paris and did not want to sell to a newcomer. By the early 1970s, it was technically viable, but still unusual, to air-ship fresh produce out of Africa. So finding suppliers was "truly an adventure!" involving bush-plane rides and long drives between villages, including one where a local chief brought out a bottle of Mumm Cordon Rouge to seal an agreement. Since then, Gallot's relations with villages in a number of different countries, including Burkina Faso, had grown "very close, very friendly, very convivial," and when he traveled to his supply countries, he visited at least some of them. But over three decades, Selection's business grew to include a pineapple plantation in Ivory Coast, green bean suppliers from southern France to Madagascar, and sizable trades in tomatoes and tropical fruits—all of which gave Gallot less time for the forays into the bush which he so clearly enjoyed.[23] In Burkina Faso, therefore, Gallot's friends were a small group of mostly urban-based businessmen, plus a prominent village-based chief. As described in chapter 3, these men contracted with groups of smallholders to produce Selection's green beans, which as of 2000 accounted for about 40 percent of the country's total green bean exports.

Gallot was one of the very few French importers who regularly pre-financed green bean production in Africa. In Burkina Faso he sent tens of thousands of dollars worth of farm inputs and cash annually to each of his suppliers (for a total of 2 million francs in 2001, or around $300,000), with the understanding that these credits would be taken out of the purchase price. In theory, every harvest and delivery of the three-month season was planned in advance, to assure Selection the steady supply that it promised clients. In practice, the volumes shipped during the 1999–2001 seasons were highly irregular. The increasingly unreliable service of Air Afrique was partly to blame, as were periodic weather incidents, but Gallot and his employees also blamed his suppliers (the Burkinabé exporters) for failing to fulfill their responsibilities. They suspected that some of them did not distribute the inputs, or pay the peasants their due, or assure that the peasants—understandably disgruntled—did not then sell Selection-financed green beans to other exporters. Chapter 3 situated such practices in Burkinabé exporters' local social networks, where resources intended for green bean production sometimes get invested instead in the re-affirmation of patronage ties and social status. From the perspective of most Rungis importers, these practices were simply typical of "black Africa," and a reason not to do much business there.

So why did Selection continue to invest in Burkina Faso? Gallot often said that it was only because his friends were there. While this claim sounds disin-genuous coming from the owner of a multimillion-dollar business, it makes sense in light of Gallot's own position in and his views of the broader trade relationships linking Africa and Europe, and Selection's role in supplying the contemporary French green bean market.

Among the Rungis importers, Gallot was one of the most outspoken critics of the "Anglo-Saxon" way of doing business in food. He showed particular scorn for the British preoccupation with hygiene, but he also expressed a certain distaste for the "businesslike" cultural legacies of British colonialism as seen in countries like Kenya.

> I think the British left behind a bit more rigor than we did. By con-trast, what you find more of in our culture, and what we left even at the level of the population was *un peu plus d'amour de choses . . .* We maintained relationship with them that is, at the end, *plus sym-pathique . . .* a relationship which sometimes leads to a little violence because that's what happens where there's passion between people. Whereas the relation I see between Britain and its former colonies is colder, it's, how should I say it? A relationship of etiquette. Not

this warmth. Their great advantage is the rigor at the level of work
. . . All the same, we have a savoir-faire, an intelligence that largely
compensates for this handicap we've had vis-à-vis the Anglo-
Saxons . . .

Gallot acknowledged that this British "rigor" had made Kenya the world's
most consistent producer of top-quality green beans, but expressed little affec-
tion for the country. By contrast, in Burkina Faso he found a commercial culture
that not only spoke his language but also, for all its frustrations, suited his
sensibilities and skills: Passionate argument and appeals to friendship and morality were accepted, even expected; official documents were treated with a
certain skepticism while personal loyalty was appreciated and sometimes re-
warded.[24] It was also a commercial culture based on peasant production. Gallot
subscribed to the belief, widely held in France, that peasant farmers could not
only better sustain the rural environment and society but also produced better
food than industrial agriculture. This belief gave Gallot confidence in the ability
of Burkinabé smallholders to meet new EU food safety regulations (in sharp
contrast with the doubts expressed by British importers and supermarket buyers). But perhaps more importantly, Gallot was confident that the Burkinabé
would continue to accept their position in his transcontinental green bean empire and, more precisely, the prices they received from him.

For ultimately the French market wanted only so much of the best. Over
the past three decades, the market for African *haricot vert* in France had become
a mass market (in part thanks to Gallot's work) but also a segmented one.
Kenya's beans, recognized for their *qualité top*, satisfied demand from the top-
end clientele (exclusive greengrocers and restaurateurs) and were priced accordingly. Everyone else, however, expected a good quality but cheaper product—almost a euro less per kilo—and that, Gallot explained, was Burkina Faso's
raison d'etre in the overall market. This reasoning did not sit well with the
Burkinabé exporters who remembered the days when their country's beans still
commanded premium prices. But given how much of current production Gallot
financed, he effectively set the price for Burkinabé green beans. Although the
exporters might complain (those not counted among his friends did so vehe-
mently), they did not want to lose his patronage altogether.

Lastly, Gallot stayed in Burkina Faso because selective and strategic investments in friendship helped him to respond not only to the market's demand
for affordable luxury but also, by the end of the 1990s, its increasingly rigorous
food safety and environmental standards. Although French produce importers,
unlike their British counterparts, did not need to prepare their suppliers for on-
site inspections by supermarket personnel or outside auditors, they did have to

be able to claim that their suppliers were in compliance with European retailer standards of "good agricultural practice," as well as EU pesticide regulations.

For Gallot's work in Burkina Faso, this meant, among other things, entrusting his ablest friends with the resources needed to adapt. By 2001, the largest single recipient of Selection financing was not one of the urban-based exporters, but rather a prominent Mossi chief who lived in a village near an irrigation scheme. The chief had some 500 local households growing green beans on land that he controlled, using seeds and farm chemicals that he distributed. While Gallot expressed exasperation with the Burkinabé exporters as a group, he had nothing but praise for the chief, who for the past several years had proven Selection's most reliable supplier in terms of both quality and quantity. His reliability did not owe to technological advantage, for the site did not even have electricity. Rather, the chief drew on both his ascribed moral authority and a formidable business savvy (aided by years of education and travel) to assure the loyalty and productivity of his growers. Gallot thus chose the chief's land to experiment with drip irrigation and non-chemical pest control, both part of the rubric of agricultural methods described in French as *culture raisonnée* ("reasonable farming"). By 2002, Selection's Web site boasted of its *culture raisonnée* in Burkina Faso, a country where, it claimed, "peasant savoir-faire and nature" combined to produce a "delicious, attractive and wholesome (*sain*)" green bean. With a little help from his friends, in other words, Gallot was able to refashion Burkina Faso's traditional advantages as a supply region— namely its low labor costs and winter time production—to keep up with the changing demands of his clientele. In turn, Gallot spoke of tentative plans to help the chief (who was Catholic) build a church in his village—a monument that would testify to the moral and material worth of both men.

The relationship between Gallot and the chief, it should be clear, is hardly typical of those between French importers and their African suppliers. But it does illustrate a broader point about trade relations couched in terms of friendship: Namely, that while it would be naive to take traders' own descriptions of these friendships at face value, it would also be wrong to assume that traders forge such preferential relations for purely strategic reasons. Instead, the discourses and practices of friendship in the market have to be situated in a broader cultural context. In this case, the value that Gallot placed on his relationship with the chief reflects not only the uncertain conditions of trade in countries such as Burkina Faso—conditions under which friendship may help to counter risk—but also French cultural norms about the work of food provisioning. These norms draw on France's own past as a peasant nation and as the birthplace of gastronomy, and they inform an idealized vision of food provisioning work as a whole, from farm to market to table. According to this ideal, the *métier* of the fresh produce trader is an honorable one, insofar as it helps to assure both the livelihood of the farmer and the satisfaction of the consumer. This ideal assumes not only that the trader possesses expert knowledge of the product, but also that the pace and scale and setting of commerce allows for the sociable display and sharing of that knowledge.

This idealized vision of the sociable and appreciative market in turn informs traders' nostalgia for *les Halles,* as well as their disdain (if not outright hostility) for supermarkets, fast food, and the perceived invasion of "Anglo-Saxon" food culture more generally. Such attitudes, as manifested in French popular support for José Bové's anti-"McDo" campaign, have been interpreted as French cultural nationalism in the face of globalization (Gordon and Meunier 2001). But this is not necessarily the same thing as opposition to globalization in any simple sense. The importers and exotic produce wholesalers at Rungis, on the contrary, have obvious stakes in an increasingly internationalized French fresh food supply. What they fear, rather, is a system of international food provisioning in which they are marginalized, if not totally obsolete.

Across the Channel, fresh produce traders like those who work at Rungis are, in fact, effectively obsolete, and importing has become a very different kind of enterprise. Although some of the differences are due to a history of laissez-faire food retailing in Britain, it would be a mistake (albeit a common one) to view the British system as a simply more advanced stage of capitalist food provisioning. As the next chapter shows, the intermediaries of the British fresh food supply operate in a qualitatively different cultural context—one shaped, again, by both historical influences and contemporary crises.

6

Britain

Brands and Standards

In February 2002, the *Financial Times* ran a full-page article on the dangers posed by excessive "food miles." It was written by the editor of *Country Life*, a magazine dedicated to the preservation of "the British way of life." Like many critics of food globalization, the author argued that the cheap food policies that originally drove the United Kingdom to import much of its food had hidden costs and posed grave risks both at home and abroad. The article noted that the United Kingdom, despite its experience of mad cow and foot-and-mouth diseases, still imported meat from countries known to be "breeding grounds for killer plagues"—in particular, species-jumping pathogens such as AIDS and the Ebola virus. Despite Britain's capacity to produce many kinds of fresh fruits and vegetables, supermarkets imported them from countries where, the article said, export farming "deprived" hungry people of land for their own food crops. The airfreight transport of such foods consumed huge quantities of fossil fuel, which drove global warming, which might, the article implied, hasten the onset of geopolitical conflict over increasingly scarce farmland. To avert this dark future, the author called on "concerned shoppers" to use their buying power to "force supermarkets" to purchase and promote more local foods. And, to make perfectly clear who was to blame for burning all these food miles, the accompanying illustration featured two cartoonish characters, one a businesslike carrot wearing the brand of Tesco, the country's biggest food retailer, and the other a Zambian green bean dressed as an ugly tourist (Aslet 2001) (see Fig. 6.1).

In turn-of-the-21st-century Britain, countryside preservationists were among the many activists who saw the African green bean and "baby veg" as symbolic of food globalization gone wrong, and who called on shoppers to help make things right. The supermarkets that stocked these petite, prepackaged vegetables intended, of course, a very different message—namely that convenient, novel fresh foods belonged in the British way of life, ideally 365 days a year. Yet this marketing strategy had a paradoxical payoff. As the supermarkets catered to, and indeed helped to cultivate, the tastes of a new

Figure 6.1.

"Clocking Up the Food Miles" by Ferguson. Reproduced Courtesy of the *Financial Times*.

generation of British "foodies," these valued consumers were starting to seek qualities in food that they, as corporate retailers, had no expertise in providing. The foodies, it turned out, were listening to, even joining forces with the activists!

The activists were also joining forces with each other, despite their diverse political priorities. With help from the popular media, they pushed the image-conscious retailers to demonstrate accountability through myriad performances of social responsibility. And although the activists' numbers were small relative to the total population of British supermarket shoppers, as outspoken "stakeholders" they wrested promises of reform from the country's food giants. These reforms would be felt in the many transnational fresh food commodity networks provisioning the birthplace of "industrial food" (Goody 1982).

In *English Culture and the Decline of the Industrial Spirit,* Martin Wiener examines Britain's longstanding tradition of "countryside" politics as one example of elite distaste for the values and aesthetics of industrialism (Wiener 1981). He argues that this distaste influenced patterns of investment, education, and business behavior in ways that contributed, ultimately, to Britain's 20th century decline as a global economic power. By the end of the century, however, the idealized visions that informed British agro-food activism—visions of a nation charged with maintaining not only a "green and pleasant land" but also an ethical post-empire—had begun to generate lucrative, albeit unintended, synergies.

On one side, the supermarkets found that the discourses and practices of corporate "social responsibility" could advance both their individual brand images and their political clout as an interest group. Demonstrating accountability, in other words, helped them carve out "competitive space" for waging ongoing battle over market share (Marsden, Harrison, et al. 1998; Hughes 1999). On the other side, nongovernmental organizations (NGOs, or in the United Kingdom, "charities") found that if they did not simply push but indeed *helped* the supermarkets to demonstrate social responsibility, they could earn the publicity and legitimacy necessary to their own political effectiveness and economic survival. Their own brand images, in other words, could benefit from the supermarkets' need to appear responsive to "stakeholder" concerns—or at least some of them. For while some NGOs focused on making the national food supply healthier, "greener," and above all more local—goals that drew quite directly on English cultural anti-industrialism—others sought to hold the corporate retailers accountable for working conditions and economic development in their overseas supply regions. These groups worked in an equally deep-rooted tradition of charity activism, one informed by Britain's history as an imperial power (Drescher 1987).

The supermarkets' reformism must also be set against the backdrop of Thatcherism and neoliberalism more broadly. Besides fueling NGO activism, state deregulation at the national and international level effectively handed over to the corporate supermarkets substantial powers of governance. Supermarket regulatory responsibility for the nation's food supply became not just possible, but expected—and expected, moreover, not just at home but also in the global South supply regions where the regulatory capacity of national governments and civil society was presumably much weaker.

These expectations weighed heavily on the minds of the intermediaries responsible for procuring fresh vegetables from Africa. They also raise questions about the cultural economy of corporate food "sourcing" in which these intermediaries worked. First, why did Britain's supermarkets come to be seen as responsible for assuring that food commodities from the former colonies were not just hygienic but also "ethical"? Second, how were certain NGOs able to influence the meanings and practices of supermarket supply chain ethics? In exploring these questions, I consider what political economic and social developments distinguished Britain's recent food history—the emergence of both "foodie" culture and an energized agro-food movement, among other things—and also what this history says about food provisioning in the industrialized world more generally. In particular, I consider the popular media's potent but also paradoxical role in food politics, especially in societies where direct knowledge of food production has grown scarce.

Third and last, how did the supermarkets assure that all their suppliers were "up to code," and how did anglophone intermediaries experience this new culture of supply chain management? Building on chapter 4, this chapter examines how ostensibly "objective" measures of supplier performance were necessarily and sometimes uneasily implemented through subjective personal (though often at-a-distance) relationships. Yet the personal nature of these relationships should not distract from their geopolitical and geo-economic significance. Rather, the technical, discursive, and social methods of managing and checking up on suppliers represented a new form of postcolonial power. It was postcolonial not simply because it was exerted in former colonies but also because it relied on certain identities and subjectivities established during the colonial era (Scott 1995; Gupta 1998). Or, in the words of one supermarket middle manager, this power relied on finding suppliers with "like minds," and these minds were easiest to find on the large, white-owned settler and corporate farms of anglophone Africa.

The supermarkets' postcolonial power enabled them to clean up down South in more ways than one. On one level, it sanitized production sites, helping to insure that Zambian "baby vegs" were untainted by bacteria, pesticides, or child labor. On another level, the supermarkets "cleaned up" by pushing certain costs and risks onto their suppliers. By doing so, they introduced new forms of vulnerability, exploitation, and exclusion in African food-exporting countries—and all supposedly to protect the interests of consumers who understandably cared more about their food than they used to. The final question, posed here but hardly possible to answer yet: Would consumers care about where and how power was exercised in their name?

Retail Rule

In January 2002, Britain's Department of Environmental and Rural Affairs (DE-FRA) released the report of its Policy Commission on the Future of Farming and Food. Six months in the making, the report generated considerable speculation among food activists and the media. Given the commission's diverse makeup—its ten members included a conservationist, organic and conventional farmers, the head of a consumer group, an economist, and, notably, the CEO of Sainsbury's—at that time the country's number-two food retailer—whose views would prevail? Although DEFRA emphasized that the members had been appointed "in a personal capacity" according to their background and expertise, the latter member obviously represented some of the most powerful actors in Britain's food supply system, namely the supermarkets.

Or maybe not. In an interview a few days after the report was released, a top-level employee of one of Sainsbury's competitors asked skeptically, "But in fact, how does one measure power?" He then pointed out that none of the British supermarkets commanded as much of the domestic or global market as the French chain Carrefour; none of them had much clout vis-à-vis multinational suppliers like Nestle; none of them, obviously, could do anything about the British climate, which limited the range of foods that the country's own farmers could supply. In short, he argued, the British supermarkets did not deserve the "concentrated assault" of criticism that farmers, charities, and even the government had leveled on them in recent years.

If this person's argument was hardly unbiased, it did make clear that simple measures of market share and earnings did not adequately describe how supermarket power was exercised and perceived. Market share alone did not explain, for example, why the British supermarkets exercised so much more influence over food production processes in faraway supply zones than did larger retailers such as Carrefour and Wal-Mart. Nor, closer to home, did it explain why the supermarkets were the targets of so many activist campaigns—many of which were not even about food per se—or why the supermarkets in turn sought the activists' approval. Nor did it explain why the national media covered supermarket competition and controversy with the ardor usually reserved for politicians or celebrities. Rather, the supermarkets' power has to be understood in light of their history as political as well as economic actors.

Their influence over British foodways as well as food policy developed in a unique geographic and regulatory context: Britain's small size and dense population enabled the top retailers to consolidate truly national (as opposed to regional) markets, and a generally laissez-faire state did little to hinder either their geographic expansion or their increasing domination of suppliers (Wrigley 1998; Marsden, Flynn et al. 2000). But the supermarkets' power reflects also how they historically responded to, and indeed cultivated the anxieties and desires of consumers who, earlier than most, were far removed from the sources of their food.

For the grocery chains (or "multiples") of the 1870s, as discussed in chapter 2, this meant selling goods that consumers could trust to be unadulterated, unvarying in quality, fairly priced, and available in their neighborhood. This formula put them in direct competition with consumer cooperatives, but at a time when demand was growing fast enough to accommodate them both (Gurney 1996). By 1920, the multiples and the cooperatives each accounted for roughly 20 percent of the country's food retail market (Jefferys 1954; Fraser 1981). While stocking similar products, they promoted very different shopping experiences and visions of consumption. Whereas the cooperatives saw consumption as a social activity aimed at building collective identity and political awareness, the commercial chains encouraged consumption as a form of self-expression, reaffirming the individual shopper's status in her household and community. The outcome of the contest is by now well known: With their advertising, appealing store design, and emphasis on service and selection, the multiples' model dominated food retailing by mid-century. Cooperatives survived by adopting many of its features (Humphery 1998).

As the multiples expanded their reach, so, too, did they seek to accommodate consumers' changing concerns and lifestyles. Good value for money, of course, remained a priority, but anxieties about old-fashioned food adulteration had lessened with the introduction of tougher laws and the growth of brand-name food manufacturing. As fewer households hired servants and more women worked outside the home, convenience became more important than ever, both in the kitchen and in the store. The model of large, self-service stores offering a wide selection of processed foods, first developed in the United States, caught on quickly in Britain in the two decades after World War II (Seth and Randall 1999).

Meanwhile, the government's postwar commitment to providing cheap and abundant food, as laid out in the 1947 Agricultural Act, assured state support for economies of scale in both food production and retailing (Self and Storing 1962, 23). In the countryside, this meant greatly increased grain and livestock production, but at the expense of more diversified local and regional farming patterns. Britain looked to other countries, especially those in Mediterranean

Europe, for more and more of its fresh fruits and vegetables. At the same time, with the decline of local farmers' markets, supermarkets took over a greater proportion of fresh produce retailing. Gradually, the products on their shelves took on characteristics suited to their own priorities of transportability and long shelf life: Softer varieties of fruit gave way to firmer ones, and more fresh produce came plastic-wrapped or bagged. Similar trends were underway in the United States, but still years away in France.

By the beginning of the 1980s, a handful of companies had begun to emerge as the country's top supermarkets (Wrigley 1998). For them, the next decade marked a golden age of high profit margins and rapid innovation. The innovations were driven partly by the retailers' need to recoup massive investments in real estate and store construction, but they greatly increased the supermarkets' ability to anticipate and satisfy consumer demand, and to parlay that satisfaction into brand loyalty (Wrigley 1992). For current purposes, three related developments proved particularly significant. First, supermarkets built regional distribution centers. Over the short term this served to cut storage and transport costs, but it also enabled the supermarkets to circumvent food wholesalers and deal directly with suppliers—that is, producers themselves or importers representing producers. This shift in turn drove many wholesalers out of business and enabled the supermarkets to intervene much more extensively in production processes than before.

Second, the supermarkets used "point of sale" information technologies (like bar code scanning) to track sales. This information facilitated "just-in-time" stocking, which reduced costs and also the likelihood that consumers would ever find a favorite breakfast cereal out of stock at their local store. It also, of course, provided the supermarkets with useful information about trends in consumer purchasing patterns, especially once "loyalty cards" linked purchases to individual consumers. This kind of retailer data collection has since become standard practice across the industrialized world, but in the 1980s it represented a major innovation.

The third development, aided by the second, came in the realm of "own brand" products. Unlike in the United States, where supermarket store brands were until quite recently considered cheap generic substitutes for major labels, the British supermarkets promoted their own brands as guarantees of quality equal if not superior to anything else on the shelf. Marks and Spencer took this idea the farthest, selling exclusively store brand goods; altogether such products came to account for more than half of all United Kingdom grocery sales by the 1990s. Store brand goods offered the supermarkets important advantages over manufacturer brands, including higher profit margins and greater control over product marketing and development (Doel 1996; Hughes 1999). More broadly, they served to build consumers' trust in their respective corporate identities—a trust they eventually invoked to justify their role as the de facto gatekeepers of the national food supply.

This gatekeeper role took shape in the 1990s, following passage of the 1990 Food Safety Law. This law incorporated the recommendations of the EU as well as the neoliberal orientation of the John Major administration, but it was also influenced by the food scares of the late 1980s, which had both undermined the public's trust in the government's regulatory capacity and heightened public awareness of the many possible ways and places where food could become unsafe (Marsden, Flynn, et al. 2000). Thus the law allowed "food businesses" of all kinds to develop their own internal "hazard analysis" systems (HACCP), but also made them legally responsible for demonstrating due diligence in the event that any of their products fell short of the governments' safety standards.

If government analysts detected dangerous bacteria or illegal pesticide residues on samples of fresh produce, for instance, a company had to show that it had done everything reasonably possible to prevent such contamination. It would need to demonstrate, in particular, that it only bought produce from growers who, in turn, provided evidence that irrigation water was clean, their worker hygiene facilities adequate, and their pesticide usage correct. The gov-

Figure 6.2.
Value-added freshness. The top British supermarkets carry an enormous assortment of "ready meals." Photo by author.

French Beans and Food Scares

ernment's policy of publishing the names of companies whose products violated legal pesticide residue levels put additional pressure on supermarkets. Given the British media's own enthusiasm for "naming and shaming," keeping the company name off the Pesticide Committee's quarterly list of residue violations became just as important as demonstrating due diligence.

In the late 1990s, Britain's supermarkets joined EUREP, a European retailer trade group committed to developing a common set of "good agricultural practice" standards for their fruit and vegetable suppliers. While product safety and quality was, as always, a top priority, EUREP also stressed the need for environmentally sustainable production methods, and in particular reduced on-farm chemical use. The resulting EUREPGAP protocol provided retailers and importers with a forty-one page checklist, and was widely considered the most comprehensive code of its kind (EUREPGAP 2000). As a retailer initiative, however, it remained voluntary, and not all the EUREP members were in much hurry to demand compliance of their suppliers. As one British supermarket employee said of the EUREP meetings he attended: "Cultures such as Scandinavia, United Kingdom, Holland to a certain extent, are very much for tightening up these standards. The Mediterranean countries—Spain, Italy, France—have tended to be more laissez-faire."

Many of Britain's small retailers and other food businesses found that the costs and technical demands required by the new generation of food safety legislation onerous if not prohibitive. But for the top supermarkets, the regulatory reforms of the 1990s provided fresh impetus and justification for practices that ultimately furthered their domination of the British grocery market. In the name of protecting consumers' right to safe and high quality food, the supermarkets disciplined their supply chains in ways that helped them to cut costs, add value, and build brand image (Marsden, Flynn, et al. 2000).

In theory, suppliers unable or unwilling to comply with the supermarkets' demands could sell their products elsewhere. The renaissance of farmers' markets, for example, offered British farmers in certain regions the opportunity to sell locally. But for many of the U.K. supermarkets' overseas suppliers, among them Zambia's produce exporters, local markets for their high-value products did not exist, and alternative overseas markets (such as most of continental Europe) did not pay enough to cover transportation and prior fixed capital costs.[1] The managers of the Zambian export firms emphasized that they had invested in state-of-the-art cold storage and pre-packing facilities precisely in order to sell to the likes of Sainsbury's and Marks and Spencer; they could not possibly survive by selling bulk beans to France. For all practical purposes, the U.K. supermarkets were, for them, the only market.

By the late 1990s, the top five of these supermarket chains accounted for 75 percent of all grocery sales and were competing primarily against each other.

Although each had a distinct class-based image—Sainsbury's and Marks and Spencer were considered more middle class, Safeway and Asda working class—all were fighting for a larger share of the total national market. And although Wal-Mart's purchase of Asda in 1999 renewed the price-cutting pressure, competition took place on several other fronts as well. Having saturated the suburbs with superstores, for example, they began building smaller shops (Tesco's "Metros" and Sainsbury's "Centrals") in urban shopping districts. They also refurbished old stores and added new services. Having saturated the airwaves with their own advertising, they recruited the country's celebrity chefs to endorse their products and use them on their enormously popular television cooking shows. Having made it possible to eat any kind of food at any time of the year, they sought to, as one supermarket manager put it, "superimpose the perception of seasonality" with promotions and in-store tastings. Last but not least, they improved their offerings in their "destination categories"—the kinds of goods that could pull shoppers into one store rather than another. Fresh produce was among these strategic foods; it was among the most profitable, bringing in higher returns per square meter of shelf space than any other major supermarket category (Blythman 2002).

By the turn of the 21st century, relatively few supermarket chains were left, compared to a half-century earlier, but they were everywhere. As a 2002 BBC documentary put it, "the supermarkets have helped convince us not only that we are what we eat, but we are where we shop." So what did a nation of supermarket shoppers look like? The documentary, titled *Trolley Trouble,* contrasted shots of decadent abundance—store shelves and kitchen tables crammed with food, feasting partygoers—with images of monoculture fields and farmers and small towns ruined by the whims of mega-retailers. The film's criticism of the country's food retailer oligopoly was melodramatic but hardly unique. The government's Competition Commission undertook its own investigation of the supermarkets' trading practices in 1999, but found no conclusive evidence that they were, as the press put it, "ripping off Britain."[2] The code of practice recommended by the Commission, intended to assure that supermarkets treated their suppliers fairly, was voluntary and limited in scope. Could anyone rein in the food giants?

The Press for Better Food

*British food culture has grown up in the past fifty years. Once, we didn't
really seem to care what we ate, just so long as it filled us up. Not any
more: from haute cuisine to high street we're now demanding the same*

high standards that others get as a matter of course. So what brought about this change? And who were the driving forces behind it?
—*The Observer, food summer special,* June 29, 2002, "50 years of Food and Drink."

The driving force behind ethical trading standards in this country are the newspapers, and the bad stories that can arise when animals, children, women, or men get abused.
—British fresh produce importer, January 2001

For much of their history, British supermarkets prided themselves on their ability to give consumers what they wanted. Given the tens of millions of customers they served each week and the resources they devoted to meeting their demands, the supermarkets' claim that they understood and protected the "consumer interest" had more than a little credibility. It convinced the government to grant them substantial powers of self-regulation under the 1990 Food Safety Act, and it arguably convinced consumers themselves that they did not need other institutions to protect their rights. So, for example, even when European unification and the food scares of the late 1980s raised questions about the future of food regulation in Britain, groups such as the Consumers Association did not see surges in membership anything like those experienced by major environmental groups during the same time period. If concerned consumers were necessarily politically organized in the 19th century (See chapter 2), it seemed they no longer needed to bother. Now they could buy whatever food quality they wanted "at the retail outlet of their choice" (Marsden, Flynn, et al. 2000, 72).

By the late 1990s, however, the supermarkets faced a food movement that intended to use consumer power to leverage change well beyond the store aisles and indeed well beyond issues of food quality. Its members included traditional consumer groups as well as defenders of longstanding domestic concerns such as farm animal welfare and child nutrition. But some of the most vocal organizations demanded that the supermarkets work with them to fight poverty and injustice in the Third World—problems that they, as sellers of groceries, had never before considered their responsibility.

Market research indicated that only about three percent of consumers regularly demonstrated their own concern about such problems by seeking out certified fair trade products or other "ethically marked" products (Browne, Harris, et al. 2000). Nonetheless, the supermarkets did not just grant the NGOs an audience but eventually agreed to work with them to develop and implement new principles and benchmarks of supply chain "good practice." In other words, they agreed to demonstrate a particular kind of accountability. They had plenty of company. As Britain's late 20th-century leaders scaled back the government's regulatory roles, all kinds of corporate and public sector organizations sought to appear accountable by drawing up codes of conduct, undergoing audits, and engaging with stakeholders (more on them later). It was a way of showing that they could be trusted, in effect, to self-govern (Shore and Wright 2000). Although some of these accountability performances were legally required (such as the demonstration of due diligence in matters of food safety), the supermarkets' efforts to demonstrate ethical conduct represented a different kind of "bulletproofing," to borrow Marilyn Strathern's apt term (Strathern 1993).[3] For the supermarkets, a top priority was to protect themselves against incriminating media coverage, which NGOs often helped to generate.

The popular media, in this sense, did not just cover the movement to reform the supermarkets, but also became central to its dynamic. This dynamic owed, first, to the historically aggressive and loosely regulated nature of the British press,[4] and second, to the media's broader influence on popular food knowledge in a country where inherited or experiential food knowledge had grown weak, at least compared to a country such as France[5] (Caraher, Lang, et al. 2000). For the supermarkets, the most obvious problem rising from the public's relative lack of such knowledge was that it made it easy for the media, and especially the tabloid press, to set off food scares (Macintyre, Reilly, et al. 1998). As one fresh produce importer explained:

> There's nothing that makes a reporter's life so easy as a food scare. Now bearing in mind that we're talking about an urbanized country. Where do people receive their news about food? Because they're not on the farm, they don't understand how they [farmers] practice. And so that if they read it in the newspaper, they see it on the TV, it must be true. And even if it might be, in the overall scheme of things, an issue that we're dealing with that's not really something to worry about, the fact that it's now hitting the media means that it is something very much to worry about. You'll find the U.K. public stampede away from any product that has a bad image.

While this remark reflects a common food industry perspective—namely that the media manipulates an ignorant and emotional public[6]—it also hints at the media's more complex role in food politics and governance. Three aspects of this role are worth mentioning here. First, certain kinds of media food coverage, such as the immensely popular "celebrity chef" cooking shows, clearly benefited the supermarkets. These shows proliferated in the 1990s, with the newer ones focused less on the step-by-step directions offered by veteran chef Delia Smith (*Ready, Steady, Cook*) and more on exotic food themes and the entertainment value of particular personalities (Jamie "Naked Chef" Oliver and the voluptuous Nigella Lawson). Surveys found that viewers rarely prepared the dishes they saw on TV, but supermarket managers reported that they would often come looking—sometimes in huge numbers—either for featured ingredients or "ready-meal" versions of the dishes (Caraher, Lang, et al. 2000). The retailers, therefore, profited from the chefs' shows and spin-off cookbooks, their endorsements of retailers' store brand goods, and, not least, from their role in encouraging viewers to try new and often pricey foods.

Second, the TV cooking shows were just one kind of "foodie media" that food activists credited with making the public care more about the quality and origins of their food. Although the celebrity chefs rarely discussed politics, other members of the food-related media openly took sides. Among them were members of the Guild of Food Writers, an organization formed in 1984 to promote debate and advocacy around food issues. Some of the Guild's members were academics, others beat journalists or freelance food writers. They covered events sponsored by food-related NGOs such as the Soil Association and looked to them for information and guidance on current controversies. In the late 1990s, for example, many NGOs linked Britain's rural economic decline to the supermarkets' globalized sourcing practices—an issue which food writers could potentially get their readers to do something about. As an opinion piece in a 1999 Guild newsletter told fellow members, "It would be difficult to stop supermarkets from sourcing from abroad, but we can, and we must, direct consumers to buy more British food." Be sure, the writer urged, "to include that one important word BRITISH in your copy" (Lloyd-Davies 1999).

The idea that bad food and bad food policy had produced a national crisis became a common and compelling theme in books such as Graham Harvey's award-winning *The Killing of the Countryside* and John Humphrys's best-selling *The Great Food Gamble* (Harvey 1997; Humphrys 2002). Both authors were well-known BBC radio personalities, and both argued that supermarkets had helped create the crisis. Harvey, for example, said that they have "followed food manufacturers along the path of standardization and uniformity . . . they have joined in the general industrialization of the countryside." For the supermarkets, however, criticism about distant history mattered little compared to negative media portrayals of their distance supply regions.

One of the most damning such portrayals appeared in *Mangetout,* a widely-viewed 1997 BBC documentary that contrasted the impoverished and precarious livelihoods of workers on a Zimbabwean horticultural export farm with the affluence and apathy of shoppers at Tesco, the farm's main U.K. client. Although the film's narrative itself did not explicitly criticize, it showed a Tesco buyer receiving royal treatment during a visit to the farm, thus emphasizing the retailer's neocolonial control over its supplier.

Five years after *Mangetout,* supermarket fresh produce managers and importers still referred to it as an example of the kind of media coverage they dreaded. Even if it did not have the "stampede" effect of a food scare, it created an image problem, and not just for Tesco. One importer said he still ran into people who knew nothing about mangetout peas except what they saw on *Mangetout,* and such people could not appreciate how the filmmaker's technique had, in his view, dramatized and distorted the truth. The resulting portrayal raised questions about all the supermarkets' dealings in their cheap-labor supply regions. And both the media and NGOs continued to raise such questions in exposés of particular commodities and companies, as well as in series such as the *Guardian's* "What Is Wrong with Our Food?"[7]

Even if media coverage of supermarkets' supply chain practices had little direct effect on people's food shopping and eating habits (except, again, in the case of food scares), supermarkets had to consider how such coverage built popular support for the organizations demanding that they change their practices. In other words, as the supermarkets assumed more de facto powers of governance, they became more concerned about how the media influenced not only "consumer behavior" in the narrowest sense—which store or which brand people chose—but also their corporate image in the eyes of a whole range of "stakeholders." As one journalist who wrote frequently (and critically) about the retailers said, "There's this bigger public opinion, where it doesn't suit them to look like bad guys."

In the late 20th century, the British supermarkets were obviously not the only large corporations that saw abusive supply chain practices exposed in the media (often with help from NGOs) or that cared about the opinions of stakeholders, however defined (Hughes 2001b).[8] Indeed, the corporate embrace of "stakeholder capitalism" received encouragement not only from politicians such as Tony Blair and Bill Clinton but also from a huge management literature advocating "triple bottom line" (financial, environmental, and social) accountability. Much of this literature argued that firms displaying responsiveness to a range of stakeholders (employees, suppliers, local communities) ultimately do better financially than those focused only on shareholder profits (Zadek 1998). This "instrumental" argument for accountability also made clear, however, that different stakeholders have different interests—especially when firms' operations are highly globalized—and that some add more value and therefore merit more attention than others (Kay 1995; Julius 1997; Sunley 1999).

Britain's supermarkets counted certain NGOs among their most influential stakeholders, not because of their size but rather because of their voice and established moral or expert authority. Through a variety of media—not just the popular press and broadcasting, but also research reports, campaign materials, even labels—these NGOs could for better or worse, sway the opinions of other valuable stakeholders, namely consumers and shareholders.[9] Given this influence, efforts to engage with such NGOs represented strategic management (Freeman 1984).

For the NGOs, however, participation in the neoliberal governance of their country's food supply posed a new set of challenges. These arose partly from the media's third and most paradoxical role in shaping public knowledge about food. As one of the defining institutions in the modern "information society," the media tempts us, as Tsoukas puts it, into believing that we can know the world through abstract, decontextualized information—whether it takes the form of a CNN news brief, a corporate annual report, or a product label—and that such information carries more authority than experiential knowledge, or *mētis* (Tsoukas 1997).

For intermediaries in the anglophone commodity network, the obligation to produce such information had a number of paradoxical consequences, as will become clear later in the chapter. For the NGOs, the most striking paradox lay between the basic goal of achieving a more just and sustainable food supply—a supply produced and distributed under complex and widely varying ecological, regulatory, and socioeconomic conditions and therefore dependent on many different actors' *mētis*—and the need to accomplish this goal through reductionist information. The NGOs both produced such information, in the form of campaign publicity, and collected it, typically through audits, in order to "objectively" assess and show progress toward their campaign goals.

As already indicated, by the end of the 1990s all kinds of organizations were generating information about organizational performance; it was a basic feature of stakeholder capitalism and the "audit explosion" that went with it.[10] Nonetheless, for the NGOs the paradox of using simple information to reform intrinsically complex systems posed at least two problems. First, it challenged the cohesion of the British "agro-food" movement itself, which by the end of the 20th century included scores of NGOs of varying political persuasion. In interviews, long-time activists emphasized how since the 1980s members of these NGOs, whether they campaigned for animal welfare, biodiversity, children's nutrition, or urban community development, learned not only how to collaborate on shared goals (for example, a moratorium on genetically modified organisms) but also how to listen to each other and respect each other's perspectives and knowledge. As experienced activists, in other words, they came to appreciate complexity (moral as well as technical) and tolerate difference (see also Lang 1997).

These skills and experiences helped the "food troublemakers," as one activist put it, command the attention of the supermarkets. But once they had won this attention, the actual process of developing specific goals and standards for supermarket reform discouraged complexity and accentuated ideological differences. These differences—especially between the "development" NGOs (sometimes referred to as the "globalizers") and the environmentalists (often "relocalizers")—were hardly fatal to the broader movement, but they did complicate the reform initiatives discussed in the following section.

Second, a basic belief motivating the agro-food activists, the advocacy media, and indeed many people in the food business itself, was that if consumers knew more about how and where their food was produced, they would care and perhaps even willingly pay more for certain values and qualities. The activists concerned about North-South inequities, in particular, believed that more information about global South food producers could help to expand consumers' "moral geographies"—that is, the scope of humanity they cared about (and had in mind while shopping)—and thus help build broad-based support for fairer forms of food globalization.[11] Yet this worthy vision was compromised by the very circulation of such information through the market economy, where NGOs needed donor support, newspapers needed to sell, and supermarkets insisted on efficiencies.[12] The information about faraway farms and workers produced for campaigns, audits, and various forms of marketing, therefore, tended again to obscure complexity, and sometimes itself contributed to new kinds of unfairness and exploitation.

The Ethical Advocates

They (the supermarkets) used to be very arrogant, and dismissed us with contempt—in a very charming way of course. But now they take the food troublemakers very seriously.
—London food activists, January 2002

The pressure comes from a very small group of people, and we respond to it as one of a raft of things we do to look socially responsible.
—U.K. supermarket social responsibility manager, January 2002

[The NGOs] do a good job and they are extreme in their opinion, but that's fair. And I think that the dialogue we have in general terms with them is healthy. And providing it is realistic, providing their aims are realistic—then to try and deliver is part of the deal. Providing it's something customers are interested in, that's part of the deal. So, our lives depend on customers and what customers think. So, if there's an extreme point of view we'd probably go and find out what customers really thought: does it really matter?
—Supermarket fresh produce manager

Christian Aid and the Ethical Trading Initiative

As both an aid agency and an advocacy group, Christian Aid's primary objective is fighting poverty, primarily in the global South. Of all the NGOs profiled here, Christian Aid adheres most closely to the activist tradition established by church-based charities in the antislavery movement (Drescher 1987). Unlike most of its predecessors, however, the group backs up its advocacy—which in recent years has covered issues ranging from international debt to biotechnology—with in-depth reports produced by a globally networked research staff and then aggressively publicized through the popular media.

Christian Aid had long encouraged consumers to buy "fair trade" labeled products, because their price premiums assured that small farmers would receive fair prices for commodities such as coffee and cocoa (Renard 2003). But given that until the late 1990s, fair trade organizations typically only dealt in a handful of commodities and only worked with "alternative" suppliers and retailers (that is, small farmer cooperatives and specialized "Third World" shops), their potential to improve labor conditions in poor food-exporting regions was limited. Any more ambitious initiative would have to target the retailers who accounted for the vast majority of Britain's sales of food imported from global south regions. As a Christian Aid spokesperson later said, it was "time for ethical business to come out of the ghetto and into the mainstream. It is no longer good enough to have just a few ethically-traded products." Such an initiative would also need the support of more mainstream consumers—those who might prefer to know that their goods were "ethically" produced but were not necessarily willing to venture out of their neighborhood supermarkets or their normal price range to buy them.

In preparation for such a campaign, Christian Aid launched a mid-1990s investigation of working conditions in several of the U.K. supermarkets' African, Asian, and Latin American supply regions. Its research turned up abundant examples of abusive labor practices (intimidation and unfair sackings of workers, unpaid overtime, pesticide exposure) as well as useful factoids (it would take fifteen centuries for a South African fruit farm laborer to earn the annual salary of Tesco's CEO), all of which appeared in a 1996 report, *The Global Supermarket* (Orton and Madden 1996).

This report "got a lot of column inches and broadcasts," according to a Christian Aid staffer, and laid the ground for stage two, "the great supermarket till collection campaign." Consumers were urged to send all their supermarket receipts, as evidence of their buying power, to Christian Aid, which sorted them by company and store. After collecting more than seventeen million pounds worth of receipts in two years, the group presented them publicly to store managers, with its staffers dressed in "media-friendly" fruit and vegetable costumes. According to a staff member, the events "generated more local media coverage than anything in Christian Aid history."

Some individuals in the supermarket and import businesses described Christian Aid's original report as "unprofessional" and counterproductive, because its exposé of child labor on farms in Peru led to the quick dismissal of a supplier, costing hundreds of Peruvian households their livelihoods. "They made fools of themselves," said one fresh produce importer of the NGO. Nonetheless, the report got results: In 1998, most of the top supermarkets agreed to join the Ethical Trading Initiative (ETI), a "multi-stakeholder alliance" organized by NGOs and trade unions and backed by the Department of International Development. Membership in the ETI committed companies, NGOs, and unions to work together to develop a code of good labor practice for their suppliers and methods of monitoring and verifying compliance.

ETI member companies were expected not only to devote financial resources and senior management personnel to the initiative, but also to incorporate its code's principles into their "core business relationships and culture." The ETI statutes, in other words, demanded that companies go beyond "cherry-picking" standards for in-house codes of practice, choosing only those that would most likely impress consumers and the media (Blowfield 1999). Yet in return for showing that they were not involved in the ETI just for PR purposes, the ETI promised companies good PR. Member companies would be able "to know for themselves and demonstrate to others" that their standards were effective.[13]

"Others" here included the NGOs that, as ETI members, became stakeholders in the initiative, giving them unprecedented access to the company personnel involved in standards and to the information they possessed. Christian Aid, in particular, became one of the three NGO representatives on the ETI board, from where it continued to monitor the supermarkets' ethical trade progress. The tone and content of its 1999 report *Taking Stock: How the Supermarkets Stack Up On Ethical Trade* reflected the group's new status as a "peripheral insider" (Taylor 1999). It combined Christian Aid's traditional critique of structural inequalities ("We will remain sceptical of prevailing social and economic systems") with detailed praise, criticism, and suggestions for each company (Christian Aid 1999).

But reporting on the supermarkets, and "media work" more generally, marked only the beginning of Christian Aid's ethical trade campaign. With the formation of the ETI came three new challenges: first, defining labor standards appropriate for a code that would, in principle, be applied globally and in many kinds of workplaces; second, determining how (and by whom) compliance with such a code should be assessed; and third (and perhaps most difficult) doing all this in committees with corporate and trade union interests. Indeed, geographer Alex Hughes' study of the initiative in 2000 found that for a self-described "multi-stakeholder alliance," the ETI was rife with suspicion and mis-understanding; in the words of one NGO representative she interviewed, the early meetings saw the "clashing of three different cultures." Company members in particular feared that the NGO members would launch "surprise attacks" by leaking damaging information about them to the media (Hughes 2001).

The first major tangible result of these meetings was the ETI Base Code. Like many other industry codes of practice, its nine provisions drew on existing conventions, such as those established by International Labor Organization (table 6.1; see also Jenkins, Pearson, et al. 2002).

The Base Code small print defines and elaborates on the basic provisions—Provision Four, for example, specifies that "there shall be no *new* recruitment of child [under-15] labor" and that member companies' suppliers should assist any existing child laborer "to enable her or him to attend and remain in quality education until no longer a child." Having developed these guidelines, however, the ETI left it to companies to decide, ideally in consultation with their suppliers, how to implement the Base Code in individual workplaces—keeping in mind that the results would eventually be subject to "independent verification" by auditors. The ETI also urged the supermarkets to "take into account" how much their suppliers would have to spend to comply with the code.

The gap between code and practice, between charity ideals and corporate imperatives, soon appeared in Zambia's horticultural export industry. As chapter 4 discussed, the supermarkets opted for a stricter ban on child labor than the ETI specified. This was not because anyone truly believed that it was always wrong for children to work—on the contrary, individual managers acknowledged that children routinely, willfully and usefully worked on farms in Africa

Table 6.1
Ethical Trading Initiative Base Code Principles

Employment is freely chosen
Freedom of association and the right to collective bargaining is respected
Working conditions are safe and hygienic
Child labor shall not be used
Living wages are paid
Working hours are not excessive
No discrimination is practiced
Regular employment is provided
No harsh or inhumane treatment is allowed

Source: Ethical Trade Initiative Web site, http://www.ethicaltrade.org/pub/publications/basecode/en/index.shtml [Dec. 21, 2003]

and, for that matter, Britain—but rather because it could be made to *look* wrong. The possibility of bad media coverage permitted no shades of gray. As one informant in the produce import business explained, "Supermarkets aim to avoid being compromised in the newspapers, and so have an effective ban on anyone under the age of sixteen." On the other hand, said the same informant, neither did the supermarkets want to appear insensitive to the reasons that child labor existed:

> ETI and supermarket brochures are very careful about their wording as they are conscious that in many parts of the world children add economically to the household, and so do not want to say publicly they discriminate against the poorest of the poor, although this is in fact what they do.

In any case, the result of the child labor ban in Zambia may have undermined rather than improved children's access to schooling. As for supermarket prices, the Zambian suppliers specifically noted that they did not take into account the costs of code compliance—with the result that many outgrowers had, by 2000, given up on export horticulture altogether, and hundreds of field laborers had lost their jobs.

Most of the research on the ETI and similar initiatives indicates that Zambia's experience with supermarket ethical trade codes was neither unique nor, for the activists involved in the ETI, surprising (Du Toit 2001; Hughes 2001a). It was clear from the beginning that the ETI would not by itself lessen the power inequalities that allowed supermarkets to impose standards and their costs on suppliers. It was also clear that monitoring compliance with the standards forbidding, for example, discrimination and "inhumane treatment" would require different methods and skills—and probably ultimately different auditors—than those employed during technical audits of food safety and quality practices. Could a British male food technologist, flown in for a forty-eight hour visit, credibly "audit" gender relations on a South African fruit farm? On the other hand, could local auditors be objective and incorruptible?

As mentioned earlier, concerns about how to audit corporate behavior were obviously not unique to the ETI or to the British business world (Power 1997). The unique structure of the ETI, however, meant that any decisions about how to "check up" on the supermarkets' overseas suppliers would have to win the approval of both corporate and NGO members—a process that would assure greater accountability but would not likely be quick or definitive. Perhaps not surprisingly, two years after the formation of the ETI, members and other participants appeared to value it at least as much, if not more, as a meeting-place and "talking shop"—where longtime antagonists might reach some "mutual understanding"—than as a route to measurably positive changes in supply chain labor conditions (Hughes 2001b, 430).

For consumers, however, discussions between NGOs and supermarkets did not by themselves add value. This was perhaps the greatest limitation of the ETI. For unlike certified "organic" or "fair trade" foods, "ethically traded" products received no label. The supermarkets used their membership in the ETI to claim the "ethical" mantle for their entire corporate identity, not just the few goods produced in compliance with ETI standards. This precluded the possibility of charging a premium for those goods—a premium that could, in turn, help suppliers cover the costs of compliance and perhaps even pay better wages.[14] The "improved labor conditions" promised by ETI had neither face nor place. Indeed, only a consumer who took the trouble to study the ETI and individual supermarket policies could determine which products were supposed to be ethically traded.

For all its shortcomings, the ETI marked a campaign triumph for Christian Aid and demonstrated the effectiveness of its media tactics. But the organization's campaigns director recalled that the supermarket campaign took place in a crowded field of NGO activism—everyone, it seemed, was getting involved in the food movement—so Christian Aid had to make sure that its own campaign received due coverage by the media. "The volume of media profile you get affects your income," he said, and there was "loads of competition" for profile. So Christian Aid does not scrimp on this front; it employs about twenty people in its press office, he said, many of them former journalists with extensive personal connections in the media world.

Race to the Top and "Brokered Engagement"

Not long after the supermarkets agreed to join the ETI, they were asked to participate in yet another ambitious multi-stakeholder project, this one aiming to "track supermarket progress towards a greener and fairer food system." The "Race to the Top" (RTTT) project was launched from garret-like offices of the London-based International Institute for Environment and Development, a think tank known for policy-oriented research on irrigation and agro-forestry. Even compared to Christian Aid's demand for "ethical" trade, this project expected a great deal from the country's top food retailers. Drawing on input from multiple advocacy groups and academics as well as the supermarkets themselves, it proposed to develop "indicators" for "benchmarking" the supermarkets in seven broad performance areas (see table 6.2). Unlike the ETI, the RTTT proposed to assess supermarkets' treatment of farmers, primarily in the United Kingdom but with some consideration of small farmers in developing

Table 6.2
"Race to the Top" Measures of Supermarket Performance

Performance Areas	Examples of indicators
Environment	Corporate commitment to environmental responsibility; energy use; waste management
Producers	Terms of trade with U.K. farmers; availability of and promotion of Fairtrade marked products
Workers	Remuneration of supermarket employees and conditions of employment; application of labor standards code of conduct
Local	Company policy on sourcing food "locally" and "locality" foods
Nature	U.K. apple and pear varieties displayed and sold in-store (as measure of commitment to biodiversity preservation); wild and farmed fish from sustainable sources
Animal	The welfare of laying hens and broiler chickens; policy on transport of farm animals
Health	Store location and pricing policy; extent to which sales support dietary guidelines

Source: Race to the Top Web site, http://www.racetothetop.org [Dec. 21, 2003]

countries. It also planned to produce "objective data and analysis" for use by policymakers, investors, campaigners, consumers, and, not least, the supermarkets themselves. Although the project intended to publicize the data, its directors emphasized that they were aiming for "brokered engagement" with the supermarkets, not a frontal "name-and-shame" attack. For that reason some protest-oriented groups, such as Friends of the Earth, declined to join the alliance. But twenty-four others did, providing an otherwise relatively obscure and technocratic initiative with much-needed "brand recognition."[15]

These organizations lent their logos and advice to the RTTT because they supported and wanted to be associated with the basic premise and methods, not because they necessarily agreed on all the goals. The fair trade organizations and Worldwide Fund for Nature, for example, wanted the retailers to help small farmers in the global South find reliable and remunerative markets for their "environmentally friendly" crops (such as shade-grown coffee and organic produce); they also wanted large farms to provide living wages and stable employment. Groups such as the Countryside Agency and the Small and Family Farms Alliance, on the other hand, wanted the supermarkets to source more of their fresh produce (*especially* organic produce) from British farmers. These "relocalizers" reserved particular criticism for the supermarkets' airfreighted fresh produce supply chains because they expended large quantities of fuel (relative to ocean shipment) on predominantly high-end or at least out of season products—products, some activists argued, that did not belong in sustainable food supply.

The RTTT directors acknowledged that in order to accommodate the different views of participating NGOs, they had produced indicators of supermarket performance that, in some cases, contradicted each other. This concerned them less, however, than the need to develop indicators that were not biased in favor of the most high-end retailers, like Marks and Spencer and Waitrose. If, for example, stores were graded simply on how many organic, fairtrade, and health-promoting products they offered, the elite stores would come out on top simply because their customers demanded and could pay for such goods. To make reasonable demands of the supermarkets, to reconcile diverse NGO agendas, to produce robust and "objective" data without alienating carefully-cultivated supermarket contacts—for the RTTT directors, such concerns assured that the process of satisfactorily developing indicators for the "Race" was anything but fast and straightforward.

Seven of the ten top supermarket chains eventually agreed to participate in the RTTT (the Co-op, Iceland, Marks and Spencer, Safeway, Sainsbury's, Somerfield, and Tesco). As a supermarket representative told one of the project's directors, "we need you." "We" had two meanings. First and by now most apparent, the supermarkets as a whole needed to show that they were cooperating with the NGOs, because the public trusted NGOs more than they did either the government or the supermarkets themselves.

But "we" also referred to the supermarkets' "social responsibility" managers, who met with the NGOs and other stakeholders as part of their job. These middle managers were often genuinely sympathetic, and in some cases had previously worked for NGOs themselves. But they had to convince their superiors that the RTTT was worthwhile. After all, the project would require the supermarkets to spend considerable time and money to collect information that might, in the end, just expose their shortcomings, and lead to further demands for reform.

The RTTT directors, aware of the supermarkets' internal divisions, tried to help the social responsibility managers develop the strongest possible case for participation. According to one such manager, this case was premised on "fear of missing out"—in other words, the bandwagon argument. By participating in the Race, a supermarket could appear at least as accountable as the competition. But unfortunately for the RTTT, the bandwagon could roll both ways. Once it came time to actually provide the requested information in 2003, only three supermarkets (Somerfield, Safeway, and the Co-op) actually did so. Meanwhile Tesco backtracked, and ASDA (the U.K.'s Wal-Mart, and by then its second largest food retailer) refused participation altogether, claiming that it would write and release its own social responsibility report. Other retailers followed their lead, and the Race to the Top was called off in January 2004. Although the project failed to gather as much information as hoped, it did expose the supermarkets' reluctance to let anyone beside themselves define the terms of transparency.

The Soil Association and "Ethically-Traded Organic"

The Soil Association, they are not government. Especially following BSE, Joe Public doesn't trust the government. You get some minister saying something is safe and there's a mad run in the opposite direction. Kiss of death that is. So government can't be trusted, supermarket can't be trusted. Suppliers can't be trusted, whether it's [Company X] or [Company Y] or whoever it might be. We have an interest in selling the products. We can't be trusted. So who do you trust? You trust a third party organization . . . The one thing that you have to admit about [the Soil Association] is that they have their hearts in the right place, and they're completely independent of everyone else.
—Fresh produce importer

The Soil Association, one of the oldest and best-known organizations involved in food advocacy in the United Kingdom, has a dual identity. Founded in 1946 by a group of politicians, writers, and farmers—a number of whom had ties to right-wing British nationalist groups—it initially focused on promoting environmental and human health through agro-ecological methods of food production, such as the use of compost. By the late 20th century, it was arguably the single most influential NGO in the United Kingdom food and agricultural reform movement. In addition, Soil Association Certification Ltd. (also known as SA Cert), a wholly-owned subsidiary of the Association, had become the country's largest organic certifier. Seventy percent of the organic food sold in the United Kingdom bore the SA label, as did many restaurants and even a few bed and breakfast establishments. Although the Association emphasized that certification revenues were "directly covenanted back to the charity for educational purposes," the separation between its advocacy work and its certification business was not always clear (Soil Association 2002, 14).

In any case, after years of food scares and farm crises in the United Kingdom, the Soil Association was well positioned on both fronts. Rarely did the media cover a story about a food or farm policy controversy without seeking its opinion; as the Association's chair boasted, the media saw it "as a reliable source of information in a haze of biotech and agribusiness spin" (Sams 2002). In addition, the Association had the ear of the government at many different levels. The charismatic director Patrick Holden met repeatedly with Tony Blair during the 2001 foot-and-mouth crisis, and claimed to be on familiar terms with the Association's "Royal Patron," Prince Charles. An SA director served on the government's "future of food and farming" Policy Commission in 2001–02, helping to assure that the commission's final report endorsed many of the Association's goals. The Association was also the official advisory service for British farmers converting to organic production. In short, said an informant in the organic import business, the Soil Association's relentless "running after microphones" year after year had paid off:

> They do a fantastic job highlighting their organization and their cause . . . As a result, ten or more years later, people trust them because they've got a consistent message . . . and historically, they've proven to be right. There are issues and concerns about the environment, about pesticides, about people's health. Foot-and-mouth and BSE, these are things that wouldn't have happened if the organic standards had been adhered to. And so when they run up to the microphone in the middle of a crisis . . . the message grips in. When they start saying sensible things now, people start paying attention to them.

Meanwhile, the U.K. organic food market was expanding by 30 to 50 percent each year, and farmers and food companies were rushing to get certified. Although by 2002 a dozen accredited agencies offered organic certification services, the Soil Association emphasized that its standards were the country's, and indeed Europe's, most rigorous, especially in the sensitive areas of animal feed and welfare. More broadly, it invoked its long history as an advocacy-oriented organization to claim that it was *the* scientific and moral authority on organics, and the SA label, therefore, *the* best guarantee of "food you can trust" (Conford 2001; Reed 2001).

The top supermarkets bought this claim, and gave SA Cert responsibility for certifying most of their organic suppliers, both in the United Kingdom and abroad. According to one long-time fresh produce importer, not only the Soil Association's history gave its certification service an advantage over its competitors; in addition, it "had the thickest manual" of organic standards. Some of the supermarkets, like Sainsbury's, also consulted regularly with Soil Association staff for advice on how to build and supply the highly lucrative organic foods market. In turn, Sainsbury's sponsored events such as the Soil Association's annual National Conference, which was typically attended by several of the retailer's employees. Although some food activists questioned the Association's cozy relationship with supermarkets and corporate organic foods manufacturers, it argued that such ties only furthered the cause. "As long as major companies demonstrate social responsibility by supporting the Soil Association, we want to encourage their involvement. Their support also helps strengthen our campaigning clout" (Soil Association 2002, 14).

One issue that the Soil Association (like the organic movement more generally) had historically said very little about was labor, either on the farm or farther down the food supply chain. Its campaign to expand organic acreage in Britain did point out that organic farms would provide more and better jobs than did existing, highly mechanized farms, and that such employment would help rebuild rural economies and communities. Its organic standards, however, included no provisions for fair treatment of workers themselves, in the United Kingdom or anywhere else.

But a few of SA Cert's clients, such as Green and Black Chocolate, already sold organic products that were also labeled by a fair trade organization, such as the Fairtrade Foundation or Traidcraft. According to an SA Cert staffer, these clients' wish for a "broader and deeper" label, combined with their willingness to finance the development of such a label, convinced the agency to draft a new set of "ethically traded organic" (ETO) standards. As with ordinary organic certification, would-be ETO producers and processors would have to pay for an initial certification visit as well as regular follow-up inspections. But the money spent on getting certified—unlike the money spent on compliance with ETI standards—would pay for a label from a known and trusted "brand name" charity, which, like the organic label, would justify a price premium.

The "ethical" provisions of the ETO standards differed from both the ETI Base Code and existing fair trade standards on a few important points. They stated, for example, that suppliers must be paid a "fair" price, but did not specify a fixed bottom price—the traditional means by which fair trade protected producers against volatile global markets. The ETO standards also covered all ingredients and all parts of a supply chain, whereas the fair trade designation on, say, a chocolate bar only covered the on-farm production of cacao. In short, these standards were broad, as SA Cert's clients wanted, and compliance would not likely come cheap. Indeed, when the ETO standards began circulating among members of the food activist community, some skeptics quietly noted that the Soil Association's new label would threaten not only the certification business of existing fair trade NGOs, but also small scale producers in the global South, who would be hard pressed to meet its complex technical standards. Then again, the Soil Association had never been in the business of encouraging long-distance food trading, and in fact the ETO standards included a "recommended best practice" of local (meaning United Kingdom) sourcing.

This conflation of *ethical* and *local* reflected not simply the Association's adherence to agro-ecological principles of food production and distribution, but also its longstanding allegiance to British agriculture (Conford 2001; Reed 2001). For although SA Cert earned revenue as an organic certifier both in the United Kingdom and abroad—and some critics suspected that revenue was an important, if not primary, motive behind the development of the ETO standards—it generated much more media coverage and political support from campaigns and events supporting British farmers. It had pushed supermarkets, for example, to adopt an organic "British First" policy, which would commit them to source organic produce from Britain rather than abroad whenever possible. The Association's highly successful "Eat organic! Buy local!" publicity campaign, launched in October 2001, even prompted a telephone call from the government's Department for International Development. DFID was concerned, according to a Soil Association staffer, that the Association was undermining DFID's own efforts to sell British citizens on the development benefits of international trade.

Ultimately, the Soil Association never brought its ETO label to market. Instead, in January 2003 it devoted its annual conference to the theme "Fair trade begins at home," and announced a joint venture with the Fairtrade Foundation to develop, on a trial basis, an organic-and-fair label. This one would be available to British producers, provided they demonstrated commitment to invest in their local communities. Whatever behind-the-scenes politicking influenced the Soil Association's decision to collaborate with Fairtrade rather than develop its own label, both NGOs publicly emphasized that the joint venture posed "many challenges," as much political as logistical (Fairtrade 2003). On the one hand, the Fairtrade Foundation wanted the label to continue to express solidarity with producers in the global South, and appreciation for the particular hardships they faced. On the other hand, the Soil Association intended to use the new label to certify "primarily U.K." products. Whether the two groups could reconcile their geographically distinct loyalties remained an open question.

It was also unclear whether they would even be able to convince the supermarkets to stock fair-and-organic products. After all, competition for shelf space was fierce, and the retailers had no patience for inconsistencies in supply quality or quantity. Would they make room for yet another NGO initiative? One longtime Soil Association staffer, expressing frank uncertainty, said it depended "on how much media interest we generate when we launch." In other words, it was taken for granted that the media coverage would determine the supermarket response.

This remark said much about the media's extraordinarily important role in the British supermarket reform movement. It also reaffirms how much the media, together with the NGOs, have helped to shape not just people's general food knowledge but also their expectations of the supermarkets. While as NGO campaign slogans these expectations were expressed as broad ideals ("greener and fairer" food), within the supermarkets' supply networks they gave rise to very specific kinds of managerial practices and commercial relationships.

Managing Suppliers

We have to make sure that the policy for pesticides is in place, for manure is in place, for water is in place, for environmental responsibility is in place and worker welfare is in place. All those issues, and I can go on listing them forever, but it's to ensure that we have a policy, we have a really clear thinking about how we buy product, from wherever in the world, in a way that delivers the intrinsic quality value to the customer, plus the confidence that in buying that product we're doing it in a legal, legitimate, honorable, honest, sensitive way.
—Supermarket fresh produce manager

Unlike in France, Britain's trade in airfreight fresh produce has no real geographic center. Most of the produce arrives at Heathrow, but from there it is quickly trucked to the supermarkets' regional distribution centers and then to individual stores. Similarly, the trade's key intermediaries, whether they work for supermarkets or import firms, operate out of offices scattered across the commercial districts and business parks of greater London. They thus have relatively little direct, day-to-day contact with either each other or products they sell. The trade has no social spaces comparable to the selling floors and bars of France's Rungis market.

Also unlike the Rungis traders, these intermediaries do not identify with a tradition of commerce, in fresh produce or anything else. If anything, the reverse: Even veterans in the supermarket fresh produce business remembered the old days of wholesale trading as a time when the fruit and vegetable supply was erratic and often poor quality, and buyer-supplier relations were ridden with distrust and deceit. They looked back on those days not with nostalgia, but rather for lessons in what not to do.

More generally, most of the main decision-makers in the import business identify themselves as managers, not traders, and this occupational role informs both their relations with each other and the kind of knowledge they employ to solve problems and handle risk. Even though they arrange all kinds of commercial exchanges on behalf of their companies, they do so in the context of programs and "partnerships" that draw on the latest thinking in corporate supply chain management (SCM), and that aims to eradicate the very uncertainties and variability associated with trade relationships, and especially with trade in fresh produce.

That said, the knowledge and skills required of these managers are by no means simply or generically managerial. By the late 1990s, as supermarkets sought to sell more value-added fresh fruits and vegetables and to protect such products from the taint of food scares and scandal, fresh produce managers had to learn about a vast range of products, regulations, and technical standards. In addition, they needed to implement their companies' SCM objectives in regions ranging from Wales to Thailand to southern Africa. Not least, they had to contend with the proliferating demands of NGOs and other stakeholders.

To carry out their responsibilities, top-level fresh produce managers drew on the counsel of others, such as food technologists, social responsibility officers, and sometimes groups such as the Soil Association. Although they did not have the same kind of everyday contact with their suppliers as did the produce buyers, their responsibility for insuring that their supply chains were committed and compliant required that they get to know the people who could bring that about, such as the managers of major export firms. Over the longer term, these relationships might become personal and friendly, but they could only be justified as long as they met broader company objectives.

Rationalization: Hierarchies and "Partnerships"

One of the broadest and most important goals of late 20th century supermarket supply chain management was "rationalization," which simply meant winnowing down the number of suppliers for each category of product in order to achieve both economies of scale and greater control over production and innovation processes (Crang, Cook, et al. 2000). One supermarket chain, for example, might source all its pre-packed baby carrots from only one or two import companies. The import companies would in turn source baby carrots from exporters in as many countries as necessary to assure a year-round supply, but again from only a small number of producers in each. One of the main British importers of African snowpeas, for example, worked with one exporter each in Kenya, Zambia, Zimbabwe, and Gambia. For common products such as apples, a supermarket would retain more suppliers, but only one would be designated the "category leader," a ranking that assured steady business but also considerable responsibility. As one supermarket fresh produce manager explained,

> Sometimes they call them category captains or category managers,
> but we describe them as category leaders because it implies being
> very proactive and leading the way in that particular category. And

they will be an expert in that category . . . They will be charged with providing us product within that category for twelve months of the year . . . and it is very much a genuine partnership because you're putting all of the product of that category into one person's hands. And you're saying to them effectively the success of that category depends on your performance. And [store X's] success is your success and [store X's] failure is your failure at the end of the day.

Although a category leader was invariably a corporate entity, this reference to "one person" says much about how produce managers actually interacted with suppliers. It is worth emphasizing, though, that only the supermarkets decided what constituted both "success" and the penalties of "failure." A successful category leader, for starters, knew where and how to procure top-quality produce year-round, even when natural or geopolitical disasters disrupted normal supplies. One supermarket manager, after describing a series of recent threats to their African green bean imports—deluges, drought, a coup attempt—said that the importer in charge of green beans would be responsible for securing emergency alternatives, such as green beans from Guatemala. "We would expect our supplier to work with us," he said, "and to be in the position of reacting to risk quickly."

For importers, this meant they had to be prepared to pay dearly for last-minute purchases. One category leader in certain high-value vegetables said that the last time bad weather in Africa forced him to buy Central American produce, "we had to ask ourselves, do we let [supermarket X] down or do we lose money?" The importer chose to take a loss of tens of thousands of pounds rather than risk losing the position of category leader. But simply supplying volume on time hardly guaranteed that he would keep this status. Profit per product also mattered. His supermarket clients looked "at the margin level earned from you versus the margin earned from your competitor," he said. "It's frightening how much information they have."

Frightening, because information about products helped supermarkets rank the companies and, implicitly, the individuals who arranged to supply them. Importers of Zambian fresh produce harbored few illusions about their "partnerships" with supermarkets. Suggestions for profitable innovation—new products or packaging, new cost-cutting measures—the supermarkets welcomed, even expected; but otherwise importers felt they had to tread carefully. One individual, for example, saw the supermarkets' refusal to bear any of the costs of "ethical trade" as unfair and ultimately unsustainable. But he said that if he expressed this view openly, his company

could very easily and quickly get itself a name as a trouble maker, and no matter how good [importers'] produce, no matter what standards they themselves hold and are trying to pursue with their suppliers, once you're a trouble maker—out, just out. [The supermarkets say] "We want people who cooperate with us, not who argue with us. Get out. Plenty more people in the queue who want to do business with us. Just fuck off."

Arguments with company policy aside, one consultant for a horticultural import firm noted that on a day-to-day level he dealt mostly with high-strung and "arrogant" supermarket buyers who responded to delivery delays or shortfalls with strings of obscenities and threats. Even if these were only idle remarks born of stress, they spoke to the highly uneven power dynamics characterizing buyer-supplier relationships. The supermarkets' rankings, moreover, extended down to the level of producers. As one supermarket produce manager explained:

> We ask the category leaders to divide their grower base into what we call premier league and first division. If you are a premier league grower, which means that you have got very high levels of compliance in health and safety and all these sorts of areas, you have shown commitment and all the rest of it, you will have first call on [store X's] orders. Any surpluses or any cutbacks that do have to occur falls on the first division. And it creates a tension, if you like, where if you're toward the bottom of the premier league you're going to improve your ability. And if you're the top of the first division you're going to be trying to improve your ability. Because they can change places . . . So all the time we are committed to the concept of continuing improvement.

"Continuing improvement," a standard mantra of certain schools of management thought,[16] could be interpreted in many ways, but in this context it describes two distinct yet related improvements. First, the supermarkets expected suppliers to contribute to the innovation process by suggesting ideas for new products and paying to develop them. This required not just on-farm experimentation, but also familiarity with trends in the U.K. market, typically acquired through trade literature or trips to Britain. So in Zambia in 2000, for example, the technical managers of Agriflora and York Farms (themselves British) were trying out lines of prepackaged pre-sliced mixed vegetables, organic vegetables, and novel varieties of "baby veg." In part they were seeking a high-value niche not yet captured by producers in Kenya or other competitor countries. But they were seeking also to portray themselves as (in the words of one supermarket manager, describing what he looked for in suppliers) "the companies and the individuals who could make things happen."

Second, as the supermarkets competed increasingly on quality rather than merely price, the "continuing improvement" of products required and justified the disciplining of producers through hierarchical treatment and the ever-present threat of getting demoted or, worse, "de-listed"—in other words, removed from a retailer's list of approved producers. As the quotation above indicates, supermarkets assessed growers not simply according to their capacity to produce in volume, to meet rigorous aesthetic and hygienic specifications, and to demonstrate an innovative spirit. These were baseline expectations. What ultimately distinguished the "premier" growers from the rest was their compliance with standards of "good practice" at all stages of food production and handling.

Checking Up: Standards and Audits

The problem with EUREPGAP is that it is so very comprehensive that if you hit farmers with it first off, they just crawl under the table and try to hide away. It's just too much for them.
—U.K. fresh produce importer, 2001

We didn't want to rush in and go and buy product from any old person, because we believed in, and still do, what we were doing. So it took us a long time to find other people [to buy from]; we would make a visit to somebody else, and would say, well, hold on, the farm, that house would have to have flush toilets, and you'd have to have a crèche for the children . . . We'd rather not do business than deal with somebody we haven't fully checked out and fully understand in terms of what they're doing. Often we turn business opportunities down, because we're very rigid, and non-compromising in what we do . . .
—U.K. fresh produce importer, 2001

For African horticultural producers supplying the U.K. supermarkets, the age of neoliberalism hardly liberated them from onerous and costly regulations. Even as their own national governments abolished protective agricultural and trade policies, export producers found that the day-to-day operation of their enterprises as well as their longer-term prospects were increasingly governed by the private standards of their overseas customers.

Whether developed in-house or drawn from industry-wide protocols (such as EUREPGAP) or stakeholder initiatives such as the ETI Base Code, standards filled page after page of the checklists that had to be filled out before a supermarket agreed to do business with a supplier, as well as during periodic audits. In addition to the many product and task-specific standards (for example, the schedule of chemical applications for specific crops), the supermarkets' concern with due diligence made traceability the meta-standard of all supply chains, and one that could only be assured by regular and meticulous record-keeping by growers and importers alike. Supermarkets let suppliers know that they would not wait for food scares to check up on their suppliers' books. Tesco, for example, formed what became known as its "hit squad," which could demand proof of compliance with standards from "any supplier, day or night" (Fearne and Hughes 2000).

This commitment to the formalized verification of standards set British supermarkets apart from their European (and North American) counterparts. Many European retailers belonged to EUREP and endorsed its principles of good agricultural practice, and they were already all subject to the same EU food safety laws regarding, for example, pesticide residues. But the sheer volume of paperwork that the British supermarkets required of their suppliers was unparalleled. For one French exotic produce importer interviewed at Rungis, it was overwhelming. He said he had considered trying to sell some of his products to a British supermarket until, earlier that day, the supermarket's import firm had faxed him the necessary forms—all fifty pages worth, which ended up in his trashcan.

Like other French importers, this man saw the British insistence on checklists as typical of the "Anglo-Saxon" preoccupation with hygiene and "everything but the taste" of food. For U.K. importers, paperwork was just an aptitude learned over time, like any other professional task. As one of them half-joked, his growers needed to learn one simple mantra: another day, another form. Another importer suggested that colonial era trade and administration had spread the British taste for "bureaucratic" forms of quality control and verification. When asked if it was easier to do business in some regions than others, he responded:

> Yes, I think countries that formerly had an association with the U.K.,
> it makes it a lot easier in implementing systems and putting treaties
> into place. We don't deal with India, but when I travel to India, it's
> incredibly bureaucratic. They like their procedures. I imagine they
> would be ideal people for actually filling in the forms and doing every-
> thing on a very bureaucratic basis and having the total traceability in
> everything being recorded. So they do help you in a particular coun-
> try. But, yes, we do find it easier, I suppose, dealing in [sub-Saharan]
> Africa than we would dealing in Egypt purely and simply because
> they are more Anglicized, I suppose, in the way that they conduct
> their business, or the way that they administrate everything within
> their country.

As we have seen, codes of conduct and traceability systems permitted supermarkets to "govern at a distance," a key indicator of modern power. But from time to time, managers or buyers made "source visits." Here, too, the U.K. retailers differed from their European counterparts, which rarely sent employees to foreign supply regions. Buyers made routine "checking up" visits to see, for example, what facilities growers had built to comply with standards for pesticide storage and worker hygiene. Managers, by contrast, undertook reconnaissance and diplomatic missions. They went looking for new suppliers—individuals and companies who could "make things happen"—and to prepare existing suppliers for new standards. As one manager put it, "I tend to go for the political dimensions . . . [when] we want to encourage something to move in a particular direction. You've got to be able to persuade the people involved that this is in their own best interests."

Importers, whose own business with the supermarkets depended on providing them with the best possible producers, helped African export companies prepare for these all-important visits. As one importer explained,

> Whenever the supermarkets visit the source, the packhouse is a key
> area of the visit . . . If the packhouse is wrong, forget the growers,
> you're not usually going to bother with the growers . . . [The super-
> markets] have got some really, really clear ideas about what they
> want to see there . . . Now the issue and difficulties that we face as
> an importer from primarily tropical countries is that the supermarkets
> wish to see U.K. standards when they travel abroad . . . They want to
> see a U.K. farm but abroad, a U.K. packhouse but abroad. And so it's
> been part of our job to put that in place.

The job of getting ready for a source visit began weeks if not months beforehand, and involved not just meticulous cleaning but also preparing documentation to answer every possible question the supermarket visitors might ask. The importer quoted above said that the supermarkets' buyers, in particular, needed to see paperwork, because unlike the managers, they tended to be "fresh out of university," and did not know how else to assess an African horticultural export enterprise. Paperwork they knew. More generally, he said, the visit had to be carefully planned in order to "keep them moving" and entertained. A typical source visit to Zambia, for example, included a safari drive.

Given the infrequency of source visits—typically every one or two years—the supermarkets' suppliers could easily slack off on some of the day-to-day procedures expected of them. The managers of Zambia's horticultural export companies acknowledged that supermarket visits occasioned extra-thorough cleaning and grounds maintenance. But otherwise, they said, it was more cost effective and less risky to incorporate compliance into the everyday routines of both management and labor.

At the relatively technical level of food safety and quality, this internalization of supermarket surveillance made "checking up" down the line less necessary. Again, it demonstrated how much the supermarkets' technical standards pervaded the culture of their supply networks. As one U.K. importer said of his Zimbabwean growers' vegetables, "We don't actually need to inspect our product when it arrives, because they know what's expected and how to run the quality controls. Everything is actually done out there. So we do have a cursory look at it, but nothing more than that. We look at one percent of it."

When it came to labor standards, however, neither supermarkets nor their suppliers wanted them left to internal monitoring, believing that the obvious conflicts of interest would undermine the credibility of everyone involved. So either importers certified in "social auditing" or private firms such as BVQI (Bureau Veritas Quality International) typically audited working conditions on supplier farms. Importers, however, were not considered sufficiently objective, the hired private auditors were prohibitively expensive, and usually neither spoke local languages. Ideally, most parties involved supported the eventual use of local auditors, but not without reservations. The problem, as one supermarket manager said, "is how to prevent them becoming corrupt."

Indeed, the more scrutiny suppliers received—not just from supermarkets themselves but also from NGOs and other potential critics—the more they had to invest in showing that they had nothing to hide. In effect, the audit process did not simply assess suppliers' performance but introduced new tests of their worth: accountability, transparency—in short, auditability. Both U.K. importers and overseas growers felt the pressures to demonstrate total openness. Consider this importers' description of the measures his company has taken since joining the ETI.

> We all have to do an annual audit, and you can say if you don't
> want it to be anonymous, but basically it is looked at by NGOs and
> by unions . . . [And] we are using independent verifiers or indepen-
> dent auditors who speak the local language and who would have
> every right to turn up with the NGO or trade union for that audit. So
> we are encouraging that, which gives greater credibility to what
> we're saying. It's not just a marketing ploy . . . also, on our Web site
> . . . basically we'll publish our independent ethical audits on the web
> literally for anybody to see.

Marilyn Strathern describes this compulsion to make an organization's insides visible to the outside as the "tyranny of transparency" (Strathern 2000b).

At first glance, the tyranny simply appears tedious and expensive, but perhaps justified if it builds credibility and thus trust. But as a number of writers on "audit culture" have noted, it may in fact do the opposite (Power 1997; Strathern 2000a). Indeed, the need to produce information "for anyone to see" may end up having all kinds of consequences that are not simply unseen, Strathern notes, but knowingly hidden.

Small Is Not Beautiful

How are you going to impose EUREPGAP on a small farm? . . . I've said from the beginning that if we don't watch out we're going to kill off the small farmer.
—Consultant to major U.K. import firm

Although the supermarkets' increasingly stringent hygiene, environmental, and ethical standards were in principle scale-neutral, in reality they favored producers who could mobilize all the financial and human resources needed not just for de facto compliance but also for demonstrating compliance through particular discourses and practices. This was the case wherever the supermarkets sourced food, including within the United Kingdom. But in their African horticultural supply regions, the bias towards larger producers was also, by virtue of the colonial past, a bias towards white-owned farms and export firms. Besides occupying much of the land best suited for irrigated, high-value export horticulture, these producers also enjoyed social and cultural advantages. As the importer quoted earlier said, the supermarkets had very clear ideas what they wanted to see in Africa—"a U.K. farm but abroad"—and it was not Africa.

As discussed in chapter 1, these expectations had dramatic consequences in Kenya, where for many years smallholders, working under contract for companies or aid projects, grew most of the country's export horticulture crops (75 percent in 1992). In fact, Kenya's green bean sector appeared to offer a rare model of "win-win" export agriculture: It gave farmers access to a premium-priced market, generated foreign exchange for Kenya, and provided Europe's markets with high quality beans, produced by the small farmers' disciplined and exceedingly cheap family labor (Jaffee 1994, 1995a). Yet by the end of the 1990s, large farm-packhouse operations dominated export horticulture not just in Kenya but also in Zimbabwe and Zambia. As one U.K. importer explained, his supermarket clients didn't boast about their role in driving smallholders out of export production. For even though they were much more comfortable dealing with Africa's large-scale, tightly managed (and typically white-owned) export farms, purchasing from smallholders had helped them cultivate political good will in Africa and a socially responsible image at home:

I think supermarkets are sort of caught between a rock and a hard place because they feel obliged to play a social role in the development of a country. So they have a warm place in their heart for smallholder schemes and encouraging them and so on. But on the other hand, they have nightmares about food safety, and food quality, and hygiene issues . . . So there is a genuine look of relief upon [the supermarket personnel's] faces, when they turn up the biggest thing, because they know it's under control. They look with interest upon the smallholders' schemes, something that's not too big and too important . . . But when it comes to mega smallholder schemes, now they get worried.

Smallholder schemes were worrisome partly because they were hard to check up on, either from a distance or on-site. The audit process presumes a degree of organizational integrity and legibility so that information can be easily collected and assessed. It does not deal well with decentralized and loosely coordinated entities, or those lacking written records. So even if smallholders could produce quality beans more cheaply than large-scale farmers, their very geographic dispersion posed, in the eyes of supermarket personnel, unduly high risks. Indeed, for one U.K. importer working in Africa, even export companies that used large-scale outgrowers (like those in Zambia) introduced too much uncertainty into supply relationships:

We don't use outgrowers, period, because . . . in terms of the traceability and due diligence, for every packet that we sell, it has a code, our supplier code, and we can trace that packet to where it's come from. And we need to know that there've not been chemicals on it, or something other. So basically, from an ethical point of view, from a due diligence point of view, and from an environmental point of view, we would like to know exactly where everything is coming from.

The problem with smallholders, however, went beyond the logistics of traceability. Importers and supermarket managers also admitted, not always comfortably, that they doubted their capacity to provide safe food. As a supermarket manager said,

Obviously there are many people . . . who are concerned about the long-term livelihood of smallholders in the marketplace . . . [but] for instance, in Zimbabwe the average smallholder plot is a sixth of a hectare. On the basis of one sixth of a hectare, does it make sense to try to train that individual as a spray operator? Who is going to provide him with the protective clothing? Can he read what is actually on the label anyway? How safe is that product going to be under those circumstances?

An importer put it even more bluntly:

> I don't want you to go away thinking I'm a racist bastard or something. They are ignorant, these people [smallholders]. That is very different from stupid, but they are ignorant. They don't have the pesticide application equipment. If they do they don't maintain it. If they do they don't know at what rate to put it on. They don't have the training . . . If you show people the bottle and give them the sprayer, the moment they get the slightest hint there's a problem they'll go and put the poison on anything.

Such remarks contrast sharply with those of French importers and Burkinabé exporters, who typically attributed smallholders' misuse of pesticides to clever corner cutting, not ignorance. Whether or not the British intermediaries' nervousness about "these people" wielding poison was justified, it showed how the rise of "audit culture" in the anglophone commodity network had not simply devalued smallholders' skills and practical knowledge (*mētis*), but also rendered them untrustworthy.[17] Most of the intermediaries in this network, therefore, saw smallholder schemes as viable suppliers to the U.K. supermarkets only if they were supervised by what one study described as "benign dictators," meaning "major, well-established" firms, capable of "assuming responsibility for the rigid enforcement of standards" (and responsible for pesticide sprayers as well) (Naidoo 1999). Zambia's Agriflora sought to portray itself as a "benign dictator" when it launched its smallholder scheme, though it was not immediately clear whether the company would be able to enforce the necessary standards or whether smallholders would abide by its dictates.

But then again, did smallholders really belong in commercial agriculture, over the long run? Putting aside the concerns of development NGOs such as Christian Aid, the fresh produce managers at two supermarkets saw the consolidation of Africa horticultural production as a positive and indeed natural evolution:

> It's no different from how Europe evolved . . . Successful exporters currently will get bigger and better, they will capture more land, however they do that. And hopefully the economy in total will become better, the infrastructure will get stronger and better and everybody will directly or indirectly benefit. That's what I'd like to think. . . .

I think there's the issue of the natural evolution in the marketplace and whether or not we should or should not be manipulating that situation. Good small growers become good medium-size growers and good medium-size growers become good large growers.

But as the marketplace demanded more and more of not just the products but also food production processes, we need to take one more perspective on the question: What made growers good?

Like Minds

If you get a good working relationship, if you get harmony in thinking, you understand each other's businesses and how those businesses work, then you get efficiencies . . . There is an affinity between the people here and the people in our supply base. There is an understanding, a bond if you like, and I think it is still very, very important. I mean you can trade with a big branded company, but if you can't get on with the people within that big branded company then you don't trade. So, that relationship, the people bit is critical. And it's critical because you have to have people of like minds that understand the business, understand the variants of producing good quality fruit, good quality vegetables. I mean, it's never easy, it's never the same day in, day out. So, it is a mindset and you're going to have to be dealing with people who understand that mindset and are prepared to put themselves out to try to deliver it, no matter how tough it is out there.
—Supermarket fresh produce manager

By the end of the 20th century, British supermarkets had many ostensibly objective methods for assessing the value of individual supply chains. From product bar codes to checklists of "good practice" to on-site visits by independent auditors, these methods yielded information that allowed supermarkets to calculate their gains not only from particular commodities (in terms of profit margins and market share) but also from the farms and firms supplying them. As Busch and Tanaka observe, this is the point of standards: to test simultaneously goods and supplier goodness, according to supposedly universal measures (Busch and Tanaka 1996).

In practice, supermarket managers assessed suppliers' worth through relationships that were far from objective, and few would claim otherwise. The previous section showed how anxieties about scares and scandals increasingly led them to see centralized, large-scale production and dictatorial management as necessary supplier attributes. In this final section I want to consider how the very need to find suppliers of "like minds" (and large scale) forged a commodity network that boasted of advanced technologies and enlightened principles, but also relied on inequities of power and wealth established during the colonial era.

Recall that the supermarket managers were responsible not only for evaluating suppliers' performance but also for developing and maintaining their "commitment." As the supermarkets demanded more and more of suppliers, this managerial responsibility required ongoing persuasion and, in a sense, translation. If growers were to be truly "on board" a supermarket's ethical trade program (or, to borrow Latour's (1987) term, "enrolled"), they had to appreciate, if not the entire historical and political context of the British ethical trade movement, then at least their client's priorities—among other things, to avoid bad publicity. It made the supermarket managers' job much easier if suppliers required relatively little translation—if, in other words, they already understood and approved of the specific standards and underlying mores of corporate social responsibility that they were expected to uphold.[18]

In sub-Saharan Africa, supermarket managers were most likely to find such individuals in former British colonies, running export farms on land formerly (or still) occupied by the families of colonial-era white settlers, and therefore managing their enterprises under a set of quite particular social and political as well as material circumstances. Whether they were born in Africa or had expatriated there, these individuals were more likely than not, by virtue of their professional (and perhaps personal) backgrounds to understand the supermarkets' vision of corporate goodness, and to have the capacity to implement it.

The managers of Zambia's Agriflora and York Farms, discussed in chapter 4, did not agree with the supermarkets' policy of making suppliers alone bear the costs of ethical standards. Still, they described the responsibilities, personal satisfactions, and the strategic priorities of their own managerial work in much the same way as their supermarket clients. They described corporate paternalism—"looking after your people"—as both ethical and politically necessary. Similarly, the outgrowers who produced baby corn and other vegetables for Agriflora recognized the political as well as economic value of modest investments in worker welfare—schools, clinics, protective clothing—well before the supermarkets mandated such provisions. For their part, supermarket managers repeatedly described displays of corporate social responsibility—such as membership in ETI, participation in the "Race to the Top"—as not only "the right thing to do," but also vital to their own legitimacy in the eyes of consumers, NGOs, and the government.

In short, personal "like-mindedness" in supply chain relationships corresponded very closely with the objectively superior value—in terms of profit margins, innovation, and auditability—that large white-run enterprises could offer supermarkets. So closely, in fact, that supermarket managers might easily describe the economic value generated by particular supply chains as a *product* of such affinities—as the "efficiencies" generated by "harmony in thinking"— without reference to the uneven power relations that enabled supermarkets to coerce growers, and growers to exploit labor. As one supermarket fresh produce manager said, "We have in this sector here a very discrete supply base, who understand us, our philosophy and our customers very well, and are therefore much more willing to buy into change than if you were going through a very fragmented, uncontrolled supply chain."

The "understandings" between supermarkets and their suppliers in sub-Saharan Africa, however, were not only reinforced by the historical legacies of colonialism, but also ultimately imperiled by them. The political-economic conditions that encouraged and enabled displays of corporate paternalism were inherently fragile. This became apparent in Zimbabwe in the late 1990s, when President Robert Mugabe re-initiated his campaign to expropriate white-owned farmland. Even before Mugabe-backed squatters began occupying white farms, tensions around white domination of commercial agriculture were higher than in either Zambia or Kenya. Not surprisingly, therefore, Zimbabwe's predominantly white Horticultural Export Council sought to appear proactive on labor standards; some of its members, for example, participated in the ETI's first pilot project.

In addition, at least a few of Zimbabwe's horticultural producers found that superior on-farm labor standards gave them a competitive advantage. As one U.K. importer said of his main Zimbabwean supplier of high-value vegetables, "What was attractive for us dealing with him and him working with us is that he had an ethical or welfare policy for his staff that was unprecedented in Africa." This policy, the importer said, offered farm laborers benefits well beyond what the ETI standards required (pensions, meals, housing for married workers, employment for spouses), and insured that they were "very, very privileged in terms of what else is going on in that country" and "very happy to work there."

Sourcing produce from Zimbabwe became more complicated, however, once Mugabe's land reclamation campaign led to economic upheaval and deteriorating diplomatic relations with the United Kingdom, the ancestral homeland of many of Zimbabwe's white farmers. Although export horticulture was initially less disrupted by the squatters' movement than maize and tobacco production, it was affected by flight cutbacks. Overall, U.K. supermarket managers had to weigh the increased uncertainties of doing business there against loyalty to suppliers who, through compliance with standards, had demonstrated goodness. But could they justify loyalty if it did not promise bottom-line benefits? One supermarket manager's explanation for his company's stance provides an ambiguous response, at best:

> There are many, many cheaper places to buy legumes from than Zimbabwe . . . The only reason we actually stay in Zimbabwe instead of going somewhere else is out of loyalty to those growers who we know have responded to what we have asked them to do, have done a bloody good job for their black Africans and don't deserve to go under . . . I would maintain there is not a supermarket buyer in this country who could not buy cheaper if he was totally promiscuous and wasn't concerned about any of these other sorts of issues that we are talking about there. You can buy competitively and improve the conditions of workers, etc. Because at the end of the day a happy work force is a productive work force. And you've seen that in Zimbabwe.

Whether or not workers on Zimbabwe's horticultural farms were "happy," they had little influence over the standards of worker welfare to which the U.K. supermarkets held their employers. But then the supermarkets' influence also proved limited, in the end. For if the reach of their governance seemed quasi-imperial, it could hardly undo the legacies of a previous imperial era. Displays of corporate paternalism did not deter Mugabe's government from seizing most of the country's white-owned farmland. Ultimately, neither the "happiness" nor the productivity of the workforce mattered much in the face of broader political conflicts.

In short, supermarket supply chain management in Africa has to be understood as a set of cultural practices that, while technocratic and standardized on paper, were in fact highly subjective. They were shaped both at the micro level by the personal nature of supply chain relationships, and at the macro level by the broader political economic conditions and cultural norms that took root during the colonial era.

The Paradoxes of Transparency

You see the benefit that [export horticulture] has on to local community . . . the benefit of regular employment, good employment, good social accountability, you look at the benefit to some of the environmental projects that are being practiced—fantastic. It's real buzzy. But how you translate that to consumer-speak in a way that they understand it? Tough.
—Supermarket fresh produce manager

I think to some degree we are victims of our own success, because we've
conditioned consumers to expect what we provide.
—Supermarket public relations director

A At the turn of the 21st century, British supermarkets competed to provide consumers with everything they might expect, and then some. In a way, this was nothing new. The very making of the mass market, after all, had depended on creating new material wants and turning them into expectations. Historically, Britain's high levels of industrialization, urbanization and dependence on food imports had enabled corporate food retailers to play a central role in this process. Contemporary British society's expectations, however, extended well beyond what the supermarkets could package and put on a shelf. Certainly shoppers still expected low food prices, and shareholders high stock prices. But the state and NGOs also expected the supermarkets to demonstrate good governance, and not just over the technical aspects of food retailing. In return for minimal state interference in their affairs, the supermarkets had to expand the old service industry dictum—that the customer is always right—to include a proliferating variety of stakeholders. "Engagement" with stakeholders became a part of brand image-building, but only as long as these commitments did not compromise the bottom line.

These conditions imposed paradoxical and sometimes uncomfortable responsibilities on the mid-level managers and importers who procured fresh produce from Africa. On one hand, in order to assure that the commodities themselves complied with the supermarkets' high standards of quality, safety, and "ethics," these intermediaries needed to cultivate personal relationships with suppliers and win their loyalty. Often they took genuine pleasure and pride in these "partnerships," and believed in their possibility to do good, albeit in ways and places not easily described in "consumer-speak." On the other hand, they had to subject these suppliers to impersonal forms of surveillance and control, reinforced by the ever-present threat of abrupt "delisting." In other words, it was not enough to "trust, but verify"; they had to verify, trust, then verify and verify again. In this sense, the intermediaries were "victims of their own success." They were victims of the "tyranny of transparency" they had helped to create, to draw again on Tsouka's and Strathern's insights (Tsoukas 1997; Strathern 2000b). The more auditable information they demanded from suppliers, they less faith they could put in any other measures of worth.

This tyranny had other victims, of course. For what transparency concealed, ultimately, was the power that made transparency possible. It concealed the vulnerability and eventual exclusion of suppliers who could not generate the right kind of information, and the necessarily dictatorial management of those who could. It obscured, moreover, the fact that the entire commodity network, for all the talk of continuing improvement, depended on the continuing availability of very cheap and flexible labor.

Sometimes this concealed information leaked out. In mid-2003, the *Guardian*'s consumer affairs correspondent wrote a long and unflattering story about Kenya's horticultural industry and, in particular, her visit to what was widely considered one of the country's most "ethical" export farms (Lawrence 2003b). One of the major complaints of the workers interviewed were the "flextime" production schedules that often required them to work twelve-hour (or longer) shifts. These schedules were determined not so much by the export companies themselves but by the supermarkets, which e-mailed orders at midday for the shipments they wanted that night. Supermarket representatives quoted in the article said that they took allegations of excessive overtime very seriously; their auditors looked for these things. The Tesco spokesman, moreover, said that his company's work with the ETI was ongoing, for what the Kenyan horticultural industry really needed was "a change of culture."

The overarching paradox of the supermarkets' ethical mission was that it imposed such demanding standards so far from the places that consumers cared about as consumers. The anthropologist Daniel Miller observed this paradox in his ethnographies of shopping in North London in the mid-1990s. Even shoppers who discussed their concerns about the environment and social justice while pushing their carts through the aisles, he noted, almost never bought "green" or "ethical" goods, even if their budgets would permit them to. Or if they did, it was out of concern about their own and their families' well-being. Miller argues that this gap between talk and action reflects not hypocrisy but rather the difference between moral and ethical shopping. Miller's North London subjects saw thrift as a moral virtue at the supermarket because, like gift shopping, it expressed care for the household. Ethical shopping, by contrast, made an abstract and usually more expensive statement about justice (Miller 2001, chapter 4). It is worth considering how supermarkets themselves have influenced societal norms of thrift, but the tendency to prioritize the near-and-dear in day-to-day provisioning is hardly unique to Britain or other mass consumer societies. The possibility of expanding care to encompass justice is one that concerned moral philosophers and, increasingly, geographers at the end of the 20th century.[19] It also raised real challenges for the intermediaries and activists engaged in shaping the future of Britain's globalized food supply.

Conclusion

Seven years after Britain's government in 1996 admitted to the potentially catastrophic human health risks of mad cow disease, fears of the deadly pathogen had faded. Scientists had neither a vaccine nor a cure for nCJD, but in early 2003 they downgraded the projected infection rates; tens of thousands of cases of nCJD now appeared unlikely. The domestic beef market had recovered, and even long-critical media commentators said it was time for beef "to have a revival" (Lawrence 2003a). Whether for reasons of safety, taste or patriotism, market surveys indicated that consumers now preferred British beef to imported meats (Mintel 2003). They also worried rather less about overall food safety. According to the government's Food Standards Agency (FSA) annual Consumer Attitudes Survey, the percentage of consumers who described themselves as "very" or "quite" concerned about food safety had dropped to 68 percent in 2002 down from 71 percent the year before.[1] This is still a lot of concern, but the government nonetheless concluded that it had "made some headway" in its efforts to win back public trust.

At the international level, however, longstanding food controversies still simmered and sometimes flared. Zambia, for example, set off a round of transatlantic name-calling in late 2002 when, despite impending famine, it refused to distribute genetically modified (GM) food aid from the United States. The U.S. trade secretary accused the "Luddite" Europeans of forcing Africans to go hungry because the Zambians, like other southern African agro-exporters, feared losing access to the European market if American GM corn contaminated their own crops. European NGOs, meanwhile, condemned the United States for using food aid to establish an African beachhead for the biotech industry (Vidal 2002; Teather 2003).

Media analysis of this controversy gave little attention to Zambian citizens' views of GM food, emphasizing instead the striking rift between American and European perspectives on GM foods and food quality more generally. As in past coverage of the transatlantic GM battle, the explanation was partly cultural (Europeans simply care more about taste than shelf life), partly social-psychological. The trauma of recent food scares, in other words, had left Europeans suspicious of "unnatural" foods even if "science" insisted they were safe. As one Greenpeace representative said, "It is not enough anymore for European consumers to have somebody with a white coat, a professional, saying it's OK." (Alverez 2003).

Popular media coverage of the GM controversy testifies to the endurance of national and even civilizational-scale characterizations of food culture, even as food commodities and cuisines travel ever farther from home. These characterizations remain widely familiar and politically potent not because they accurately describe a society's day-to-day foodways, but rather because they tap into familiar identities and express ideals that, for whatever reason, still resonate. These ideals are clearly about more than eating; they are also about how people should treat nature, as well as each other, as members of communities and polities of different scales, and as producers, consumers, and sellers of food.

This book has aimed to show how such ideals, as expressions of different nations' shared histories and values, informed the cultural norms and practices of particular transnational food commodity networks. I have argued that the origins of these ideals can be traced historically, and that they took shape under particular conditions of structural power. I have emphasized that the francophone and anglophone networks' cultures of commerce differed from one another not simply because the French and the British food cultures differ—or, for that matter, because the Burkinabé and Zambian agro-export regions do— but rather because the networks themselves produced and sustained difference. They produced, in other words, their own culture (Appadurai 1986). Before considering why this point matters well beyond the world of transnational green bean trading, it is worth very briefly reviewing the history, norms, and practices that distinguished these two networks and held each one together.

The Francophone Trade

The fresh vegetable trade between Burkina Faso and Paris centered on a single crop known for the hard work it demands from producers and for the familiar pleasure it offers French consumers. A New World legume that the French claimed as their own, the "French" green bean also became familiar to the Burkinabé, who learned to grow it under conditions of forced labor. Later the green bean became a quintessential development crop, expected to generate not only foreign exchange, but also rural jobs and food security. These expectations informed not only the contract relations between peasants and exporters but also those between exporters and French importers. In this sense the perceived need for peasant-based rural development defined both the moral mission and the constraints of the entire francophone network.

French fresh produce importers assessed green bean quality primarily as aesthetics: color, uniformity, flawless surface, apparent freshness. They were picky because they knew their customers would be. The importers did not begrudge this pickiness; discerning taste was rather a source of professional and national pride. They did, however, resent the French supermarkets' growing proclivity for paperwork, which they saw as an "Anglo-Saxon" form of quality control. For them, the obligation to fill out forms as "proof" of compliance with supermarket standards appeared not just unnecessary but indeed an affront to their own expertise. Still, compared to their British counterparts, the French importers did not worry much about the supermarkets actually checking up on them. This gave them greater autonomy to decide how, and with what suppliers, they would meet changing EU regulations and market standards. They adapted in ways that reflected partly their enduring confidence in the capacities of peasant producers, and partly French consumers' enduring confidence in the wholesomeness of fruits and vegetables, foods associated more with grandparents' gardens than with the sordid practices of agro-industry.

Burkinabé green bean growers and exporters shared French importers' sense of professional pride in the provisioning of aesthetic quality, even if they did not see the diminutiveness expected of green beans as a particularly attractive quality in their own foods. What they resented was that the French market's aesthetic standards grew stricter even as the market grew more crowded and less remunerative. The exporters also resented their financial dependence on French importers, which constrained not only their bargaining power but also their capacity to distribute patronage and win loyalty from their peasant growers.

Historical linkages and common experiences fostered certain common sentiments among people whose positions in the francophone network—as growers, exporters, and importer/wholesalers—were otherwise very different. First, they shared a sharp nostalgia for the days when profits were higher and customers more appreciative. Second, they shared a sense that they had neither much control over or confidence in the people and things on which their earnings depended. This was a self-perpetuating problem, because it encouraged actors to protect themselves against risk in ways that often further undermined both their control over others and their own reliability. Combined with long-standing, mutually-held stereotypes that characterized other actors as inherently untrustworthy ("sly" peasants, "corrupt" exporters, ruthless "wolf-like" importers) this climate of uncertainty also fostered a "cheat or be cheated" mentality.

Third, under these conditions, participants in the francophone network placed great value on friendship, as both a means to and a measure of professional success. The fact that most participants worked for themselves or for their families' companies encouraged this priority. Careers hinged not on company targets or share prices or brand-name recognition, but rather on actors' own capacities to command the loyalties of others, regardless of what else went wrong. It is worth emphasizing, however, that some actors were much better positioned, as the old book title put it, to win friends and influence people. The relationship between the "green bean king" and the chief, described at the end of chapter 5, is a case in point.

The francophone green bean trade was in many respects an old-fashioned commodity network. With its many small-scale actors, its lack of coordination between production and retail distribution, and its reliance on personal trust relations rather than institutional audits to assure quality and manage risk, the trade appeared anachronistic compared to British supermarkets' "rationalized" supply chains. Yet this trade endured because certain intermediaries were able to negotiate the "disjuncture and difference" of the contemporary global cultural economy (Appadurai 1990). More precisely, they learned to operate in a network where quality norms were understood because of certain historical ties— between peasant producers and the urban business elite, between colony and colonizer—and where the very bases of trust and risk could not be taken for granted. The capacity to do business and forge friendships in culturally diverse realms paid off in ways that could not always be tallied, but which helped to explain why intermediaries persevered in seemingly unprofitable commercial enterprises. Still, it is important to remember how this capacity to trade transculturally drew on and reinforced intermediaries' social power—power rooted in gender ideologies, patronage, and postcolonial race relations—in ways that allowed for the exploitation and exclusion of the less powerful.

The Anglophone Trade

The fresh vegetable trade between Zambia and the United Kingdom dealt in novelty and depended on perpetual innovation. None of the vegetables that Zambia sells to Britain are "traditional" to either country, but that was precisely their point. In Zambia, a non-traditional export industry meant new jobs and skills; new opportunities for commercial farmers; a new niche in the world economy, after the fall of King Copper. In Britain, prepackaged baby vegetables appealed to "foodie" consumers seeking fresh and stylish alternatives to the archetypal canned peas of the traditional British diet—yet which, like the canned peas, they could find at their supermarket in a convenient form and bearing a familiar brand label.

For all the emphasis on newness, the very geography of Zambia's horticultural export industry betrayed its debt to colonial-era land policies. Given the region's enduring tensions around white landownership, it was only politic for the horticultural industry management to downplay this lineage, and identify instead with the tradition of corporate paternalism instituted by the colonial-era mining companies. Yet "looking after your people" became increasingly complicated and costly as British supermarkets demanded compliance with ever broader and more stringent array of "ethical" standards.

In era when advocacy groups and neoliberal governments alike were demanding that corporations display social responsibility, the British supermarkets' adoption of ethical standards was not by itself unusual. Nonetheless, compared to supermarkets in continental Europe and the United States, they faced unusual pressures not merely to adopt codes of conduct but also to involve a wide range of non-governmental "stakeholders" in the cleaning up of their supply chains. While the British government encouraged the supermarkets' display of accountability, the national media mandated it. Given their intense battle for market share, the top food retailers sought to avoid being "named and shamed" at all costs—even if it meant that some of the "ethical" standards they adopted had little relevance in overseas supply regions.

Similar concerns framed the supermarkets' handing of food safety, for they knew that media-fueled food scares could do more all-around damage (to sales, stock prices, brand image, and individual careers) than even child labor exposés. Supermarket managers and importers attributed the danger of food scares to consumer ignorance and the media's taste for food-borne scandal. They addressed this danger, like the NGOs' demands for ethical sourcing, through strict standards of "good practice" and regular auditing.

"Rituals of verification" became part of the daily work of intermediaries in the anglophone network, and they posed challenges as much social as technical. Adhering to the latest theories of supply chain management (SCM), the supermarkets sought "committed partnerships" with suppliers in order to minimize the uncertainties and inconsistencies associated with old-fashioned produce trading. Yet while SCM discourses described these partnerships as "win-win" arrangements, only certain kinds of suppliers stood a chance of winning the title of "category leader," and their victories were never secure. A hygienic or ethical offense could be grounds for de-listing—a constant disciplinary threat in all realms of Zambia's horticultural export industry.

Company managers in this industry took obvious pride in their ability to meet whatever standard their supermarket clients set before them. Expatriates themselves, they nonetheless boasted of what they brought Zambia: a technologically sophisticated, environmentally responsible export industry; thousands of jobs; worker welfare standards as high as any in southern Africa, a "brand image" for the country's products, and hard currency for its coffers.

All these payoffs helped to justify, in their own eyes, the stressful managerial work involved in supplying some of the world's most demanding supermarkets. Yet as those supermarkets raised their standards while holding prices flat, it was not clear how much longer outgrowers and other Zambians would share the managers' faith in the industry's beneficence and revolutionary potential.

If the anglophone fresh vegetable network represented the future of transnational fresh produce sourcing, it relied on relationships that were not only colonial in origin but also tribal in their social content. In other words, the actors controlling the key resources and decision-making power in this network—growers, export company managers, importers, and supermarket produce managers—claimed broadly similar ethnic and in many cases educational and professional backgrounds, whether they had been raised in Britain or Africa. The commonalities would matter little, if at all, in Britain, but in Zambia (as in other former British settler colonies) they defined a small and culturally "European" (meaning white and typically Anglo) community whose members reaffirmed their Europeanness through their choice of churches, schools, social clubs, and holiday trips abroad. British supermarket managers and their importers, on their visits to Zambia, became temporary members of this community. Yet this was not a tribe defined simply by whiteness or European ancestry or economic privilege. Its members also shared a commitment to high technical and ethical standards as forms of "bulletproofing" against challenges to their relatively exclusive control over a lucrative commodity network. In this latter objective, the Zambia-United Kingdom fresh vegetable network, for all its technical and managerial sophistication, had more in common with traditional ethnic trade diasporas than did the Burkina Faso-France green bean trade.

What Difference Does Difference Make?

So why ask about cultural difference in a globalized food economy?[2] At one time such an inquiry might have simply produced useful evidence that globalization is not a vast homogenizing force, driving the McDonaldization of the world (Ariès 1997). But geographers and anthropologists, among others, made this point some time ago.[3] So, too, have they shown how the marketing of cultural difference in food ("exotic" fruit, ethnic cuisine) while perhaps encouraging more cosmopolitan eating habits, still obscures the exploitation involved in bringing consumers "the world on a plate" (Cook and Crang 1996).

Cultural analysis sheds some light on persistent controversies surrounding the global reach (or attempted reach) of certain kinds of food. Research on different societies' opposition to genetically modified foods, in particular, has helped debunk the claim that such opposition is rooted in public ignorance and irrational fear; it has also helped show why small farmers' concerns still resonate in countries with hardly any farmers left, small or otherwise. In addition, and as I have tried to show throughout this book, attention to culture helps to illuminate both the immediate political crises and the longer-term commercial changes set off by turn-of-the-century food scares.

Yet the larger goal here was to take cultural analysis beyond a reading of headline events and supermarket labels, and to show how it illuminates the very workings of contemporary globalized food power. The book began from the assumption that this power has historical roots, operates through relationships between specific actors—among them a wide variety of transnational intermediaries—and is manifested in the workaday norms and practices that get food from farm to table. The driving question behind the comparison of two transnational food commodity networks was not whether cultural difference is coming or going but rather what work it does—and what power it expresses—in specific situations.

The anthropologist Eric Wolf posed this question in many of his writings; so did Sidney Mintz in his study of the British taste for sugar (Mintz 1986; Wolf 1999; Wolf and Silverman 2001). But it has become ever more salient in a world where culture all too often serves to naturalize and rationalize the widening gap between global (and for that matter local) rich and poor.[4] The food trades and controversies examined in this book provide many examples of power at work in different cultural forms; here I want to conclude by examining three of them.

First, consider the power relations inherent in the very existence of fresh produce commodity networks that feed the high end fresh food market. Power on a hemispheric scale sounds abstract, but it takes concrete form at check-out counters in the global North, where better-off consumers have acquired the buying power to purchase fresh produce, whether "traditional" (green beans) or "ethnic" (baby corn), any day of the year. This power has not only increased enormously over time, as the real costs of food have dropped, but also relative to the poorest countries in the global South, whose people have so little buying power that they are rarely even described as consumers.[5] The news coverage of the genetically modified food aid controversy mentioned earlier was fairly typical in its assumption that people who do not have much power to buy food also do not have culturally-informed opinions about its safety and quality.

In any case, the airfreight fresh produce trade that developed during the last third of the twentieth century could be seen as a natural extension of wealthy metropolitan markets' ceaseless appetite for new products and supply regions. But consumer taste for this kind of freshness is no more natural than the association of the French bean with France. As Appadurai has argued, creating demand for "the pleasure of ephemerality"—that is, for the novel, the fashionable, and the fresh—has been central to the "disciplining" of the modern consumer (Appadurai 1996, 83). The pleasure found in the ephemeral, edible or otherwise, is rarely merely sensual; often it is social and performative (Guthman 2003). More to the point, it is the pleasure that comes from displaying cultural capital, or what Bourdieu called distinction (Bourdieu 1984), Extra-fine counter-seasonal green beans and pre-packaged "baby veg" rank among the fresh foods of distinction in some societies. But they have become available to these societies' consumers owes only because of the availability of other societies' cheap labor.

Put somewhat differently, consumer buying power in the global North, expressed through purchases of high-value fresh vegetables, offers modest economic gains, at best, for peasant producers and farm laborers in the global South. But such gains ultimately depend on their own lack of such power—and more precisely, their need to work very hard for very little, relative to the earnings of those who consume their goods. As I discuss momentarily, the fact that the South-North food trades are uncomfortably inequitable does not mean that they should be reeled in; this solves nothing. The point here is simply that the power to consume tasteful freshness year-round does not simply derive from technological progress. This power resides in the structural inequalities of the world economy.

Second and related, consider what power adheres in movements to counter food globalization through renationalization and re-localization. As chapter 6 discussed, the scientific arguments for food re-localization in the United Kingdom tended to focus on the ecological costs of "food miles:" that is, the fossil fuels consumed and pollution generated by long-distance transport, and the land degradation engendered by monocropping in export production zones (Sustain 2001). Although the "food miles" math is more complicated than it might seem, these ecological arguments were not without merit.[6] But fuel efficiency has never been among the main selling points of local and national food, in Britain or anywhere else. Rather, the marketing of food as local or national appeals to assumptions about the qualities of place-based foodways and, more fundamentally, to people's affinities for and identification with place itself.[7]

These affinities, if not "natural," are certainly well taught, and reinforced by the local routines of day-to-day life. So it is understandable that they might help to sell food at times when the integrity of places and their foodways appear threatened, both by specific events (like the foot-and-mouth outbreak) and by the institutions associated with globalized food culture (like multinational retailers, fast food chains, or the WTO). In the case of local food, it is also easy to understand why farmers' markets and other forms of sociable food exchange have seen such a renaissance in Britain and the United States, the countries that pioneered self-service supermarket shopping. Such initiatives offer not only the aforementioned "pleasures of ephemerality," but also an opportunity for consumers to shop morally, because their purchases support producers and a place they have come to care about. Daniel Miller's ethnography of North London shopping, discussed at the conclusion of chapter 6, identified thrift as a moral virtue in shopping because it expressed care for household members (Miller 2001). Shoppers considered ethical purchases, by contrast, not only unthrifty but also calculated, cold, even *un*caring—even if they were genuinely concerned about the injustices that ethical products were supposed to address. Yet if we understand care simply as "a felt concern for others, and for community with them" (Baier 1987, 43) then the popularity of farmers' markets and other local food initiatives suggests that, under at least some circumstances, people's shopping does indeed express care extending beyond the household.

I belabor this point partly to emphasize that I am not attacking local food initiatives such as farmers' markets (quite the opposite), and partly to highlight a basic challenge facing ethical trade initiatives. Can more than a tiny minority of consumers "feel community" with food producers in distant and foreign places? This question requires (and has already received) some creative thinking.[8] But I also want to emphasize—to come back to the original question of the power inherent in movements to bring food supply "back home"—that the very capacity to express care through local food purchases is unevenly distributed on all kinds of scales (Smith 1998, 32). Again, food activists in Britain and elsewhere have helped to bring markets and gardens to inner-city "food deserts," as well as to the equally inedible monoculture landscapes of the American Midwest.[9] But in countries such as Burkina Faso and Zambia, most people's capacity to express care through their choice of food commodities, whether for household members or local farmers, is limited. This is partly because they have little money, partly because of limited retail options, and partly because their local markets may be dominated by cheap imports ranging from U.S. soybean oil to EU milk powder to South African apples.

The historical origins of these inequalities between local food markets in North and South is closely linked to the origins of the North's national foodways. Recall that whatever integrity these foodways appear to possess owes to the power of certain institutions and social actors to draw borders and define value. In Britain and France, this drawing of national food borders took place first and most decisively at a time when both countries were carving out their African empires and consolidating control over commodity networks that would enrich their industries, merchants, and governments. In this sense, the political and economic power mobilized to define and protect British and French foodways cannot be separated from its imperial roots. More specifically, this power cannot be separated from the colonial and postcolonial development policies that pulled many African localities—through coercion if not overt violence—into transnational trade networks that, for all their current injustices, are still vital to many people's livelihoods. Until their own local and regional economies generate per capita earnings of more than a dollar a day, these people do not stand to benefit from the global North's movements to bring the food supply "back home." Put somewhat differently: The localist and nationalist conceptions of care implicit in such movements, for all their good intentions, will not address (and may in fact perpetuate) the injustices of uneven development that made such movements even imaginable in the first place.

Lastly, consider the power expressed in the institutional responses to late 20th century anxieties about food safety and quality. Again, beyond instinctive fears of poison and other acute food harm, these anxieties are not natural; even within the relatively confined region of Western Europe, they have taken culturally specific forms. Nonetheless, they have driven national governments, multilateral organizations, and multi-billion-dollar food retailers to initiate far-reaching reforms in food governance at many levels. Not unlike the anti-adulteration laws passed a century earlier, some of these reforms were long overdue, and in at least certain sectors proved effective; witness the recovery of Britain's beef market. In both centuries, the eventual willingness of food retailers, manufacturers, and regulatory agencies to undertake reform testified to the power of food activists, once strategically allied, not merely to push through new laws or product innovations but indeed to transform the basic norms and day-to-day practices that constitute cultural economies of national (and increasingly European) food provisioning.[10]

The more recent reforms, however, have stretched far beyond national and continental borders, into food-producing regions remote in every way from the industries that produced mad cows and dioxin chickens. They have subjected these regions' export producers to regimes of "good practice" that are harmonized in form but culturally specific in their content and implementation. To be specific: Supermarket codes of conduct draw on conventions and "science-based" standards established by multilateral institutions such as the International Labor Organization and CODEX, the WTO's food standards agency. This makes them seem unassailably universal and objective—in short, culture-less. But these codes are imposed on African horticultural farms in order to manage culturally-constituted anxieties back at home, and by intermediaries whose own views and actions are informed by those anxieties, as well as, of course, by the lopsided nature of buyer-supplier power relations. Not least, these intermediaries' tools of accountability—codes, checklists, audits—are themselves products of an "audit culture" attached less to a particular nationality or industry than to the age of neoliberalism.

This era saw all kinds of organizations and networks adopt such tools; their displays of accountability both facilitated and were fueled by a shift towards privatized or semi-privatized governance that quickly became global in scope (Power 1997; Strathern 2000a). Yet the stakes were especially high—and the consequences especially far reaching—in the realm of European and above all British food provisioning, where the rise of neoliberal governance coincided with and in some ways contributed to heightened anxieties about the safety and quality of food. By the early 21st century, the top British supermarkets had incorporated the norms and practices of audit culture into their African fresh vegetable supply chains more thoroughly than had their counterparts across the Channel. But French supermarkets were subject to the same European Commission regulations, as well as to increasingly similar demands for transparency.[11] So French fresh produce importers, however much they disliked what they perceived as the Anglo-Saxon invasion of their profession, would eventually have to show that their green beans were as traceable as those in any Tesco.

Given the magnitude of irresponsibility and overall accountability revealed in the wake of the BSE crisis, such developments are not surprising, and they are in some ways positive. They may, for example, encourage more research and investment into agricultural practices such as integrated pest management (or *culture raisonée*), which would benefit farmers and farm laborers as much as they would consumers. Yet the spread of the corporate supermarkets' approach to assuring food safety, quality, and ethics is also cause for concern for at least three reasons. First, they employ codes of best practice as well as unwritten expectations that have been developed largely without the input of farm laborers and small-scale farmers, who have consequently been subject to hygienic and "ethical" standards that are not necessarily meaningful or appropriate. Such standards may in fact serve no purpose other than to "bulletproof" the corporate retailers and exporters who implement them. Many of the intermediaries who worked for such firms in Zambia and Britain readily admitted, for example, that they did not think that banning under-16 child labor on African horticultural farms was always the right thing to do—especially in a country where adolescent AIDS orphans might have their households to support—but in the interests of avoiding a media scandal, they had to do it anyway.

Second, just as transparency conceals the power relations that produce it (chapter 6), so too can specific standards serve to disguise and legitimate prejudice and discriminatory practices. As chapter 5 showed, racist stereotypes abounded in the conversations of French produce traders at Rungis. But they were expressed relatively openly, and acted upon in varied ways. They did not always stop people from doing business with one another. This meant that the African exporters subject to such stereotypes could confront or at least work around them; they could learn how to survive in the "wolves' den," as one exporter described it. This kind of overt prejudice was in no way defensible, in other words, but it could be defended against. British supermarkets' codified, "science-based" standards of hygiene and agricultural best practice, by contrast, excluded Kenyan smallholders from their supply chains for reasons that were both nonnegotiable and, on the face of it, perfectly reasonable. The standards were supposed to protect consumers' right to safe and high quality food, after all. But the supermarket personnel who used these standards had quite particular ideas about what kinds of suppliers could be trusted to produce such food. They came to Africa looking for "a U.K. farm, but abroad;" they wanted to find suppliers with "like minds." Standards, in other words, do not necessarily make prejudice go away; they can also cloak it in scientific rationale and managerial euphemism.

Third and last, the increasing reliance on codified measures of goodness in food and food provisioning work has devalued and threatens to destroy all kinds of practical knowledge, or *mētis*. The loss of agrarian *mētis* is already well advanced in many parts of the world, not only because farming populations have diminished but also because farmers have been forced to abandon what they know in favor of what a contract tells them to do (Scott 1998). So, too, has much practical knowledge about handling food disappeared, especially in industrialized countries. As Scott notes, the loss of such knowledge is not always to be mourned if accompanied by material improvements and greater freedoms in peoples' lives (see also Weber 1976). But it is not clear that this would be the case if codified standards of goodness destroy the most invisible but still vital food provisioning *mētis,* namely that of the intermediaries. The use of such standards to assess both people and their goods threatens to put more and more of the food supply in the hands of actors who know everything about category management and nothing about the taste of a good carrot; who know how to audit but not how to intuit. It threatens to erode the social basis of trust in food trade networks, and especially in those networks spanning long distances and varied social and cultural contexts. Such a loss would not merely rob certain professions of their day-to-day pleasures; it would also set back the efforts of those now calling for standards to make transnational food trading more ethical. This project cannot proceed by the book, and especially not a book controlled by a handful of corporate retailers. If food globalization is to proceed humanely, it will depend not on codes but on knowledgeable humans who, in the face of their differences and uncertainties, can put aside anxieties and trust each other.

Notes

1. As Beck showed in *Risk Society,* such anxieties are not limited to food alone, but rather apply to the many kinds of "modern" risks that cannot be easily detected or assessed, and therefore cannot be managed in the same way as relatively tangible risks, such as hunger. Wynne has rightly pointed out that in the case of genetically modified organisms, popular anxiety has turned into public distrust of government and science because the public expects not perfect protection from risk, but rather acknowledgement of uncertainty. See Beck 1992, Wynne 2001.

2. The smell came from a rodenticide used on some of the beverage company's shipping pallets, not from the cola itself. Thanks to an immediate recall and a massive PR campaign, Coca Cola won back consumer's confidence relatively quickly.

3. The United States will not import meat from countries where livestock are vaccinated against hoof-and-mouth disease because the vaccine makes it impossible to differentiate symptom-free carriers of the virus from uninfected animals.

4. Japan's ban on U.S. apples was overturned in 1999 after the WTO, in response to a complaint lodged by the United States, ruled that the apples posed no risk of infestation. *Seattle Times,* July 30 1999. "More apple, cherry varieties will be allowed into Japan," p. C2.

5. The WTO's Agreement on Sanitary and Phytosanitary Measures "recognises that governments have the right to take sanitary and phytosanitary measures but that they should be applied only to the extent necessary to protect human, animal or plant life or health and should not arbitrarily or unjustifiably discriminate between Members where identical or similar conditions prevail." http://www.wto.org/english/docs_e/legal_e/ursum_e.htm#bAgreement [Dec. 20, 2003].

6. For a methodological discussion of how cultural economy analysis applies to the study of food commodity networks, see Dixon 1999, Crang, Dwyer, et al. 2003. Other useful discussions of cultural economy analysis include Appadurai 1990, Ray and Sayer 1999, and Du Gay and Pryke 2002.

7. For example, Cohen 1971, Gregoire 1986, Clark 1994, Evers and Schrader 1994.

8. On organizational culture, see Frost 1991, Hamada and Sibley 1994, Alvesson 2002.

9. See for example Kaplan 1984, Tilly 1985, Messer 1984, Walton and Seddon 1994.

Farming is also, of course, a source of cultural and in particular national identity; agrarian ideals continue to provide arguments for agricultural protectionism even in countries where less than five percent of the population still farms. Farmers' perceived role in preserving a nation's countryside and rural culture gives potency to these ideals, as does their role in feeding the nation.

10. For example, Busch and Juska 1997, Whatmore and Thorne 1997, Murdoch and Miele 1999, Morgan and Murdoch 2000.

11. Classic but still revelant critiques of pesticide intensive export agriculture include Weir, Schapiro, et al. 1981; Murray, Hoppin, et al. 1990; Thrupp, Bergeron, et al. 1995.

12. The most important of these was the European Retailer Association's Protocol (EUREPGAP) which outlined "best practices" for FFV producers supplying the EU market. See www.eurep.org [Dec. 20, 2003].

13. For example, Marcus 1998, Mitchell 1997, Hughes and Cormode 1998, Marcus 1998, Parry 1998, Hughes, 1999.

14. In 2000 there were also several smaller rose growers, operating on approximately two hectares apiece, but many of them had recently gone out of business.

15. As Alex Hughes's research on the Kenya-United Kingdom cut flower commodity network has demonstrated, Foucault's ideas about governmentality, or "the mentalities of government," are useful for understanding how transnational commodity networks regulate their own activities through voluntary codes of conduct that NGOs have both advocated and helped to develop. See Hughes 2000, Hughes 2001a.

16. The literature on local food initiatives in the United States and Western Europe is by now huge. Examples include Winters 1983, Murdoch and Miele 1999, Hinrichs 2000, Holloway and Kneafsey 2000, Parrott, Wilson, et al. 2002, Allen, Fitzsimmons, et al. 2003, Weatherell, Tregear, et al. 2003.

17. See, for example, Marsden and Wrigley 1996, Marsden, Flynn, et al. 2000.

18. On the persistence of these stereotypes within the context of the European Union, see McDonald 1997, McDonald 2000.

19. General discussions of this kind of colonial power can be found in Bhabha 1994, Scott 1995, Young 2001. See also Hansen 1992.

Chapter 2

1. Congres International d'Hygiene de Paris 1889. Compte Rendu des Seances. Paris: Librairie J-B Baillière et Fils. Discourse Prononcé à la séance generale d'ouverture. Par M. le professeur Brouardel, p. 6.

2. In Britain in particular, mid-19th century political opinion favored an "informal empire" of trade in Africa. For a very concise discussion of how opinion turned in favor of formal colonial occupation, see Chamberlain 1999. A rather different argument can be found in Robinson and Gallagher 1961. For an overview of 19th century African economic history prior to European conquest, see Freund 1998.

3. On how these anxieties manifested themselves in both Britain and colonial societies, see McClintock 1995.

4. The role of botanical gardens in imperialism is the subject of a large literature. See for example Brockway 1979, Browne 1996, Bourget and Bonneuil 1999, Drayton 2000.

5. European assumptions about which Africans needed which tools and what knowledge about food and hygiene were highly gendered. See for example Hansen 1992, Moore and Vaughan 1994.

6. For a more general discussion see chapter 4 of Rau 1991. See also Watts 1983, Davis 2001.

7. Among them were Nott 1856, Knox 1862. See also Livingstone 1999.

8. This debate was also pertinent to United States imperialism in the Philippines; see Anderson 1996b.

9. It was widely believed that the fruits themselves caused tropical fevers. On the earlier recommendations see, Arnold 1996, 64; also Curtin 1989. On late 19th and early 20th century tropical hygiene, see Giles 1904, Livingstone 1999.

10. As Peters (2001) notes, the French in France took to canned food with great reluctance, but bought them eagerly—at least as their budgets allowed—in Vietnam. See also Bruegel 2002.

11. On famine in postcolonial Africa see De Waal 1997. The United Nation's annual Human Development Index provides some of the most useful statistics. See also Millstone and Lang 2003.

12. To be fair, the 19th century "pure food" movement in the United States also had its share of muckrakers, but they got a somewhat later start. Young 1989.

13. Polanyi's (2001) ideas about the "protective movements" generated by the great transformation are obviously relevant here.

14. The historical literature on British food supply is extensive; Burnett's (1966) chapters on food adulteration and quality are particularly useful. See also Drummond and Wilbraham 1958, Oddy and Miller 1976, Geissler and Oddy 1993.

15. For example, *Deadly Adulteration* 1830, Mitchell 1848. Portrayals of food adulteration also took more literary forms; see Stern, 2003.

16. Much more has been written about the glories of 19th century French food than about its impurities. See, for example, Aron 1975 and Pitte 1991. For a rather less glowing account see chapter 7 of Zeldin 1980.

17. Extraits des *Annales d'hygiene publique et de medicine legale*. 1856. Tome 32, Part 2. "Sur les alterations et falsifications des substances alimentaires."

18. Among the practical guides: *Tricks of Trade* 1856, Marcet 1856, Hassall 1857.

19. Punch, 1851, Vol. XX. Cited in Drummond and Wilbraham 1958, 294.

20. Reports from Select Committee on Adulteration of Food, etc., Third Report, H.C. 379 (1856), viii, 1. Cited in Burnett 1966, 192–93.

21. Clause I, Adulteration of Food and Drinks and of Drugs Act, 1872; cited in French and Phillips 2000, 34.

22. These debates continued for decades at international conferences, and were detailed in publications such as France's *Annales de Falsification*. Dairy products were the source of ongoing controversy, partly because cows from different regions produced milk with different levels of butterfat; some producers argued that if they were not allowed to add preservatives to their butter, it would not be commercially viable. *Compte*

rendu des travaux du 1ere Congrès International pour la Repression des Fraudes Alimentaires et Pharmaceutiques, Geneve, 8–12 Septembre 1908, p. 99. See also French and Phillips 2000.

23. M. Rouchet, participant at the Congrès International de Geneve 1908. Cited in Pagès 1909, 90.

24. Joseph Ruau, *Compte rendu des travaux du 1ere Congrès International pour la Repression des Fraudes Alimentaires et Pharmaceutiques,* Geneve, 8–12 Septembre 1908, p. 54.

25. Reprinted in Brizon and Poisson 1913; cited in Furlough and Strikwerda 1999, 39.

26. For example, Gemahling 1912, Curtil 1933, Martin-Saint-Léon 1911.

27. On the history of French and British vegetarianism, see Ouédraogo 1999.

28. Grimod de la Reyniere 1803–12, Carême 1833, Brillat-Savarin 2000 (1825). "Meditation 13" proposes the gastronomic class test.

29. Cited on p. 365, Peltre and Thouvenot 1987. The chef also wrote the famous *Guide Culinaíre* (Escoffier, Gilbert, et al. 1921).

30. Joseph Favre. 1890. "Of hygienic cuisine and the necessity of cooking schools," *Congrès Internationale d'hygiène et de demographie à Paris.* Paris: Bibliothèque des Annales Economiques, p. 102.

31. Following the government's adoption of a plan to stimulate rural economic growth in 1879, more than 16,000 km of railroad tracks were laid down. Transportation construction and improvements overall consumed more than 9 billion francs over the next several years (Weber, 1976, 210; Clozier 1963).

32. *Annales des Falsifications,* May 1911; *Fraudes et Falsifications: Traité Théorique et Pratique.* F. Monier, (procureur de la Republique près le Tribunal de la Seine), F. Chesney, (Judge) E. Roux (Chef de la repression des frauds au Ministère de la Ag.). Larose & Forcel, Paris, 1909.

33. *Vendémaiaire,* March 15, 1908, quoted in Hamelle 1913.

34. On this disillusionment see Ferguson 1999.

CHAPTER 3

1. On how development in this sense has shaped agrarian identities and practices, see Gupta 1998.

2. Actually there was some debate over the borders of what the Colonial Minister Albert Sarraut called "useful Africa." He believed it included some inland regions; others argued that French development efforts should focus on the continent's useful "edges." On this debate see Cooper 1996.

3. On the scientific objectives of French colonialism see Latour 1988, Bonneuil 1991, Osborne 1994.

4. Osborne (1994) argues that while British colonialism was motivated more by the need for new markets and settler regions than French colonialism, the latter was driven (though obviously not exclusively) by the drive for scientific progress.

5. See for example Hill 1963, Copans 1988. On French colonial debates about how well the cocoa and groundnut models applied to agricultural commercialization in French colonies, see Roberts 1996.

6. "Note: Economie Génerale de l'A.O.F.," prepared by Services Economiques, enclosed in correspondence from Sarraut to Governor-General, French West Africa, 22 August 1932, 17G 364, Archives du Sénégal. Quoted in Cooper 1996, 33–34. The assumption that peasant societies' "traditions" were ancient, unchanging, and necessary to the stability of these societies also guided British colonial policymaking. See chapter 2 of Berry 1993.

7. On these ideas as they apply to Africa, see the preface of Delavignette 1931, Muller 1984. On the recent history of the French peasantry, see Wright 1964, Weber 1976.

8. "Note: Economie Génerale de l'A.O.F.," prepared by Services Economiques, enclosed in correspondence from Sarraut to Governor-General, French West Africa, 22 August 1932, 17G 364, Archives du Sénégal. Quoted in Cooper 1996, 33–34.

9. The region does have gold deposits, but these did not begin to be exploited until the late 20th century. Jeune Afrique 1993.

10. Le Gouveneur-général de l'Afrique occidentale francaise à Messieurs les Lieutenant-gouveneurs des Colonies du Groupe, Circulaire Relative à l'application de l'arrêté du 6 mars 1924, organisant la production des textiles en Afrique occidentale francaise, 15 Mars 1924, p. 170. Cited in Roberts 1996, 148.

11. Archives du Sénégal Haute-Volta Service Agricole Rapport Annuel 1925.

12. Archives du Sénégal HV SARAA 1929.

13. Archives du Sénégal RA 1932.

14. "Rapports sur: les cultures indigenes maraichères; les essais de culture, la culture intensive, les industries agricoles." 1903. Archives du Sénégal R5.

15. Some of these vegetables, such as tomatoes, were brought to Africa from South America centuries earlier by the Portuguese.

16. Archives de Bobo-Dioulasso *Journal de Cercle, 1919–22*.

17. Based on interviews conducted with several elders in the village of Sakaby, 1993–94.

18. The literature on West African women's role in vegetable and other kinds of food marketing is extensive. See for example Sudarkasa 1973, Diouf 1981, Robertson 1984, Schilter 1991, Clark 1994.

19. Cited in Bassolet 1992, 73.

20. Large-scale schemes appealed not only to the engineers who designed them but also to donor and recipient governments. For donor governments, irrigation schemes, dams, and other technically ambitious forms of development aid served, in part, as ammunition in the contest for African Cold War allies. For recipient governments, large projects furthered domestic political ends, insofar as they testified to a government's progress towards development and, more concretely, created plum jobs for political appointees. Bates 1981.

21. For examples of projects that fared poorly because of lack of attention to local gender relations, see Conti 1979, Mackintosh 1989, Carney and Watts 1990, Schroeder and Watts 1991, Schroeder 1999.

22. After a gradual and uneven decline in annual rainfall from the 1960s through the late 1980s, rainfall averages began to increase in the late 1990s. For critiques of the "spreading Sahara" assumption, see Swift 1996, Fairhead and Leach 1998.

23. See Bassolet 1992, Savadogo and Wetta 1993.

24. Le Ministre du Commerce et de l'Approvisionnement du Peuple/Le Ministre de l'Action Paysanne/Le Ministre de l'Agriculture et de l'Elevage, "reglementation de la profession d'exporteur des fruits et légumes," signed October 30, 1990.

25. Interview with Nazaire Paré, Director of Studies and Prospectives, Burkina Faso Office Nationale du Commerce Exterieur, July 4, 1994.

26. In addition, other parts of the EU were importing increasing quantities of beans from Ethiopia and Egypt, mostly via Belgium. COLEACP 2001.

27. Production of coffee, shrimp, and counter-seasonal fruit also boomed.

28. On West African ethnic trade networks, see Cohen 1969, Gregoire 1986, Gregoire and Labazée 1993.

29. See for example Grandmaison 1969, Sudarkasa 1973, Brooks 1976, Cordonnier 1982, Eames 1988.

30. According to the United Nation's annual human development index, the female literacy rate in Burkina Faso is one of the lowest in the world, at 14.9 percent in 2003.

31. "Household" laborers may or may not be family members, and family members often expect payment, if not necessarily daily, then at the end of the season.

32. Selling food deemed unsafe for human consumption is a crime punishable by imprisonment in France, but if residues are detected, an importer is more likely to be warned than charged.

33. One exporter, with help from his French client (the "green bean king" described in chapter 5) was experimenting with integrated pest management (IPM), which would reduce chemical pesticide use.

34. The cheating methods bear some resemblance to the "weapons of the weak" described by James Scott in his discussion of "everyday" forms of peasant resistance (1985), but if they bring in cash or cut expenses, they also have everyday practical utility.

35. Historically, rural communities in Burkina Faso (especially in the predominantly Mossi regions) have depended on remittances from household members working in town or in Ivory Coast. Local trade and artisanal activities also provide at least seasonal income for many men and women. However, household members' individual incomes are not always pooled.

36. The World Bank has also provided aid for small-scale irrigation development. "World Bank finances pilot irrigation project in Burkina Faso," News Release 99/2070/AFR, World Bank, Washington, D.C. January 12, 1999.

37. Historically, the Ivory Coast's cocoa farms and urban service jobs offered relatively good employment prospects for Burkinabé migrants, but civil conflict and government-endorsed anti-immigration sentiment in 2002–03 dimmed these prospects considerably, and in fact forced many Burkinabé to flee the country.

38. As yet there is little research on modern African foodways, and much of it focuses on the "Westernization" of diet. See however Goody 1982, Kouman 1987, Requier-

Desjardins 1989, Aymard, Grignon, et al. 1993, Menozzi 1993, Ikpe 1994, SYFIA 1994, Freidberg 2003.

39. On the ways that such conditions can change over time as well as be perceived differently in different social and cultural contexts, see Asano-Tamanoi 1988, Wells 1996.

CHAPTER 4

1. "Zambian women, doomed to life on a rockpile." *New York Times,* August 2, 1996. "Two-faced copper." *New Internationalist,* issue 312, May 1999.

2. Great Britain Colonial Office 852/1/15004/1, Maize, Northern Rhodesia, 12/11/ 1935. Cited in Vickery 1986, 210.

3. *History of Mazabuka,* typescript, Livingstone Museum. Cited in Vickery 1986, 93; *So this was Lusaka,* 1959, Lusaka Publicity Association. Cited in Gann 1964, 140.

4. In the town of Luanysha, the European death rate from all causes dropped from 13.23 per 1,000 in 1930 to 9.9 in 1938; for African workers it dropped from 34.6 to 6.6 (Gann 1964, 210).

5. *Northern News.* January 7, 1956, p. 4; cited in Kallman 1999, 80.

6. As Stoler and Cooper (1997, p. 5) observe, "In colonial societies as in Europe, "racial survival" was often seen to be precariously predicated on strict adherence to cultural—and specifically gendered—prescriptions." On how Southern Rhodesian hygiene concerns shaped commodity culture, see Burke 1996. For a more general discussion of European colonial communities, see Stoler 2002.

7. Originally the Colonial Development Corporation, the CDC was founded in 1948. In 1999 it was converted into a public limited company, as part of Tony Blair's efforts to promote "public private partnerships." Its name was later changed again to CDC Capital Partners. http://www.cdcgroup.com/about_us/timeline.asp [Dec. 20, 2003]

8. The flower industry standards are discussed in Hughes 2000.

9. Zambia Agricultural Sector Performance 1997–98. Institute of Economic and Social Research, prepared for MAFF, published December 1999, p. 93. Eighty-three percent of the rural population was below the poverty line, and 56 percent of the urban.

10. Agriflora figures from data provided for VINET. http://www.nri.org/vinet [Jan. 26, 2004]. York Farm figures provided by the company's technical manager.

11. The Zambian horticultural industry did see a small influx of farm managers and other skilled workers from Zimbabwe, where production on some horticultural farms was disrupted by squatter occupations. On the other hand, the Zambian industry's own labor force was hit hard by HIV/AIDS.

12. On the contemporary expressions of these expectations, and how they have been disappointed, see Ferguson 1999. On corporate paternalism in export agriculture, see Du Toit 1998.

13. Dexterity, or "nimble fingers," has long been used to explain why women and girls are the preferred labor force for Third World export industries such as garment and semiconductor assembly. Ong 1987.

14. On how different codes of practice have incorporated these considerations, see Tallontire, Dolan, et al. 2001.

15. This is a pseudonym.

16. Strathern 1999, 2000a, Strathern 2000b, Hughes 2001a.

17. SA 8000 and Social Accountability International: www.sa-intl.org [Dec. 21, 2003]. COLEACP Harmonized Framework, 2000: http://www.coleacp.org/fo_internet/en/cadre/document.html [Dec. 21, 2003]. For an overview and comparison of these codes see Tallontire, Dolan, et al. 2001, Jerkins, Pearson, et al. 2002.

18. U.K. Food Safety Act 1990, Defence of due diligence, section 21.

19. Industrial and Labour Relations Act 1993, Section 15, Funeral Assistance.

20. The huge profit growth owed partly to the rise of the Euro against the dollar; the company incurs dollar costs but receives Euro revenue. "Taking Stock: Barbican Asset Management." *Zimbabwe Independent,* December 14, 2001. In 2003, the Industrial Development Corporation of South Africa Limited (IDC) made a $4 million equity investment in Agriflora, lowering the TZI share of ownership. "South African Loan to Zambia's Agriflora Gets World Bank Guarantee." Just-Food.com June 30, 2003.

21. The horticultural industry's low wages appeared particularly inadequate when famine threatened Zambia in 2001–02. According to a March 2002 article in the Zambian press (Phiri 2002), workers and even a district chief took their complaints about inadequate pay to the Agriflora management. The company had responded to the widespread hunger by paying most workers partially in tins of maize, which reduced their take-home pay. The middle manager quoted in the article responded to the chief's complaint: "We agree that poverty levels are very high and people cannot survive on these salaries but I am not ready to pay them more . . . Where am I going to get the money? My company has to make a profit, otherwise it will be closed."

CHAPTER 5

1. For perspectives on these changes from inside and outside the French culinary establishment, see Lazareff 1998, Bové, Dufour, et al. 2001. See also Ariès 1997.

2. My understanding of *mētis* draws on James Scott's (1998) discussion of the term, which emphasizes the importance of *mētis* for "responding to a constantly changing human and natural environment" (313) whether in the fields, the kitchen (where the "environment" is effectively the stovetop) or the market. Scott contrasts *mētis* with the epistemic knowledge (or what the Greeks called *techne*) typically acquired through texts and formal education. Some occupations have always required both forms of expertise (engineers, heart surgeons); in transnational fresh produce trading, the codes of "good practice" discussed in chapters 4 and 6 represent new forms of *techne* that intermediaries must learn, atop older codes of product grades and standards. See also Marglin (1996) on threats to peasant knowledge. Both Scott and Marglin draw on Nussbaum's (2001) discussion of *mētis* in Greek philosophy. On the rise of modern food retailing, see Fraser 1981.

3. Contrary to appearances, there is no direct etymological relationship between the

two terms. *Métier* derives from the Latin term ministerium, as in to serve. *Dictionnaire Historique de la Langue Francaise,* 1992 1235–6. Paris: Dictionnaires Le Robert.

4. Cultural economy analysis presumes that economic activity is not just *embedded* in the relationships and cultural norms of particular networks, but rather that the economic and the cultural are mutually constituted through these relationships. Du Gay and Pryke 2002.

5. See for example Abolafia 1998.

6. On this point see Stoler and Cooper 1997. Development is a crucial postcolonial "encounter" where identities are mutually constituted. See for example Gupta 1998.

7. Duby, Wallon, et al. 1975. For a comparative perspective on French and British rural histories, see Boudiguel and Lowe 1989.

8. This is a huge literature, but for changes over time see, for example, Hémardinquer 1970, Grignon 1986. On the regional and social diversity of diet and foodways in France, see Grignon 1986, Grignon and Grignon 1986, Calvo 1997, Calvo 2002. The series *Inventaire du patrimoine culinaire de la France* (P. Albin Michel/Conseil National des Arts Culinaires) provides examples of regional recipes, including those from overseas possessions such as Guadeloupe.

9. This is a point made clear by Miller's (2001) ethnography of British shoppers.

10. This statement is not accurate. Potentially lethal strains of E-coli, while more often found in meat, can also contaminate fruits and vegetables.

11. A 2002 survey found that 41 percent of the population put their trust in farmers, as opposed to 15 percent in supermarkets and 4 percent in the government. "Enquête exclusive *CSA-L'Expansion:* Même à la table, le grand retour de la France d'en bas," *L'Expansion,* juillet-août 2002, 71.

12. Agro-industry has found inroads into fresh produce packaging via salad mix in the United States as well. See Guthman 2003.

13. In 1999, supermarkets, hypermarkets, and "hard discount" stores together accounted for 67.7% of fresh fruit and vegetable sales by volume. CTIFL Diagramme de la distribution 1999. www.ctifl.fr [Jan. 27, 2004].

14. Women's employment increased from 45.3 percent to 80 percent for women age 25–29; from 39 percent to 76 percent for women age 30–34, and from 41 percent to 75.6 percent for women age 40–44. Grignon and Grignon 1999.

15. Per capita frozen food consumption in France was 66 pounds in 2001, versus 4 pounds in 1960. Sciolino 2002.

16. *Les Halles* was perhaps an especially vivid example of how markets are never separate from the rest of social life, as they are often treated in neoclassical economics. Granovetter 1985.

17. By the end of World War II, traders in the meat, fish, and dairy pavilions did have refrigerated storage, as did the independent wholesale houses. But many of the fruit and vegetable sellers, in particular those outside the pavilions, did not. Chemla 1994, 88.

18. *France-Soir,* 20 January 1970. "L'horaire de jour" à Rungis permettra usagers des Halles d'avoir une vie normale."

19. This man was approaching middle age and came from a wholesaling family; younger managers are more likely to have studied management or business.

20. For this reason the British supermarkets and importers advise their African suppliers to be on the lookout for undercover journalists.

21. Women owners and managers are somewhat more common among the wholesalers than the importers.

22. One importer interviewed at Rungis in 1999 had begun taking digital photographs of merchandise upon arrival, and sending the images to his suppliers, precisely to resolve uncertainties about its condition. Of course, this technical innovation would be useless to suppliers without the appropriate computer hardware and software—which, in Burkina Faso, would have been most, if not all, of the exporters.

23. Between 1999 and 2001, I met with Gallot several times, both at Rungis and in Burkina Faso, and also interviewed all his Burkinabé suppliers.

24. On the Selection Web site, a statement by Gallot lists "courtesy, efficacy, combativeness, and reliability" as the company's working principles.

CHAPTER 6

1. Many smaller Kenyan fresh vegetable exporters could still find buyers among the U.K. wholesalers who supplied the country's "ethnic" markets and other smaller retailers. Some of these buyer-supplier arrangements were based on family ties. Jaffee 1995a; Barrett, Ilbery, et al. 1999.

2. "Supermarkets Given All Clear." BBC News, October 10, 2000. http://news.bbc .co.uk/1shhi/business/965665.stm [Feb. 8 2004].

3. Strathern (1999) employs "bulletproofing" to describe university departments' use of mission statements and audits. She draws an analogy between these "weapons" and painted shields employed by warriors in Papua New Guinea, in part because both defensive forms rely on self-depictions intended not only to impress others but also to show "how impressed we are with ourselves." She considers how these weapons are turned inwards—that is, how they become part of internal disciplinary regimes. This is certainly the case for the standards and audits employed in the supermarkets' fresh vegetable supply chains. See also Shore and Wright 2000.

4. The British press is also unusual in that all the major papers have national as opposed to regional or metropolitan markets. See Sparks 1999; Eldridge, Kitzinger, et al. 1997; Davis 2002.

5. On the historical role of the press and other media in shaping French and British food knowledge, see Mennell 1996.

6. The food industry perspective has much in common with other industries confronted with what they see as "irrational" public fear of their products, for example genetically modified organisms and nuclear power. See Wynne 2001.

7. "What is wrong with our food?" *Guardian Unlimited*. http://www.guardian.co .uk/food/0,2759,178225,00.html [Dec. 20, 2003]. See also Hughes 2001.

8. Freeman's definition of stakeholders as "any individual or group who can affect, or who is affected by, the actions, policies, practices or goals of the corporation" testifies to how widely this term can be interpreted. Freeman 1984, cited in Sunley 1999.

9. For an example of how the business community relies on NGO measures of "social" performance, see Moore 2001.

10. See for example Power 1997, Crang 2000, Strathern 2000b, Strathern 2000a.

11. On moral geographies see Smith 1998 and 2000. Daniel Miller (2001) argues that most shoppers' moral geographies do not extend past the household, where both thrift and indulgence are moral virtues because they express care for household members. This explains, he argues, why even shoppers who express concern about more distant injustices do not regularly purchase goods that are supposed to help address them (for example, fair trade goods).

12. Though see Daniel Miller's (2003) discussion of how the Internet might help bring producers and consumers into more direct and thus meaningful contact.

13. ETI: www.ethicaltrade.org [Dec. 21, 2003].

14. It should be noted that labels are not the answer to everything. As Julie Guthman's work on organic agriculture has demonstrated, the lure of the price premium (or what she describes as rent) has led large-scale farms into organic production, thereby driving down prices. On the other hand, fair trade standards guarantee producers a price floor. See Raynolds 2000, Guthman 2002, Renard 2003, Guthman 2004.

15. These include the British Independent Fruit Growers' Association, the Centre for Food Policy, Compassion in World Farming, the Countryside Agency, Council for the Protection of Rural England, English Nature, Fairtrade Foundation, Farm Animal Welfare Network, Farmers Link, Forum for the Future, Marine Conservation Society, Marine Stewardship Council, National Federation of Women's Institutes, New Economics Foundation, Royal Society for the Protection of Birds, Small and Family Farms Alliance, Sustain, Traidcraft Exchange, Transport 2000, Transport and General Workers' Union, Shop, Distributive and Allied Workers Union, World Society for the Protection of Animals, and WWWF-UK. The Soil Association joined RTTT in May 2003.

16. It is particularly associated with Total Quality Management. See Tenner and DeToro 1992, Mouradian 2002.

17. Tsoukas describes *mētis* in the context of "expert systems," in which surgeons and engineers as well as peasants work. He observes, "The paradox is that the more information on the inner workings of an expert system observers seek to have, the less practitioners are trusted, the less likely it is for the benefits of the specialized expertise to be realized." Tsoukas 1997, 835.

18. Actor-network theory emphasizes how the cohesion of networks of all kinds depends on actors' acceptance of particular "stories," for example, the story of why corporate social responsibility is necessary and good. One measure of actors' power is how effectively they can tell and convince others of these stories. See Law 1986, Whatmore and Thorne 1997.

19. See, for example, O'Neill 1996, Tronto 1993, Clement 1996, Carbridge 1993, Proctor and Smith 1998, Smith 1998, Smith 2000.

Conclusion

1. Food Standards Agency Consumer Attitudes to Food survey, February 17, 2003.

2. Credit due to Michael Watts (1994b) for this apt phrasing.

3. Two collections which illustrate how this point applies to food in particular: Goodman and Watts 1997, Watson 1997.

4. The late 20th century resurgence of "cultural" explanations for poverty is perhaps best illustrated by Landes 1998. Somewhat similar assumptions are found in Fukuyama 1995.

5. The production of fresh fruits and vegetables within the wealthy countries of the global North also relies, of course, on farm laborers who have migrated from much poorer countries in the global South.

6. Local foods are not necessarily more environmentally friendly if, for example, they are raised in heated greenhouses or if they are transported to market in many small, old, polluting vehicles (like those that small farmers often own). Over long distances, Sustain's (2001) "food miles" research rightly notes that ocean transport is far more fuel efficient than airfreight, and sometimes fresh produce travels on passenger flights, especially when (as in Burkina Faso) it is shipped in relatively small quantities.

7. On initiatives that appeal to local affinities, see Allen, Fitzsimmons, et al. 2003, Weatherell, Tregear, et al. 2003, Winter 2003, Holloway and Kneafsey 2000. Two collections exploring the relationships between food and national identity are Scholliers 2001, Belasco and Scranton 2002.

8. Supermarkets, fair trade organizations, scholars, and even lobstermen have all looked into the possibilities offered by the Internet. Supermarket managers discussed with me the easiest and arguably least effective means of connecting consumers with producers, namely short video clips of farmers on company Web sites. Given that this involves no communication, it differs little from an ordinary advertisement. Alternatively, Daniel Miller suggests noncommercial chat rooms and Web cameras as means of both educating consumers (school children especially) and facilitating real-time communication. See Miller 2003. On the use of the Internet to connect lobster fishermen and consumers, see Zezima 2003.

9. Many of the food projects in the United Kingdom are coordinated by Sustain: the Alliance for Better Food and Farming. http://www.sustainweb.org [Dec. 21, 2003]. On food projects in Iowa, see Hinrichs 2003.

10. Melanie DuPuis (2000) argues that contemporary "reflexive" consumers—those who seek and analyze information about goods and consume accordingly—can effect change even when they are not organized. See also Gabriel and Lang 1995, French and Phillips 2000.

11. On the European Union regulations pertinent to food retailers, see Marsden, Flynn, et al. 2000. Among the findings of the 2001 "General State of Food" project (chapter 5) was that consumers wanted more information about how their food was made.

Works Cited

Abolafia, Mitchel. 1998. "Markets as Cultures: An Ethnographic Approach." In *The Laws of the Markets,* ed. Michel Callon, 69–85. Malden, Mass.: Blackwell.

Abrahamsen, Rita. 2003. "African Studies and the Postcolonial Challenge." *African Affairs* 102:189–210.

Accum, Friedrich Christian. 1966. *A Treatise on Adulterations of Food and Culinary Poisons.* London: J. Mallett.

Adas, Michael. 1989. *Machines as the Measure of Men: Science, Technology, and Ideologies of Western Dominance.* Ithaca, N.Y.: Cornell University Press.

Allen, Patricia, Margaret Fitzsimmons et al. 2003. "Shifting Plates in the Agrifood Landscape: The Tectonics of Alternative Agrifood Initiatives in California." *Journal of Rural Studies* 19: 61–75.

Alvarez, Lizette. "Consumers in Europe Resist Gene-Altered Foods." *New York Times,* February 11, 2003, p. 3.

Alvesson, Mats. 2002. *Understanding Organizational Culture.* London: Sage.

Anderson, Benedict R. 1991. *Imagined Communities: Reflections on the Origin and Spread of Nationalism.* London: Verso.

Anderson, Warwick. 1992. "Climates of Opinion: Acclimatization in Nineteenth-Century France and England." *Victorian Studies* 35(2) 134–57.

———. 1996a. "Disease, Race, and Empire." *Bulletin of the History of Medicine* 1 (Spring): 62–67.

———. 1996b. "Immunities of Empire: Race, Disease, and the New Tropical Medicine, 1900–1920." *Bulletin of the History of Medicine,* 1 (Spring): 94–118.

Andriatiana, Mamy. 1998. "Les Boeufs Malgaches Vont Devoir Montrer Leur Papiers." *Syfia International,* http://www.syfia.com/fr/ [July 15, 2003].

Appadurai, Arjun. 1986. "Introduction: Commodities and the Politics of Value" In *The Social Life of Things: Commodities in Cultural Perspective,* ed. Arjun Appadurai, 3–63. Cambridge: Cambridge University Press.

———. 1990. "Disjuncture and Difference in the Global Cultural Economy." *Public Culture* 2(2): 1–24.

———. 1996. *Modernity at Large: Cultural Dimensions of Globalization.* Minneapolis, Minn.: University of Minnesota Press.

Ariès, Paul. 1997. *Les Fils de Mcdo: La Mcdonaldisation du Monde.* Paris: Harmattan.

Arnold, David. 1996. *The Problem of Nature: Environment, Culture, and European Expansion*. Oxford: Blackwell.

Aron, Jean Paul. 1975. *The Art of Eating in France: Manners and Menus in the Nineteenth Century*. London: Owen.

Arthur, Charles. "Origins of BSE May Be Found in Herds of the African Plains." *The Independent*, August 1, 1997.

Asano-Tamanoi, Mariko. 1988. "Farmers, Industry and the State: The Culture of Contract Farming in Spain and Japan." *Comparative Studies in Society and History* 30(3):432–52.

Aslet, Clive. "Clocking Up Food Miles." *Financial Times Weekend*, February 23–24, 2002.

Aymard, M., C. Grignon, et al., Eds. 1993. *Le Temps de Manger: Alimentation, Emploi du Temps, et Rythmes Sociaux*. Paris: Maison des Sciences de l'Homme.

Baier, A. C. 1987. "The Need for More Than Justice." *Canadian Journal of Philosophy* 13: 41–56.

Baret, C., F. Janet-Catrice, et al. 1999. "Grandes Surfaces Alimentaires: Vers le Modele Americain en Matière de Services?" *INSEE Premiere* 686: 1–4.

Barham, E. 2003. "Translating Terroir: The Global Challenge of French AOC Labeling." *Journal of Rural Studies* 19(1): 127–38.

Barrett, Hazel, Brian Ilbery, et al. 1999. "Globalization and the Changing Networks of Food Supply: The Importation of Fresh Horticultural Produce from Kenya into the UK." *Transactions of the Institute of British Geographers* 24: 159–74.

Barrientos, Stephanie, Ed. 1999. *Women and Agribusiness: Working Miracles in the Chilean Fruit Export Sector*. New York: St. Martin's Press.

Bassolet, Boubié, 1992. *Le Programme d'Ajustement du Secteur Agricole (PASA) au Burkina Faso: Principales Orientations et Propositions d'Activités de Recherche*. Document de travail 2. CEDRES/Université de Ouagadougou.

Bates, Robert H. 1981. *Markets and States in Tropical Africa: The Political Basis of Agricultural Policies*. Berkeley: University of California Press.

Bayart, Jean-Francois. 1993. *The State in Africa: Politics of the Belly*. New York: Longman.

Beardsworth, A. D. 1990. "Trans-Science and Moral Panics: Understanding Food Scares." *British Food Journal* 92(5):1–16.

Beck, Ulrich. 1992. *Risk Society: Towards a New Modernity*. London: Sage.

Belasco, Warren James, and Philip Scranton, eds. 2002: *Food Nations: Selling Taste in Consumer Societies*. New York: Routledge.

Berry, Sara. 1993. *No Condition Is Permanent: The Social Dynamics of Agrarian Change in Subsaharan Africa*. Madison: University of Wisconsin Press.

Bhabha, Homi K. 1994. *The Location of Culture*. New York: Routledge.

Binger, Louis-Gustave. 1892. *Du Niger au Golfe de Guinée, par le Pays de Kong et le Mossi*. Paris: Hachette.

Blowfield, Mick. 1999. "Ethical Trade: A Review of Development and Issues." *Third World Quarterly* 20(4): 753–70.

Blythman, Joanna. "Strange Fruit." *The Guardian*, September 7, 2002.

Bois, M. D. 1924. "La Culture Des Plantes Potagères Dans Les Pays Chauds." *Journal officiel de Madagascar et Dependances*.

Bonneuil, Christophe. 1991. *Des Savants Pour l'Empire: La Structuration des Recherches Coloniales au Temps de "La Mise En Valeur des Colonies Francaises" 1917–1945.* Paris: Editions d'ORSTOM.

Bosch, Ellie. 1985. *Les Femmes de Marché de Bobo-Dioulasso.* Leiden: Centre de Recherche et de Documentation Femmes et Developpement.

Boudiguel, Maryvonne, and Philip Lowe, Eds. 1989. *Campagne Francaise, Campagne Britannique: Histoires, Images, Usages au Crible des Sciences Sociales.* Paris: Harmattan.

Bourdieu, Pierre. 1984. *Distinction: A Social Critique of the Judgment of Taste.* Cambridge: Harvard University Press.

Bourget, Marie-Noëlle, and Christophe Bonneuil. 1999. "De l'Inventaire du Monde à la Mise en Valeur du Globe. Botanique et Colonisation (Fin XVII Siècle-Début XXE Siècle)." *Revue Francaise d'Histoire d'Outre-Mer* 86:5–38.

Bové, Jose, Francois Dufour, et al. 2001. *The World Is not for Sale: Farmers against Junk Food.* London: Verso.

Boyd, William, and Michael Watts. 1997. "Agro-Industrial Just-in-Time: The Chicken Industry and Postwar American Capitalism." In *Globalising-Food: Agrarian Questions and Global Restructuring,* ed. D. Goodman and M. Watts, 192–225. New York: Routledge.

Brelsford, William Vernon. 1965. *Generations of Men: The European Pioneers of Northern Rhodesia.* Salisbury: Stuart Manning.

Bridge, Gary. 1997. "Mapping the Terrain of Time-Space Compression: Power Networks in Everyday Life." *Environment and Planning D-Society & Space* 15(5): 611–26.

Brillat-Savarin, Jean Anthelme. 2000 (1825). *The Physiology of Taste, or Meditations on Transcendental Gastronomy.* Washington, D.C.: Counterpoint.

Brizon, Pierre, and Ernest Poisson. 1913. *La Coopération.* Paris: A. Quillet.

Brockway, Lucile. 1979. *Science and Colonial Expansion: The Role of the British Royal Botanic Gardens.* New York: Academic Press.

Brooks, George E. 1976. "The *Signare* of Saint-Louis and Gorée: Women Entrepreneurs in Eighteenth-Century Senegal." In *Women in Africa,* ed. Nancy Hafkin and Edna Bay, 19–44. Stanford, Calif.: Stanford University Press.

———. 1993. *Landlords and Strangers: Ecology, Society, and Trade in Western Africa, 1000–1630.* Boulder, Colo.: Westview Press.

Browne, A., P.J.C. Harris, et al. 2000. "Organic Production and Ethical Trade: Definition, Practice and Links." *Food Policy* 25: 69–89.

Browne, Janet. 1996. "Biogeography and Empire." In *Cultures of Natural History,* ed. Nicholas Jardine, James A. Secord, and E. C. Spary, 305–21. Cambridge: Cambridge University Press.

Bruegel, Martin. 2001. "A Bourgeois Good? Sugar, Norms of Consumption and the Labouring Classes in Nineteenth-Century France." In *Food, Drink and Identity: Cooking, Eating and Drinking in Europe since the Middle Ages,* ed. Peter Scholliers, 99–118. Oxford: Berg.

———. 2002. "How the French Learned to Eat Canned Food, 1809–1930s." In *Food*

Nations: Selling Taste in Consumer Societies, ed. Warren Belasco and Philip Scranton, 113–30. New York: Routledge.

Burawoy, Michael. 1972. *The Colour of Class on the Copper Mines, from African Advancement to Zambianization.* Manchester: Manchester University Press for the Institute for African Studies, University of Zambia.

Burke, Timothy. 1996. *Lifebuoy Men, Lux Women: Commodification, Consumption and Cleanliness in Modern Zimbabwe.* Durham, N.C.: Duke University Press.

Burnett, John. 1966. *Plenty and Want: A Social History of Diet in England from 1815 to the Present Day.* London: Nelson.

Busch, Lawrence 2000. "The Moral Economy of Grades and Standards." *Journal of Rural Studies* 16(3):273–83.

Busch, Lawrence and Keiko Tanaka. 1996. "Rites of Passage: Constructing Quality in a Commodity Subsector." *Science Technology & Human Values* 21(1): 3–27.

Busch, Lawrence, and Arunas Juska. 1997. "Beyond Political Economy: Actor-Networks and the Globalization of Agriculture." *Review of International Political Economy* 4(4):668–708.

Calvo, Emmanuel. 1997. "Toujours Africans et Déjà Français: La Socialisation des Migrants Vue à Travers Leur Alimentation." *Politique Africain* 67:48–55.

———. "Changements Alimentaires, Changements De Société." 2002. *POUR* 175: 68–76.

Camborde, Philippe. 1997. "L'Installation de Félix Potin à Paris: Le Choix d'un Métier." In *La Révolution Commerciale en France,* ed. Jacques Marseille, 71–90. Paris: Le Monde Editions.

Caraher, Martin, Tim Lang, et al. 2000. "The Influence of TV and Celebrity Chefs on Public Attitudes and Behavior among the English Public." *Journal for the Study of Food and Society* 4(1):27–46.

Carême, Marie Antonin. 1833. *L'Art de la Cuisine Francaise au Dix-Neuvieme Siecle.* Paris: J. Renouard.

Carney, Judith, and Michael Watts. 1990. "Manufacturing Dissent: Work, Gender and the Politics of Meaning in a Peasant Society." *Africa* 60: 207–41.

Chamberlain, Muriel Evelyn. 1999. *The Scramble for Africa.* New York: Longman.

Chan, Man-Kwun, and Bill King. 2000. *Review of the Implications of Changes in EU Pesticide Legislation on the Production and Export of Fruits and Vegetables from Developing Country Suppliers.* NRI Report No. 2525. Chatham, U.K.: University of Greenwich, Natural Resources Institute.

Chemla, Guy. 1994. *Les Ventres de Paris: Les Halles, La Villette, Rungis: L'histoire du Plus Grand Marché Du Monde.* Grenoble, France: Glenat.

Christian Aid. 1999. *Taking Stock: How the Supermarkets Stack up on Ethical Trade.* London: Christian Aid.

Clark, Gracia. 1994. *Onions Are My Husband: Survival and Accumulation by West African Market Women.* Chicago: University of Chicago Press.

Clement, Grace. 1996. *Care, Autonomy, and Justice: Feminism and the Ethic of Care.* Boulder, Colo.: Westview Press.

Clozier, René. 1963. *Géographie de la Circulation.* Paris: Génin.

Codron, Jean-Marie. 1996. *Les Stratégies d'Approvisionnement de la Grande Distribution en Produits Frais: Le Cas des Fruits de Contresaison.* Série Etudes et Recherches no. 105. Montpelier, France: INRA-ESR.

Cohen, Abner. 1969. *Custom and Politics in Urban Africa: A Study of Hausa Migrants in Yoruba Towns.* Berkeley: University of California Press.

———. 1971. "Cultural Strategies in the Organization of Trading Diasporas." In *The Development of Indigenous Trade and Markets in West Africa,* ed. Claude Meillassoux, 266–81. Oxford: Oxford University Press.

COLEACP 2001. *EU Imports of Fresh Fruits and Vegetables from 1994 until 2000.* Rungis France: CSIF.

Colin, Josette. 1998. *Je Me Souviens des Halles.* Paris: Parigramme.

Collins, E.J.T. 1993. "Food Adulteration and Food Safety in Britain in the 19th and Early 20th Centuries." *Food Policy:* 95–109.

Compaore, Viviane et al. 1987. *Burkina Faso: Développement des Cultures Irriguées.* Ouagadougou: CILSS/Club du Sahel.

Conford, P. 2001. *The Origins of the Organic Movement.* Edinburgh: Floris Books.

Conklin, Alice L. 1997. *A Mission to Civilize: The Republican Idea of Empire in France and West Africa, 1895–1930.* Stanford, Calif.: Stanford University Press.

Conti, Anna. 1979. "Capitalist Organization of Production through Non-Capitalist Relations: Women's Role in a Pilot Resettlement in Upper Volta." *Review of African Political Economy* 15/16: 75–92.

Cook, Ian. 1994. "New Fruits and Vanity: Symbolic Production in the Global Food Economy." In *From Columbus to Conagra: The Globalization of Agriculture and Food,* eds. A Bonanno et al., 232–48. Lawrence: University of Kansas.

———. 1995. "Constructing the Exotic: The Case of Tropical Fruit." In *A Shrinking World?* eds. J. Allen and C. Hamnett. Oxford: Open University Press.

Cook, Ian, and Philip Crang. 1996. "The World on a Plate: Culinary Culture, Displacement and Geographical Knowledges." *Journal of Material Culture* 1(2): 131–53.

Cooper, Frederick. 1996. *Decolonization and African Society: The Labor Question in French and British Africa.* Cambridge: Cambridge University Press.

Copans, Jean. 1988. *Les Marabouts de l'Arachide: La Confrerie Mouride et les Paysans du Sénégal.* Paris: L'Harmattan.

Coquery-Vidrovitch, Catherine. 1972. *Le Congo au Temps des Grandes Compagnies Concessionnaires, 1898–1930.* Paris: Mouton.

Corbridge, Stuart. 1993. "Marxisms, Modernities, and Moralities: Development Praxis and the Claims of Distant Strangers." *Environment and Planning D-Society & Space* 11: 449–72.

Cordonnier, Rita. 1982. *Femmes Africaines et Commerce: Les Revendeuses de Tissu de la Ville de Lomé.* Paris: ORSTOM.

Cowan, Cathal. 1988. "Irish and European Consumer Views on Food Safety." *Journal of Food Safety* 18: 275–95.

Crang, Philip. 2000. "Organisational Geographies: Surveillance, Display and the Spaces of Power in Business Organisation." In *Entanglements of Power. Geographies of Domination/Resistance,* ed. Joanne Sharp, 204–18. New York: Routledge.

Crang, Philip, Ian Cook, et al. 2000. "Have You Got the Customer's Permission? Category Management and Circuits of Knowledge in the UK Food Business." In *Knowledge, Space, Economy,* ed. J. R. Bryson, 242–60. New York: Routledge.

Crang, Philip, Claire Dwyer, et al. 2003. "Transnationalism and the Spaces of Commodity Culture." *Progress in Human Geography* 27(4): 438–56.

Csergo, Julia. 1999. "The Emergence of Regional Cuisines." In *Food: A Culinary History,* eds. Jean-Louis Flandrin and Massimo Montanari, 500–15. New York: Penguin.

Curtil, Evariste. 1993. *Des Maisons Francaises d'Alimentation à Succarsales Multiples.* Thesis, Universite de Dijon, Faculté de Droit.

Curtin, Philip D. 1989. *Death by Migration: Europe's Encounter with the Tropical World in the Nineteenth Century.* Cambridge: Cambridge University Press.

———. 1998. *Disease and Empire: The Health of European Troops in the Conquest of Africa.* Cambridge: Cambridge University Press.

Datta, Kusum. 1988. "Farm Labor, Agrarian Capital and the State in Colonial Zambia: The African Labour Corps, 1942–52." *Journal of Southern African Studies* 14(3): 371–92.

Davis Aeron. 2002. *Public Relations Democracy: Public Relations, Politics and the Mass Media in Britain.* Manchester: Manchester University Press.

Davis, Dorothy. 1966. *A History of Shopping.* London: Routledge.

Davis, Mike. 2001. *Late Victorian Holocausts: El Niño Famines and the Making of the Third World.* London: Verso.

Deadly Adulteration and Slow Poisoning Unmasked; or Disease and Death in the Pot and Bottle, by an Enemy to Fraud and Villany. 1830. London: Sherwood, Gilbert & Piper.

de Benoist, Joseph-Roger E. 1987. *Eglise et Pouvoir Colonial au Soudan Francais: Les Relations entre les Administrateurs et les Missionaires Catholiques dans la Boucle du Niger, de 1885 à 1945.* Paris: Karthala.

Delavignette, Robert 1931. *Les Paysans Noirs.* Paris: Stock.

de Montjoye, Emannuelle. 1980. *L'Evangile au Pays Bobo.* Bobo-Dioulasso: Service de Publications, Diocese de Bobo-Dioulasso.

Destaminil. 1844. *Le Cuisinier Français Perfectionné, Contenent les Meillieures Prescriptions de la Cuisine Ancienne et Moderne.* Paris: B. Renault.

De Waal, Alexander. 1997. *Famine Crimes: Politics and the Disaster Relief Industry in Africa.* Bloomington: Indiana University Press.

Diouf, Made Bande. 1981. "Restauranteurs in the Dakar Industrial Area: The Cooking-Pot War." *Cahier d'Etudes Africaine* 21(81–83): 237–50.

Dixon, Jane. 1999. "A Cultural Economy Model for Studying Food Systems." *Agriculture and Human Values* 16(2): 151–60.

Dodge, Doris Jansen. 1977. *Agricultural Policy and Performance in Zambia: History, Prospects, and Proposals for Change.* Berkeley: Institute of International Studies, University of California.

Doel, Christine. 1996. "Market Development and Organizational Change: The Case of the Food Industry." In *Retailing, Consumption and Capital: Towards the New Retail*

Geography, eds. Neil Wrigley and Michelle Lowe, 48–67. Harlow, England: Longman.

Dolan, Catherine, John Humphrey, et al. 1999. *Horticulture Commodity Chains: The Impact of the UK Market on the African Fresh Vegetable Industry.* Working Paper 96. Brighton, England: Institute of Development Studies.

Drayton, Richard Harry. 2000. *Nature's Government: Science, Imperial Britain, and the "Improvement" of the World.* New Haven: Yale University Press.

Drescher, Seymour. 1987. *Capitalism and Antislavery: British Mobilization in Comparative Perspective.* Oxford: Oxford University Press.

Drummond, Jack Cecil, and Anne Wilbraham. 1958. *The Englishman's Food: A History of Five Centuries of English Diet.* London: J. Cape.

Duby, Georges, Armand Wallon, et al. 1975. *Histoire de la France Rurale.* Paris: Seuil.

Du Camp, Maxime. 1873. *Paris, ses Organs, ses Functions et sa Vie dans la Seconde Moitié du XIX Siècle.* Paris: Librairie Hachette.

Ducrocq, Cedric. 1996. *Distribution Alimentaire: Enjeux Stratégiques et Perspectives 1994–1998.* Paris: Les Echos.

Du Gay, Paul, and Michael Pryke. 2002. *Cultural Economy: Cultural Analysis and Commercial Life.* London; Sage.

Dumont, R. 1978. *Paysans Ecrases, Terres Massacrées.* Paris: Laffont.

DuPuis, E. Melanie. 2000. "Not in My Body: Rbgh and the Rise of Organic Milk." *Agriculture and Human Values* 17(3): 285–95.

Du Toit, Andries 1998. "The Fruits of Modernity: Law, Power and Paternalism in Western Cape Fruit and Wine Farms." In *South Africa in Transition: New Theoretical Perspectives,* eds. A. Norval and D. Howarth, 149–64. London: MacMillan.

———. 2001. "Ethical Trading: A Force for Improvement, or Corporate Whitewash?" *ODI Resource Perspectives* (71): 1–4.

Eames, Elizabeth. 1988. "Why the Women Went to War: Women and Wealth in Ondo Town, Southwestern Nigeria." In *Traders Versus the State,* ed. Gracia Clark, 81–97. Boulder, Colo.: Westview Press.

Edwards, Nancy Jocelyn. 1997. "Patriotism à Table: Cookbooks, Textbooks and National Identity in Fin-De-Siecle France." *Proceedings of the Annual Meeting of the Western Society for French History* 24:245–54.

Eldridge, J.E.T., Jenny Kitzinger, et al. 1997. *The Mass Media and Power in Modern Britain.* Oxford: Oxford University Press.

Englebert, Pierre. 1996. *Burkina Faso: Unsteady Statehood in West Africa.* Boulder, Colo.: Westview Press.

Escoffier, A., Philéas Gilbert, et al. 1921. *Le Guide Culinaire: Aide-Mémoire de Cuisine Pratique.* Paris. E. Flammarion.

Ethical Trading Initiative. *Purpose, Principles, Programme.* Available online at www.ethicaltrade.org [Dec. 21, 2003].

"EU Bans Kenya Fish." 1998. *Mail & Guardian,* June 18. Available online http://www.chico.mweb.co.za/mg/africa_archive/kenya_archive.html [February 4, 2004].

EUREPGAP. 2000. *Control Points and Compliance Criteria.* Available online at www.eurep.org [Dec. 21, 2003].

Evers, Hans-Dieter, and Heiko Schrader. Eds. 1994. *The Moral Economy of Trade: Ethnicity and Developing Markets*. New York: Routledge.

Eymard, Isabelle. 1999. "De la Grande Surface au Marché: À Chacun ses Habitudes." *INSEE Premiere* 636: 1–4.

Fairhead, James, and Melissa Leach. 1998. *Reframing Deforestation: Global Analyses and Local Realities with Studies in West Africa*. New York: Routledge.

Fairtrade Foundation. *Public Statement on Collaboration between the Fairtrade Foundation and the Soil Association*. January 13, 2003.

Fauré, Yves-A., and Pierre Labazée. 2000. *Petits Patrons Africains: Entre l'Assistance et le Marché*. Paris: Karthala.

Fearne, Andrew, and David Hughes. 2000. "Success Factors in the Fresh Produce Supply Chain: Insights from the UK." *British Food Journal* 102(10): 760–72.

Ferguson, James. 1999. *Expectations of Modernity: Myths and Meanings of Urban Life on the Zambian Copperbelt*. Berkeley: University of California Press.

Ferguson, Priscilla Parkhurst. 1998. "A Cultural Field in the Making: Gastronomy in 19th Century France." *American Journal of Sociology* 104(3): 597–641.

Filby, Frederick. 1934. *A History of Food Adulteration and Analysis*. London: George Allen & Unwin.

Fine, Ben. 1994. "Towards a Political Economy of Food." *Review of International Political Economy* 1(3): 519–45.

Finlay, Mark. 1995. "Early Marketing of the Theory of Nutrition: The Science and Culture of Leibig's Extract of Meat." In *The Science and Culture of Nutrition, 1840–1940,* ed. Harmke Kamminga and Andrew Cunningham, 48–76. Atlanta: Rodopi.

Fitzsimmons, Margaret, and David Goodman. 1998. "Incorporating Nature: Environmental Narratives and the Reproduction of Food." In *Remaking Reality: Nature at the Millenium,* eds. Bruce Braun and Noel Castree, 194–220. New York: Routledge.

Foucault, Michel, Graham Burchell et al. 1991. *The Foucault Effect: Studies in Governmentality*. London: Harvester Wheatsheaf.

Fox, Nicols. 1997. *Spoiled: The Dangerous Truth About a Foodchain Gone Haywire*. New York: Basic Books.

Francois, Pierre. 1927. "Pour une Politique de l'Alimentation." *Les Cahiers du Redressement Francais* 11: 1–53.

Franke, R., and B. Chasin. 1980. *Seeds of Famine: Ecological Destruction and the Development Dilemma in the West African Sahel*. Montclair, N.J.: Allanheld & Osmun.

Fraser, W. Hamish. 1981. *The Coming of the Mass Market, 1859–1914*. Hamden, Conn.: Archon Books.

Freeman, R. 1984. *Strategic Management: A Stakeholder Approach*. London: Pitman.

Freidberg, Susanne. 1996a. *Making a Living: A Social History of Market-Garden Work in the Regional Economy of Bobo-Dioulasso, Burkina Faso*. PhD diss., University of California-Berkeley.

———. 1996b. "Tradeswomen and Businessmen: The Social Relations of Contract Gardening in Southwestern Burkina Faso." *Journal of African Rural and Urban Studies*. 3(3):137–76.

————. 2001. "To Garden, to Market: Gendered Meanings of Work on an African Urban Periphery." *Gender, Place and Culture* 8(1): 5–24.

————. 2003. "French Beans for the Masses: A Modern Historical Geography of Food." *Journal of Historical Geography* 29(3): 445–62.

French, Michael, and Jim Phillips. 2000. *Cheated Not Poisoned? Food Regulation in the United Kingdom, 1875–1938.* Manchester: Manchester University Press.

Freund, Bill. 1998. *The Making of Contemporary Africa: The Development of African Society since 1800.* Boulder, Colo.: Rienner.

Friedland, William. 1994a. "The Global Fresh Fruit and Vegetable System: An Industrial Organization Analysis." In *The Global Restructuring of Agro-Food Systems,* ed. Philip McMichael, 173–89. Ithaca N.Y.: Cornell University Press.

————. 1994b. "The New Globalization: The Case of Fresh Produce." In *From Columbus to Conagra: The Globalization of Agriculture and Food,* eds. A. Bonanno et al. 210–31. Lawrence: University of Kansas Press.

Friedland, William H., Amy E. Barton, et al. 1981. *Manufacturing Green Gold: Capital, Labor, and Technology in the Lettuce Industry.* Cambridge: Cambridge University Press.

Friedman, Marilyn. 1993. *What Are Friends For?: Feminist Perspectives on Personal Relationships and Moral Theory.* Ithaca, N.Y.: Cornell University Press.

Friedmann, Harriet. 1982. "The Political Economy of Food: The Rise and Fall of the Postwar International Food Order." In *Marxist Inquiries: Studies of Labor, Class and States,* ed. Michael Burawoy and T. Skocpol. Chicago: University of Chicago Press.

————. 1993. "The Political Economy of Food: A Global Crisis." *New Left Review* 197: 29–57.

Frost, Peter J. 1991. *Reframing Organizational Culture.* London: Sage.

Fukuyama, Francis. 1995. *Trust: The Social Virtues and the Creation of Prosperity.* New York: Free Press.

Furlough, Ellen. 1991. *Consumer Cooperation in France: The Politics of Consumption, 1834–1930.* Ithaca, N.Y.: Cornell University Press.

Furlough, Ellen, and Carl Strikwerda, Eds. 1999. *Consumers against Capitalism?: Consumer Cooperation in Europe, North America, and Japan, 1840–1990.* Lanham, Md.: Rowman & Littlefield.

Gabriel, Yiannis, and Tim Lang. 1995. *The Unmanageable Consumer: Contemporary Consumption and Its Fragmentation.* London: Sage.

Galbraith, John S. 1974. *Crown and Charter: The Early Years of the British South Africa Company.* Berkeley: University of California Press.

Gann, Lewis H. 1964. *A History of Northern Rhodesia, Early Days to 1953.* London: Chatto & Windus.

Garrett, Laurie. 1994. *The Coming Plague: Newly Emerging Diseases in a World Out of Balance.* New York: Farrar Straus and Giroux.

Gatti, Silvia, Raul Green, et al. 1997. "Contraintes Reglementaires et Logiques Commerciales: Le Cas de France, de l'Italie et de l'Espagne." Colloque SFER. *Grande Distribution Alimentaire,* 22–23 Mai, Montpelier, France, 521–39.

Geissler, Catherine, and Derek J. Oddy, Eds. 1993. *Food, Diet, and Economic Change Past and Present*. New York: St. Martin's Press.

Gemahling, Paul. 1912. "La Concentration Commerciale sans Grands Magasins." *Revue d'Economie Politique* 26: 170–92.

Gervais, Raymond. 1987. "Creating Hunger: Labor and Agricultural Policies in Southern Mossi, 1919–1940." In *African Population and Capitalism,* ed. Denis Cordell and Joel Gregory, 109–21. Boulder Colo.: Westview.

Giles, George Michael. 1904. *Climate and Health in Hot Countries*. London: John Bale, Sons & Danielsson.

Goodman, David, and Michael Redclift. 1991. *Refashioning Nature: Food, Ecology and Culture*. New York: Routledge.

Goodman, David, and Michael Watts, Eds. 1997. *Globalising Food: Agrarian Questions and Global Restructuring*. New York: Routledge.

Goody, Jack. 1982. *Cooking, Cuisine and Class: A Study in Comparative Sociology*. Cambridge: Cambridge University Press.

Gordon, Philip H., and Sophie Meunier. 2001. *The French Challenge: Adapting to Globalization*. Washington, D.C.: Brookings Institution Press.

Grandmaison, C. 1969. "Activities Economiques des Femmes Dakaroises." *Africa* 34: 138–51.

Granovetter, Mark. 1985. "Economic Action and Social Structure: The Problem of Embeddedness." *American Journal of Sociology* 91: 481–510.

Gray, Richard. 1960. *The Two Nations: Aspects of the Development of Race Relations in the Rhodesias and Nyasaland*. Oxford: Oxford University Press.

Gregoire, Emmanuel. 1986. *Les Alhazai de Maradi (Niger): Histoire d'un Groupe de Riches Marchands Saheliens*. Paris: ORSTOM.

Gregoire, Emmanuel, and Pierre Labazée, Eds. 1993. *Les Grands Commercants d'Afrique de l'Ouest*. Paris: Karthala-ORSTOM.

Grignon, Claude. 1986. "Alimentation et Region." *Cahiers de Nutrition et de Dietetique* 21(5): 38–89.

Grignon, Claude and Cristine Grignon. 1986. "Alimentation et Stratification Sociale." *Cahiers de Nutrition et de Dietetique* 21(5): 40–49.

Grignon, Claude, and Christine Grignon. 1999. "Long Term Trends in Food Consumption: A French Portrait." *Food and Foodways* 8(3): 151–74.

Grimod de la Reyniere, A. B. Laurent. 1803–12. *Almanach des Gourmands, Servant de Guide dans les Moyens de Faire Excellente Chere; Par un Vieil Amateur*. Paris: Chez Maradan.

Gupta, Akhil. 1998. *Postcolonial Developments: Agriculture in the Making of Modern India*. Durham, N.C.: Duke University Press.

Gurney, Peter. 1996. *Co-Operative Culture and the Politics of Consumption in England, 1870–1930*. Manchester: Manchester University Press.

Guthman, Julie. 2002. "Commodified Meanings, Meaningful Commodities: Re-Thinking Production-Consumption Links through the Organic System of Provision." *Sociologia Ruralis* 42(4): 295–311.

————. 2003. "Fast Food/Organic Food: Reflexive Tastes and the Making of 'Yuppie Chow'." *Social and Cultural Geography* 4(1): 45–58.

————. 2004. *Agrarian Dreams? The Paradox of Organic Farming in California.* Berkeley: University of California Press.

Guy, Kolleen. 2001. "Wine, Champagne, and the Making of French Identity in the Belle Epoque." In *Food, Drink and Identity: Cooking, Eating and Drinking in Europe since the Middle Ages,* ed. Peter Scholliers, 163–77. Oxford: Berg.

Hamada, Tomoko, and Willis E. Sibley, Eds. 1994. *Anthropological Perspectives on Organizational Culture.* Lanham, Md.: University Press of America.

Hamelle, Paul. 1913. "La Crise Viticole." *Annales des Sciences Politiques.*

Hansen, Karen Tranberg. 1989. *Distant Companions: Servants and Employers in Zambia, 1900–1985.* Ithaca, N.Y.: Cornell University Press.

————. 1992, Ed. *African Encounters with Domesticity.* New Brunswick, N.J.: Rutgers University Press.

Hardy, Anne. 1999. "Food, Hygiene, and the Laboratory. A Short History of Food Poisoning in Britain, Circa 1850–1950." *Social History of Medicine* 12(2): 293–311.

Harris, S. 1992. *Kenya Horticultural Subsector Survey.* Nairobi: Kenya Export Development Project.

Harris-Pascal, Carla, John Humphrey et al. 1998. *Value Chains and Upgrading: The Impact of UK Retailers on the Fresh Fruit and Vegetables Industry in Africa.* Sussex, U.K. Institute for Development Studies.

Hart, Keith. 1988. "Kinship, Contract and Trust: The Economic Organization of Migrants in an African City Slum." In *Trust: Making and Breaking Cooperative Relations,* ed. Diego Gambetta, 176–93. New York: Blackwell.

Hartwick, Elaine. 1998. "Geographies of Consumption: A Commodity-Chain Approach." *Environment and Planning D-Society & Space* 16(4): 423–37.

Harvey, David. 1989. *The Condition of Postmodernity: An Enquiry into the Origins of Cultural Change.* New York: Blackwell.

Harvey, Graham. 1997. *The Killing of the Countryside.* London: Jonathan Cape.

Hassall, Arthur Hill. 1857. *Adulterations Detected; or, Plain Instructions for the Discovery of Frauds in Food and Medicine.* London: Longman Brown Green Longmans and Roberts.

Hassall, Arthur Hill, and Lancet Analytical Sanitary Commission. 1855. *Food and Its Adulterations; Comprising the Reports of the Analytical Sanitary Commission of "the Lancet" for the Years 1851 to 1854 Inclusive, Revised and Extended: Being Records of the Results of Some Thousands of Original Microscopical and Chemical Analyses of the Solids and Fluids Consumed by All Classes of the Public.* London: Longman Brown Green and Longmans.

Haugerud, Angelique, Margaret Priscilla Stone et al. 2000, Eds. *Commodities and Globalization: Anthropological Perspectives.* Lanham, Md.: Rowman & Littlefield.

Headrick, Daniel R. 1981. *The Tools of Empire: Technology and European Imperialism in the Nineteenth Century.* Oxford: Oxford University Press.

Heffernan, Michael J. 1994. "The French Geographical Movement and the Forms of

French Imperialism, 1870–1920." In *Geography and Empire,* eds. Anne Godlewska and Neil Smith, 92–114. Oxford: Blackwell.

Heller, Chaia. 2002. "From Scientific Risk to Paysan Savoir-Faire. Peasant Expertise in the French and Global Debate over GM Crops." *Science as Culture* 11(1): 5–37.

Hémardinquer, Jean Jacques. 1970. *Pour une Histoire de l'Alimentation.* Paris: A. Colin.

Henson, Spencer, and Julie Caswell. 1999. "Food Safety Regulation: An Overview of Contemporary Issues." *Food Policy* 24: 589–603.

Hill, Polly. 1963. *The Migrant Cocoa-Farmers of Southern Ghana: A Study in Rural Capitalism.* Cambridge: Cambridge University Press.

Hinrichs, Claire. 2000. "Embeddedness and Local Food Systems: Notes on Two Types of Direct Agricultural Markets." *Journal of Rural Studies* 16(3): 295–303.

———. 2003. "The Practice and Politics of Food System Localization." *Journal of Rural Studies* 19(1): 33–45.

Holloway, L., and M. Kneafsey. 2000. "Reading the Space of the Farmers' Market: A Preliminary Investigation from the UK." *Sociologia Ruralis* 40(3): 285–99.

Hughes, Alex 1999. "Constructing Competitive Spaces: On the Corporate Practice of British Retailer-Supplier Relationships." 31(5): 819–39.

———. 2000. "Retailers, Knowledges and Changing Commodity Networks: The Case of the Cut Flower Trade." *Geoforum* 31(2): 175–90.

———. 2001a. "Global Commodity Networks, Ethical Trade and Governmentality: Organizing Business Responsibility in the Kenyan Cut Flower Industry." *Transactions of the Institute of British Geographers* 26(4): 390–406.

———. 2000b. "Multi-Stakeholder Approaches to Ethical Trade: Towards a Reorganization of UK Retailers' Global Supply Chains." *Journal of Economic Geography* 1: 421–37.

———. Forthcoming. "Responsible Retailers? Ethical Trade and the Strategic Re-Regulation of Cross-Continental Food Supply Chains." In *Cross-Continental Agri-Food Chains: Structures, Actors and Dynamics in the Global Food System,* ed. Neils Fold and B. Pritchard. New York: Routledge.

Hughes, Alex, and L. Cormode. 1998. "Researching Elites and Elite Spaces." *Environment and Planning A* 30(12): 2098–2100.

Humphery, Kim. 1998. *Shelf Life: Supermarkets and the Changing Cultures of Consumption.* Cambridge: Cambridge University Press.

Humphrey, John, and Hubert Schmitz. 2001. "Governance in Global Value Chains." *IDS Bulletin* 32(3): 19–29.

Humphrys, John. 2002. *The Great Food Gamble.* London: Hodder & Stoughton.

Husson, Armand. 1875. *Les Consommations de Paris.* Paris: Librairie Hachette.

Ikpe, Eno Blankson. 1994. *Food and Society in Nigeria: A History of Food Customs, Food Economy and Cultural Change 1900–1989.* Stuttgart: Franz Steiner.

Islam, Nurad. 1990. *Horticultural Exports of Developing Countries: Past Performances, Future Prospects, and Policy Issues.* Washington: International Food Policy Research Institute.

Jaffee, Steven. 1994. "Contract Farming in the Shadow of Competitive Markets: The Experience of Kenyan Horticulture." In *Living under Contract: Contract Farming and*

Agrarian Transformation in Sub-Saharan Africa, ed. Peter D. Little and Michael J. Watts, 97–139. Madison: University of Wisconsin Press.

———. 1995a. "The Many Faces of Success: The Development of Kenyan Horticultural Exports." In *Marketing Africa's High-Value Foods: Comparative Experiences of an Emergent Private Sector,* ed. Steven Jaffee and John Morton, 319–74 Dubuque, Iowa: Kendall/Hunt.

———. Ed. 1995b. *Marketing Africa's High-Value Foods: Comparative Experiences of an Emergent Private Sector.* Dubuque, Iowa: Kendall/Hunt.

Jaffee, Steven, and P. Gordon. 1993. *Exporting High-Value Food Commodities: Success Stories from Developing Countries.* Discussion Paper 198. Washington, D.C.: World Bank.

Jagger, A. M. 1995. "Towards a Feminist Conception of Moral Reasoning." In *Morality and Social Justice: Point/Counterpoint,* ed. James P. Sterba, 115–46. Lanham, Md.: Rowman & Littlefield.

Jaillette, Jean-Claude. 2000. *Les Dossiers Noirs de la Malbouffe.* Paris: Albin Michel.

Jefferys, James B. 1954. *Retail Trading in Britain, 1850–1950.* Cambridge: Cambridge University Press.

Jenkins, Rhys Owen, Ruth Pearson et al., Eds. 2002. *Corporate Responsibility and Labour Rights: Codes of Conduct in the Global Economy.* London: Earthscan.

Jeune Afrique. 1993. *Atlas du Burkina Faso.* Paris: Les Editions J.A.

Joly, Pierre-Benoit, and Claire Marris. 2001. *"Que Voulons-Vous Manger?" Les Etats Généraux de l'Alimentation: Enseignments d'une Expérience de Mise en Débat Public Des Politiques Alimentaires.* Ivry-sur-seine, France: INRA-STEPE.

Julius, Deanne. 1997. "Globalization and Stakeholder Conflicts: A Corporate Perspective." *International Affairs* 73(3): 453–69.

Jullian, Marcel, and Charles Meyer. 1983. *Histoire de France des Commercants.* Paris: R. Laffont.

Kallman, Deborah. 1999. "Projected Moralities, Engaged Anxieties: Northern Rhodesia's Reading Publics, 1953–1964." *The International Journal of African Historical Studies* 32(1): 71–117.

Kambou-Ferrand. 1993. *Peuples Voltaïques et Conquête Coloniale 1885–1914, Burkina Faso.* Paris: Harmattan.

Kaplan, Robert. 1994. "The Coming Anarchy: How Scarcity, Crime, Overpopulation, Tribalism, and Disease are Rapidly Destroying the Social Fabric of Our Planet" *Atlantic Monthly* February, 273: 44–76.

Kaplan, Steven L. 1984. *Provisioning Paris: Merchants and Millers in the Grain and Flour Trade During the Eighteenth Century.* Ithaca, N.Y.: Cornell University Press.

Kaunda, Kenneth D. 1971. *Humanism in Zambia and a Guide to Its Implementation.* Lusaka: Zambia Information Services.

Kautsky, Karl. 1988. *The Agrarian Question.* London: Zwan Publications.

Kay, J. A. 1995. *Foundations of Corporate Success: How Business Strategies Add Value.* Oxford: Oxford University Press.

Kern, Stephen. 1983. *The Culture of Time and Space 1880–1918.* Cambridge: Harvard University Press.

Kitching, Gavin. 1980. *Class and Economic Change in Kenya: The Making of an African Petite Bourgeoisie*. New Haven, Conn.: Yale University Press.

Knox, Robert. 1862. *The Races of Men: A Philosophical Enquiry into the Influence of Race over the Destinies of Nations*. London: H. Renshaw.

Kouman, O. Joseph. 1987. *La Place du Maraichage dans l'Economie Paysanne du Burkina Faso: Le Périmetre de Loumbila*. MA thesis, University of Ouagadougou.

Kuster, Sybille. 1999. *African Education in Colonial Zimbabwe, Zambia and Malawi: Government Control, Settler Antagonism and African Agency, 1890–1964*. Hamburg: Lit.

La Fontaine, Jean. 1975. "Unstructured Social Relations: Patrons and Friends in Three African Societies." *The West African Journal of Sociology and Political Science* 1(1): 51–81.

Lageat, Robert. 1993. *Des Halles au Balajo*. Paris: Editions de Paris.

Landes, David S. 1998. *The Wealth and Poverty of Nations: Why Some Are So Rich and Some So Poor*. New York: W.W. Norton.

Lang, Tim. 1997. "Going Public: Food Campaigns During the 1980s and Early 1990s." In *Nutrition in Britain: Science, Scientists and Politics in the Twentieth Century*, ed. D. F. Smith, 238–60. New York: Routledge.

Lang, Tim, and Geof Rayner, Eds. 2002. *Why Health Is the Key to the Future of Food and Farming*. London: UK Public Health Association, Chartered Institute of Environmental Health, Faculty of Public Health Medicine, National Heart Forum, and Health Development Agency.

Larmet, Gwenaël. 1999. *L'Organisation des Pratiques d'Approvisionnement Alimentaire*. Document de travail. Paris: Institut National de la Recherche Agronomique.

Latour, Bruno. 1987. *Science in Action: How to Follow Scientists and Engineers through Society*. Cambridge: Harvard University Press.

———. 1988. *The Pasteurization of France*. Cambridge: Harvard University Press.

Latour, Bruno, and Steve Woolgar. 1979. *Laboratory Life: The Social Contruction of Scientific Facts*. London: Sage.

Law, John. 1986. "On Methods of Long-Distance Control: Vessels, Navigation and the Portuguese Route to India." *Sociological Review Monograph* 32: 234–63.

Lawrence, Felicity. 2003a. "Food for Thought . . . Guide for Eating with a Clear Conscience." *The Guardian Unlimited*, February 20.

———. 2003b. "Growers' market." *The Guardian*, May 17.

Lazareff, Alexandre. 1998. *L'Exception Culinaire Francaise*. Paris: Albin Michel.

Le Clézio, Jean-Marie Gustave. *Les Geants*. Paris: Gallimard.

LeMelle, J. P. 1995. *Evaluation d'un Project de Relance de la Filière Fruits et Legumes du Burkina Faso*. Ouagadougou: Caisse Francaise de Developpment.

"Les Halles, Marché Mondiale." 1925. *Science Illustrée*.

Lever, Christopher. 1992. *They Dined on Eland: The Story of the Acclimatisation Societies*. London: Quiller Press.

Levidow, Les, and Claire Marris. 2001. "Science and Governance in Europe: Lessons from the Case of Agricultural Biotechnology." *Science and Public Policy* 28(5): 346–60.

Little, Peter D., and Michael J. Watts, Eds. 1994. *Living under Contract: Contract Farming*

Works Cited

248

and Agrarian Transformation in Sub-Saharan Africa. Madison: University of Wisconsin Press.

Little, Peter, and Catherine Dolan. 2000. "What It Means to Be Restructured: Non-Traditional Commodities and Structural Adjustment in Sub-Saharan African." In *Commodities and Globalization: Anthropological Perspectives,* ed. Angelique Haugerud, Margaret Priscilla Stone, and Peter D. Little, 59–78. Lanham, Md.: Rowman & Littlefield.

Livingstone, David. 1858. *Missionary Travels and Researches in South Africa: Including a Sketch of Sixteen Years' Residence in the Interior of Africa, and a Journey from the Cape of Good Hope to Loanda on the West Coast; Thence across the Continent, Down the River, Zambesi, to the Eastern Ocean.* New York: Harper & Brothers.

Livingstone, David N. 1999. "Tropical Climate and Moral Hygiene: The Anatomy of a Victorian Debate." *British Journal of the History of Science* 32: 93–110.

Lloyd-Davies, Victoria. 1999. "New Season for British Food." *Guild of Good Writers E-Newsletter* 1(6): www.glw.co.uk [Dec. 21, 2003].

Macintyre, Sally, Jacquie Reilly et al. 1998. "Food Choice, Food Scares, and Health: The Role of the Media." In *The Nation's Diet: The Social Science of Food Choice,* ed. Anne Murcott, 228–49. New York: Longman.

Mackintosh, Maureen. 1989. *Gender, Class, and Rural Transition: Agribusiness and the Food Crisis in Senegal.* London: Zed Books.

Mahende, E. 1997. "European Union Market Tough for African Fruits." *PanAfrican News Agency,* October 7. http://allafrica.com/ [July 16, 2003].

Mamdani, Mahmoud. 1996. *Citizen and Subject: Contemporary Africa and the Legacy of Late Colonialism.* Princeton, N.J.: Princeton University Press.

Mamère, Noël, and Jean-François Narbonne. 2001. *Toxiques Affaires: De la Dioxine à la Vache Folle.* Paris: Editions Ramsey.

Marcet, William. 1856. *On the Composition of Food and How It Is Adulterated: With Practical Directions for Its Analysis.* London: J. Churchill.

Marcus, George. 1998. "Ethnography in/of the World System: The Emergence of Multi-Sited Ethnography." In *Ethnography through Thick and Thin,* ed. G. Marcus, 79–104. Princeton, N.J.: Princeton University Press.

Marglin, Stephen A. 1996. "Farmers, Seedsmen, and Scientists: Systems of Agriculture and Systems of Knowledge." In *Decolonizing Knowledge: From Development to Dialogue,* eds. Frédérique Apffel-Marglin and Stephen A. Marglin, 185–248. New York: Oxford University Press.

Marris, Claire. 1999. "Between Consensus and Citizens: Public Participation in Technology Assessment in France." *Science Studies* 12(2): 3–32.

———. 2001. "Swings and Roundabouts: French Public Policy on Agricultural GMOs since 1996." *Politeia* 60: 22–37.

Marsden, T., and N. Wrigley. 1996. "Retailing, the Food System and the Regulatory State." In *Retailing, Consumption and Capital: Towards the New Retail Geography,* eds. N. Wrigley and M. S. Lowe, 33–47. Harlow, U.K.: Longman.

Marsden, Terry. Andrew Flynn, et al. 2000. *Consuming Interests: The Social Provision of Foods.* London: UCL Press.

Marsden, Terry, Michelle Harrison, et al. 1998. "Creating Competitive Space: Exploring the Social and Political Maintenance of Retail Power." *Environment and Planning A* 30: 481–98.

Marshall, Andrew. 2001. "Britain Debates Immigrants, Racism and Curry Chicken." *Christian Science Monitor,* April 26.

Martin-Saint-Léon, E. 1911. *Le Petit Commerce Francais, sa Lutte pour la Vie.* Paris: J. Gabalda.

Mbembé, J. A. 2001. *On the Postcolony.* Berkeley: University of California Press.

McClintock, Anne. 1995. *Imperial Leather: Race, Gender and Sexuality in the Colonial Contest.* New York: Routledge.

McDonald, Maryon. 1997. "The Construction of Difference: An Anthropological Approach to Stereotypes." In *Inside European Identities: Ethnography in Western Europe,* ed. Sharon MacDonald, 219–36. New York: Berg.

———. 2000. "Accountability, Anthropology and the European Commission." In *Audit Cultures: Anthropological Studies in Accountability, Ethics, and the Academy,* ed. Marilyn Strathern, 106–32. New York: Routledge.

McMichael, Philip. 2000. "Global Food Politics." In *Hungry for Profit: The Agribusiness Threat to Farmers, Food, and the Environment,* ed. Fred Magdoff, John Bellamy Foster, and Frederick H. Buttel, 125–44. New York: Monthly Review Press.

McMillan, James F. 1992. *Twentieth-Century France: Politics and Society 1898–1991.* London: E. Arnold.

Mennell, S. 1996. *All Manners of Food: Eating and Taste in England and France from the Middle Ages to the Present.* Chicago: University of Illinois Press.

Menozzi, Marie-Jo. 1993. *Le Bouillion Cube, un Goût de Modernité?* D.E.A. de Sciences Sociales, Paris: Université Rene Descartes (Sorbonne).

Messer, Ellen. 1984. "Anthropological Perspectives on Diet." *Annual Review of Anthropology* 13: 205–49.

Miller, D., and J. Reilly. 1995. "Making an Issue of Food Safety: The Media, Pressure Groups, and the Public Sphere." In *Eating Agendas: Food and Nutrition as Social Problems,* ed. D. Maurer and J. Sobal, 305–36. New York: Aldine de Gruyter.

Miller, Daniel. 2001. *The Dialectics of Shopping.* Chicago: University of Chicago Press.

———. 2003. "Could the Internet Defetishize the Commodity?" *Environment and Planning D-Society & Space* 21: 359–72.

Millstone, Erik. 1991. "Consumer Protection Policies in the E.C.: The Quality of Food." In *Technology and the Future of Europe: Global Competition and the Environment in the 1990s,* ed. Christopher Freeman, Margaret Sharp, and William B. Walker, 330–44. London: Pinter.

Millstone, Erik and Tim Lang. 2003. *The Penguin Atlas of Food: Who Eats What, Where and Why.* New York: Penguin.

Mintel. 2003. "Patriotic British See Demand Outstripping Supply for Home Grown Produce." Mintel News Release, January 2003. Available online at www.mintel.com [Dec. 21, 2003].

Mintz, Sidney. 1986. *Sweetness and Power: The Place of Sugar in Modern History.* New York: Penguin.

————. 1994. "Eating and Being: What Food Means." In *Food: Multidisciplinary Perspectives,* ed. Barbara Harriss-White, 102–15. Cambridge, U.K.: Basil Blackwell.

Mitchell, James Clyde. 1951. "A Note on the Urbanization of Africans on the Copperbelt." *Human Problems in British Central Africa* 12: 20–27.

————. 1969. "The Concept and Use of Social Networks." In *Social Networks in Urban Situations,* ed. C Mitchell, 1–50. Manchester: Manchester University Press.

Mitchell, John. 1848. *Treatise on the Falsifications of Food, and the Chemical Means Employed to Detect Them.* London: H. Baillier.

Mitchell, Katharyne. 1997. "Transnational Discourse: Bringing Geography Back In." *Antipode* 29(2): 101–14.

Mitchell, Vincent-Wayne and Michael Greatorex. 1990. "Consumer Perceived Risk in the U.K. Food Market." *British Food Journal* 92(2): 16–22.

Monbiot, George. "Sins of the Superstores Visited on Us." *The Guardian,* February 27, 2001.

Monceau, Christine, Elyane Blanche-Barbat, et al. 2002. "La Consommation Alimentaire Depuis Quarante Ans." *INSEE Premiere* 846, 1–4.

Moore, Geoff. 2001. "Corporate Social and Financial Performance: An Investigation of the U.K. Supermarket Industry." *Journal of Business Ethics* 34: 299–315.

Moore, Henrietta L., and Megan Vaughan. 1994. *Cutting Down Trees: Gender, Nutrition, and Agricultural Change in the Northern Province of Zambia, 1890–1990.* Portsmouth, N.H.: Heinemann.

Moreau-Rio, Marie-Anne. 1999. "Crises Alimentaires et Environnementales: Les Fruits et Légumes Aussi!" *Infos-Ctifl* 151: 20–24.

Morgan, K., and J. Murdoch. 2000. "Organic vs. Conventional Agriculture: Knowledge, Power and Innovation in the Food Chain." *Geoforum* 31(2): 159–73.

Mouradian, George. 2002. *The Quality Revolution: A History of the Quality Movement.* Lanham, Md.: University Press of America.

Muller, Pierre. 1984. *Le Technocrate et le Paysan: Essai sur la Politique Francaise de la Modernization de l'Agriculture.* Paris: Les Editions Ouvrieres.

Murdoch, Jonathan. 1997. "Inhuman/Nonhuman/Human: Actor-Network Theory and the Prospects for a Nondualistic and Symmetrical Perspective on Nature and Society." *Environment and Planning D-Society & Space* 15(6): 731–56.

Murdoch, Jonathan, and Mara Miele. 1999. " 'Back to Nature': Changing 'Worlds of Production' in the Food Sector." *Sociologia Ruralis* 39(4): 465–83.

Murray, Douglas L., Polly Hoppin, et al. 1990. *Pesticides and Nontraditional Agriculture: A Coming Crisis for U.S. Development Policy in Latin America?* Austin, Tex.: Institute of Latin American Studies, University of Texas at Austin.

Naidoo, D. 1999. "Report Back Workshop on Enhancing the Development Impact of Export Horticulture in Sub-Saharan Africa." Cedara Report N/A/99/2. Pietermaritaburg, South Africa: Cedara Agricultural Development Institute.

Naylor, Simon. 2000. "Spacing the Can: Empire, Modernity and the Globalisation of Food." *Environment and Planning A* 32: 1625–39.

Nott, Josiah. 1856. "Thoughts on Acclimation and Adaptation of Races to Climate." *American Journal of Medical Science* 5: 24.

Nussbaum, Martha Craven. 2001. *The Fragility of Goodness: Luck and Ethics in Greek Tragedy and Philosophy.* Cambridge: Cambridge University Press.

Oddy, Derek J., and Derek S. Miller. 1976. *The Making of the Modern British Diet.* London: Rowman and Littlefield.

O'Neill, Onora. 1996. *Towards Justice and Virtue: A Constructive Account of Practical Reasoning.* Cambridge: Cambridge University Press.

Ong, Aihwa. 1987. *Spirits of Resistance and Capitalist Discipline: Factory Workers in Malaysia.* Albany, N.Y.: SUNY Press.

Orton, L., and P. Madden. 1996. *The Global Supermarket: Britain's Biggest Shops and Food from the Third World.* London: Christian Aid.

Osborne, Michael A. 1994. *Nature, the Exotic, and the Science of French Colonialism.* Bloomington: Indiana University Press.

Otsuki, V. Tsunehiro, and John S. Wilson, et al. 2001. "Saving Two in a Billion: Quantifying the Trade Effect of European Food Safety Standards on African Exports." *Food Policy* 26(5): 495–514.

Ouedraego, Moussa. 1995. "Histoire et Consequences de l'Introduction du Maraichage en Zone Soudano-Sahélienne au Burkina Faso." In *Innovations et Sociétés: Quelles Agricultures? Quelles Innovations?,* ed. Jean-Pierre Chauveau and J.M. Yung, 257–63. Montpelier, France: CIRAD.

Ouédraogo, Arouna. 1999. "The Social Genesis of Vegetarianism to 1859." In *Food, Power and Community,* ed. Roberg Dare, 154–66. Adelaide, Aus.: Wakefield Press.

Page, Brian, and Richard Walker. 1991. "From Settlement to Fordism: The Agro-Industrial Revolution in the American Midwest." *Economic Geography* 67(4): 281–315.

Pagès, G. 1909. *Les Falsifications des Denrées Alimentaires et la Loi du 1er Août 1905.* Doctorat, Université de Montpelier Faculté de Droit.

Palmer, Robin. 1983. "Land Alienation and Agricultural Conflict in Colonial Zambia." In *Imperialism, Colonialism and Hunger: East and Central Africa,* ed. Robert I. Rotberg, 89–112. Lexington, Mass.: Lexington Books.

Parrott, N., N. Wilson, et al. 2002. "Spatializing Quality: Regional Protection and the Alternative Geography of Food." *European Urban and Regional Studies* 9(3): 241–61.

Parry, Bronwyn. 1998. "Hunting the Gene-Hunters: The Role of Hybrid Networks, Status, and Chance in Conceptualising and Accessing 'Corporate Elites'." *Environment and Planning A* 30(12): 2147–62.

Paulus, Ingeborg. 1974. *The Search for Pure Food.* Oxford, U.K.: Martin Robertson.

Paxton, Robert O. 1997. *French Peasant Fascism: Henry Dorgère's Greenshirts and the Crises of French Agriculture, 1929–1939.* New York: Oxford University Press.

Peltre, Jean, and Claude Thouvenot, Eds. 1987. *Alimentation et Régions.* Nancy, France: Presses Universitaires de Nancy.

Peters, Erica J. 2001. "National Preferences and Colonial Cuisine: Seeking the Familiar in French Vietnam." *Proceedings of the Annual Meeting of the Western Society for French History* 27: 150–59.

Peters, Tom F. 1996. *Building the Nineteenth Century.* Cambridge, Mass.: MIT Press.

Petrini, Carlo. 2003. *Slow Food: The Case for Taste.* New York: Columbia University Press.

Phiri, Brighton. "Chief Sinazongwe Castigates Agriflora over Poor Working Conditions." *The Post,* March 22, 2002.

Pitte, Jean-Robert. 1991. *Gastronomie Francaise: Histoire et Géographie d'une Passion.* Paris: Fayard.

———. 1999. "The Rise of the Restaurant." In *Food: A Culinary History,* ed. Jean-Louis Flandrin and Massimo Montanari, 471–80. New York: Penguin.

Poher, Ernest. 1912. *Le Commerce des Produits Agricoles.* Paris: Librairie J.-B. Bailliére et Fils.

Polanyi, Karl. 2001. *The Great Transformation: The Political and Economic Origins of Our Time.* Boston, Mass.: Beacon Press.

Powell, Douglas Alan, and William Leiss. 1997. *Mad Cows and Mother's Milk: The Perils of Poor Risk Communication.* Montreal: McGill-Queen's University Press.

Power, Michael. 1997. *The Audit Society: Rituals of Verification.* Oxford: Clarendon Press.

Preston, Richard. 1994. *The Hot Zone.* New York: Random House.

Proctor, James D., and David Marshall Smith, Eds. 1999. *Geography and Ethics: Journeys in a Moral Terrain.* London: Routledge.

Prudhomme, Claude. 1927. *La Question des Halles et la Problème Actuel du Ravitaillement de Paris.* Paris: Librairie Gènèrale de Droit & de Jurisprudence.

Pynson, Pascale. 1987. *La France à Table, 1960–1986.* Paris: Editions la Découverte.

Raffoul, Michel. "A La Reconquête du Client Perdu." *Le Monde Diplomatique,* Fevrier 2000.

RAP Market Information Bulletin.1995. *World Market for Fresh and Baby Canned Corn.* Available online at http://www.iit.edu/~tulsanu/gaurav.html [February 13, 2004].

Ratzan, Scott, Ed. 1998. *The Mad Cow Crisis: Health and the Public Good.* New York: New York University Press.

Rau, Bill. 1991. *From Feast to Famine: Official Cures and Grassroots Remedies to Africa's Food Crisis.* London: Zed Books.

Ray, Larry J., and R. Andrew Sayer. 1999. *Culture and Economy after the Cultural Turn.* London: Sage.

Raynolds, Laura. 2000. "Re-Embedding Global Agriculture: The International Organic and Fair Trade Movements." *Agriculture and Human Values* 17: 297–309.

Reardon, Tom, Jean-Marie Codron et al. 2001. "Global Change in Agrifood Grades and Standards: Agribusiness Strategic Responses in Developing Countries." *International Food and Agribusiness Management Review* 2: 421–35.

Reed, Matt. 2001. "Fight the Future! How the Contemporary Campaigns of the UK Organic Movement Have Arisen from Their Composting of the Past." *Sociologia Ruralis* 41(1): 131–45

Renard, Marie-Christine. 2003. "Fair Trade: Quality, Market and Conventions." *Journal of Rural Studies* 19(1): 87–96.

Requier-Desjardins, Denis. 1989. *L'Alimentation en Afrique.* Paris: Karthala.

Richardin, Edmond. 1914. *L'Art du Bien Manger.* Paris: Editions d'art et de litterature.

Roberts, Andrew. 1976. *A History of Zambia.* New York: Africana Pub. Co.

Roberts, Richard L. 1996. *Two Worlds of Cotton: Colonialism and the Regional Economy in the French Soudan, 1800–1946.* Stanford, Calif.: Stanford University Press.

Robertson, Claire. 1984. *Sharing the Same Bowl.* Bloomington: Indiana University Press.

Robinson, Ron, and John Gallagher, Eds. 1961. *Africa and the Victorians: The Climax of Imperialism in the Dark Continent.* New York: St. Martin's Press.

Rostow, W. W. 1960. *The Stages of Economic Growth, a Non-Communist Manifesto.* Cambridge: Cambridge University Press.

Roux, Eugene. 1913. "La Repression des Fraudes: Hier et Aujourd'hui." *Annales des Falsifications (Bulletin Internationale de la Repression des Fraudes),* 37–49.

Sachs, Carolyn E. 1996. *Gendered Fields: Rural Women, Agriculture, and Environment.* Boulder, Colo.: Westview Press.

Sams, Craig 2002. "Viewpoint." *Organic Products.* January: 9.

Sankara, Thomas. 1988. *Sankara Speaks: The Burkina Faso Revolution 1983–87.* New York: Pathfinder.

Sano, Hans-Otto. 1988. *Agricultural Policy Changes in Zambia During the 1980s.* Working Paper 88.4. Copenhagen: Center for Development Research.

Sanyal, Biswapriya 1987. "Urban Cultivation Amidst Modernization: How Should We Interpret It?" *Journal of Planning Education and Research* 6: 197–207.

Sarraut, Albert. 1923. *La Mise en Valeur des Colonies Francaises.* Paris: Payot.

Saul, Mahir. 1986. "Development of the Grain Market and Merchants in Burkina Faso." *Journal of Modern African Studies* 24(1): 127–53.

Savadogo, Kimseyinka, and Claude Wetta. 1993. "The Impact of Self-Imposed Adjustment: The Case of Burkina Faso, 1983–9." In *Africa's Recovery in the 1990s: From Stagnation and Adjustment to Human Development,* ed. G. A. Cornia, R. van der Hoeven, and T. Mkandawire, 53–71. New York: St. Martin's Press.

Schilter, Christine. 1991. *L'Agriculture Urbaine à Lomé: Approches Agronomique et Socioéconomique.* Paris: Karthala.

Scholliers, Peter. 2001. *Food, Drink and Identity: Cooking, Eating and Drinking in Europe since the Middle Ages.* Oxford: Berg.

Schreuder, Deryck Marshall. 1976. "The Cultural Factor in Victorian Imperialism: A Case-Study of the British 'Civilizing Mission'." *The Journal of Imperial and Commonwealth History* 4: 283–317.

Schroeder, Richard A. 1999. *Shady Practices: Agroforestry and Gender Politics in the Gambia.* Berkeley: University of California Press.

Schroeder, Richard, and Michael Watts. 1991. "Struggling over Strategies, Fighting over Food: Adjusting to Food Commercialization among Mandinka Peasants." *Research in Rural Sociology and Development* 5: 45–72.

Schwartz, Alfred. 1995. "La Politique Coloniale de Mise en Valeur Agricole de la Haute-Volta (1919–1960)." In *La Haute-Volta Coloniale: Témoignages, Recherches, Regards,* eds. Gabriel Massa and Y.G. Madiega, 263–91. Paris: Karthala.

Sciolino, Elaine. "Fois Gras in the Freezer? Just Don't Tell Anyone." *New York Times,* December 19, 2002.

Scott, David. 1995. "Colonial Governmentality." *Social Text* 43: 191–220.

Scott, James. 1976. *The Moral Economy of the Peasant: Rebellion and Subsistence in Southeast Asia.* New Haven, Conn.: Yale University Press.

————. 1985. *Weapons of the Weak: Everyday Forms of Peasant Resistance*. New Haven, Conn.: Yale University Press.

————. 1998. *Seeing Like a State: How Certain Schemes to Improve the Human Condition Have Failed*. New Haven, Conn.: Yale University Press.

Self, Peter, and Herbert J. Storing. 1962. *The State and the Farmer*. London: George Allen & Unwin.

Sen, Amartya. 1981. *Poverty and Famines: An Essay on Entitlement and Deprivation*. Oxford: Clarendon Press.

Seth, Andrew, and Geoffrey Randall. 1999. *The Grocers: The Rise and Rise of the Supermarket Chains*. London: Kogan Page.

Shears, Peter, Fran Zollers, et al. 2001. "Food for Thought: What Mad Cows Have Wrought with Respect to Food Safety Regulation in the EU and UK." *British Food Journal* 103(1): 63–87.

Shore, Cris, and Susan Wright. 2000. "Coercive Accountability: The Rise of Audit Culture in Higher Education." In *Audit Cultures: Anthropological Studies in Accountability, Ethics, and the Academy*, ed. Marilyn Strathern, 57–89. New York: Routledge.

Shorto, Russell. 2004. "A Short-Order Revolutionary." *New York Times Magazine,* January 11, 18–21.

Sidaway, James. 2002. "Postcolonial Geographies: Survey-Explore-Review." In *Postcolonial Geographies,* ed. Alison Blunt and Cheryl McEwan, 11–28. New York: Continuum.

Sklar, Richard L. 1975. *Corporate Power in an African State: The Political Impact of Multinational Mining Companies in Zambia*. Berkeley: University of California Press.

Slinn, Peter. 1971. "Commercial Concessions and Politics During the Colonial Period: The Role of the British South Africa Company in Northern Rhodesia 1890–1964." *African Affairs* LXX, 385–84.

Smith, David M. 1998. "How Far Should We Care? On the Spatial Scope of Beneficence." *Progress in Human Geography* 22(1): 15–38.

Soil Association. 2002. "A Question of Organics." *Living Earth* 213: 14–15.

Spang, Rebecca L. 2000. *The Invention of the Restaurant: Paris and Modern Gastronomic Culture*. Cambridge: Harvard University Press.

Sparks, C. 1999. "The Press." In *The Media in Britain: Current Debates and Developments,* eds. Jane C. Stokes and Anna Reading, 42–60. New York: St. Martin's Press.

Speirs, Mike. 1991. "Agrarian Change and the Revolution in Burkina Faso." *African Affairs,* 90: 89–110.

Stanziani, Alessandro. 2003. "La Construction de la Qualité du Vin, 1880–1914." In *La Qualité des Produits en France (XVIII–XXème Siècles),* ed. Alessandro Stanziani, 123–150. Paris: Editions Belin.

Stern, Rebecca. 2003. " 'Adulterations Detected': Food and Fraud in Christina Rossetti's 'Goblin Market." *Nineteenth-Century Literature* 57(4): 47–51.

Stevens, Chris. 2001. "Value Chains and Trade Policy: The Case of Agriculture." *IDS Bulletin* 32(3): 46–59.

Stoler, Ann Laura. 2002. *Carnal Knowledge and Imperial Power: Race and the Intimate in Colonial Rule*. Berkeley: University of California Press.

Stoler, Ann Laura, and Frederick Cooper. 1997. "Between Metropole and Colony: Rethinking a Research Agenda." In *Tensions of Empire: Colonial Cultures in a Bourgeois World*, eds. Frederick Cooper and Ann Laura Stoler, 1–56. Berkeley: University of California Press.

Stone, Glenn D. 2002. "Both Sides Now: Fallacies in the Genetic-Modification Wars, Implications for Developing Countries, and Anthropological Perspectives." *Current Anthropology* 43(5): 611–30.

Strathern, Marilyn. 1998. "Bulletproofing: A Tale from the UK." Documents: Artifacts of Modern Knowledge, conference convened by Annelise Riles, Center for Law, Culture and Social Thought, Northwestern University.

———. Ed. 2000a. *Audit Cultures: Anthropological Studies in Accountability, Ethics, and the Academy*. New York: Routledge.

———. 2000b. "The Tyranny of Transparency." *British Educational Research Journal* 26(3): 309–21.

Sudarkasa, Niara. 1973. *Women and Work: A Study of Yoruba Women in the Marketplace and the Home*. Ann Arbor: University of Michigan.

Sunley, Peter. 1999. "Space for Stakeholding? Stakeholder Capitalism and Economic Geography." *Environment and Planning A* 31(12): 2189–2205.

"Supermarkets Given All Clear." BBC News. 2000. October 10. Available online at http://news.bbc.co.uk/1/hi/business/965665.stm

Sustain 2001. *Eating Oil: Food Supply in a Changing Climate*. London: Sustain.

Suzanne, Alfred. 1894. *La Cuisine Anglaise et sa Patisserie*. Paris: L'Art Culinaire.

Swift, Jonathan. 1996. "Desertification: Narratives, Winners and Losers." In *The Lie of the Land: Challenging Received Wisdom on the African Environment*, ed. Melissa Leach and Robin Mearns, 73–90. New York: Heinemann.

SYFIA, Ed. 1994. *l'Afrique, Côté Cuisines: Regards Africains sur l'Alimentation*. Paris: Syros.

Sylvander, Bertil. 1995. "Conventions de Qualité, Concurrence, et Coopération: Cas du Label Rouge' dans la Filière Volailles." In *La Grande Transformation de L'agriculture: Lectures Conventionnalistes Et Regulationnistes*, ed. Gilles Allaire and Robert Boyer, 73–96. Paris: Economica.

Tallontire, Anne, Catherine Dolan, et al. 2001. *Gender Issues and Ethical Trade: A Mapping of the Issues in African Horticulture*. Working Paper. Chatham, UK: Natural Resources Institute.

Tanaka, Keiko, and Lawrence Busch. 2003. "Standardization as a Means for Globalizing a Commodity: The Case of Rapeseed in China." *Rural Sociology* 68(1): 25–45.

Taylor, Marilyn. 1999. "Influencing Policy: A UK Voluntary Sector Perspective." In *International Perspectives on Voluntary Action*, ed. David Lewis, 182–201. London: Earthscan.

Teather, David. "US Trade War Threat as Europe Bars GM Crops." *Guardian*, January 10, 2003.

Tenner, Arthur R., and Irving J. DeToro. 1992. *Total Quality Management: Three Steps to Continuous Improvement*. Reading, Mass.: Addison-Wesley.

The Tricks of Trade in the Adulterations of Food and Physic: With Directions for Their Detection and Counteraction. 1856. London: Bogue.

Thompson, Victoria E. 1997. "Urban Renovation, Moral Regeneration: Domesticating the Halles in Second-Empire Paris." *French Historical Studies* 20(1): 87–109.

Thrift, Nigel. 1996. *Spatial Formations*. London: Sage.

Thrupp, Lori Ann, Gilles Bergeron, et al. 1995. *Bittersweet Harvests for Global Supermarkets: Challenges in Latin America's Agricultural Export Boom*. Washington, D.C.: World Resources Institute.

Tilly, Louise A. 1985. "Food Entitlement, Famine, and Conflict." In *Hunger and History: The Impact of Changing Food Production and Consumption Patterns on Society*, ed. Robert I. Rotberg, 135–52. Cambridge: Cambridge University Press.

Trolley Trouble. BBC 2. April 24, 2002.

Trollope, Anthony. 1973. *South Africa*. Cape Town: A. Balkema.

Tronto, Joan C. 1993. *Moral Boundaries: A Political Argument for an Ethic of Care*. New York: Routledge.

Trubek, Amy B. 2000. *Haute Cuisine: How the French Invented the Culinary Profession*. Philadelphia: University of Pennsylvania Press.

Truhaut, R., and R. Souverain. 1963. *Food Additive Control in France*. Rome: Food and Agriculture Organization.

Tsoukas, Haridimos. 1997. "The Tyranny of Light. The Temptations and the Paradoxes of the Information Society." *Futures* 29(9): 827–43.

Vaughan, Meghan. 1987. *The Story of an African Famine*. Cambridge: Cambridge University Press.

Vickery, Kenneth Powers. 1986. *Black and White in Southern Zambia: The Tonga Plateau Economy and British Imperialism, 1890–1939*. Westport, Conn.: Greenwood Press.

Vidal, John. "Africa Famine Nations Resist GM Food Aid." *Guardian* September 11, 2002.

Walvin, James. 1997. *Fruits of Empire: Exotic Produce and British Taste, 1660–1800*. Houndmills, Basingstoke, U.K.: Macmillan Press.

Watson, James L. 1997. *Golden Arches East: McDonald's in East Asia*. Stanford, Calif.: Stanford University Press.

Watts, Michael. 1983. *Silent Violence: Food, Famine, and Peasantry in Northern Nigeria*. Berkeley: University of California Press.

———. 1994. "Life under Contract: Contract Farming, Agrarian Restructuring, and Flexible Accumulation." In *Living under Contract: Contract Farming and Agrarian Transformation in Sub-Saharan Africa*, eds. Peter Little and Michael Watts, 21–77. Madison: University of Wisconsin Press.

———. 1994. "What Difference Does Difference Make?" *Review of International Political Economy* 1(3): 564–69.

Weatherell, Charlotte, Angela Tregear, et al. 2003. "In Search of the Concerned Consumer: UK Public Perceptions of Food, Farming and Buying Local." *Journal of Rural Studies* 19(2): 233–44.

Weber, Eugen Joseph. 1976. *Peasants into Frenchmen: The Modernization of Rural France, 1870–1914.* Stanford, Calif.: Stanford University Press.

Weir, David, Mark Schapiro, et al. 1981. *Circle of Poison: Pesticides and People in a Hungry World.* San Francisco: Institute for Food and Development Policy.

Weismantel, Mary. 1993. "Enfants et Soupes, Hommes et Taureaux: Les Répas et le Temps pour les Femmes de Zumbagua." In *Le Temps de Manger: Alimentation, Emploi du Temps, et Rythmes Sociaux,* eds. M. Aymard, C. Grignon, and F. Sabban, 151–82. Paris: Maison des Sciences de l'Homme.

Wells, Miriam J. 1996. *Strawberry Fields: Politics, Class, and Work in California Agriculture.* Ithaca, N.Y.: Cornell University Press.

Wetherell, Iden. 1979. "Settler Expansionism in Central Africa: The Imperial Response of 1931 and Subsequent Implications." *African Affairs* 78(311): 210–27.

Whatmore, S., and L. Thorne. 1997. "Nourishing Networks: Alternative Geographies of Food." In *Globalising Food: Agrarian Questions and Global Restructuring,* eds. D. Goodman and M. Watts, 287–304. New York: Routledge.

White, Howard. 1997. "Zambia in the 1990s as a Case of Adjustment in Africa." *African Development Review* 9(2): 56–87.

Wiener, Martin J. 1981. *English Culture and the Decline of the Industrial Spirit, 1850–1980.* Cambridge: Cambridge University Press.

Williams, Raymond. 1975. *The Country and the City.* London: Paladin.

Williams, S., and R. Karen. 1985. *Agribusiness and the Small-Scale Farmer: A Dynamic Partnership for Development.* Boulder, Colo.: Westview.

Wilson, Godfrey. 1941. *An Essay on the Economics of Detribalization in Northern Rhodesia.* Livingstone, Northern Rhodesia: Rhodes-Livingstone Institute.

Winter, Michael. 2003. "Embeddedness, the New Food Economy and Defensive Localism." *Journal of Rural Studies* 19(1): 23–32.

Winters, Christopher. 1983. "The Classification of Traditional African Cities." *Journal of Urban History* 10(1): 3–31.

Wolf, Eric R. 1999. *Envisioning Power: Ideologies of Dominance and Crisis.* Berkeley: University of California Press.

Wolf, Eric R. and Sydel Silverman. 2001. *Pathways of Power: Building an Anthropology of the Modern World.* Berkeley: University of California Press.

World Bank. 1989. *Sub-Saharan Africa. From Crisis to Sustainable Growth: A Long Term Perspective Study.* Washington, D.C.: World Bank.

Wright, Gordon. 1964. *Rural Revolution in France. The Peasantry in the Twentieth Century.* Stanford, Calif.: Stanford University Press.

Wrigley, Neil 1992. "Sunk Capital, the Property Crisis, and the Restructuring of British Food Retailing." 24(11): 1521–27.

———. 1998. "How British Retailers Have Shaped Food Choice." In *The Nation's Diet: The Social Science of Food Choice,* Anne Murcott, 112–28. New York: Longman.

Wynne, Brian. 2001. "Creating Public Alienation: Expert Cultures of Risk and Ethics on Gmos." *Science as Culture* 10(4):445–81.

Young, James Harvey. 1989. *Pure Food: Securing the Federal Food and Drugs Act of 1906.* Princeton, N.J.: Princeton University Press.

Young, Robert. 2001. *Postcolonialism: An Historical Introduction*. Oxford: Blackwell.

Zadek, S. 1998. "Balancing Performance, Ethics, and Accountability." *Journal of Business Ethics* 17(13): 1421–41.

ZEGA. 2000. *Zega Code of Conduct*. Lusaka, Zambia: ZEGA.

Zeldin, Theodore. 1980. *France 1848–1945: Taste and Corruption*. Oxford: Oxford University Press.

Zezima, Katie "A Ghost at the Table: A Distant Lobsterman." *New York Times,* July 24, 2003.

Zola, Emile. (1873). 1996. *The Belly of Paris*. Trans. E.A. Vizetelly. Los Angeles: Sun & Moon Press.

Index

Accountability, 5,28,29, 169, 180, 186, 201, 215, 221–222
Accum, F.C., 39
Activism, agro-food, 7–8, 22–23, 167–169, 177–178, 181–193
Actor-network theory (ANT), 11–12
Adulteration, food. *See* food adulteration
Aflotoxin, 8
Africa
  European colonization of, 34–38, 56
  non-traditional export commodities, 13–14
  portrayed as disease-ridden "hot zone," 8
  postcolonial scholarship and, 30
Agence Francaise de Developpement (AFD), 74–74, 87–88
Agrarian change *See* foodways
Agricultural Act of 1947 (Britain), 172–173
Agriculture. *See also* contract farming, peasant, outgrowers, smallholders
  in colonial Upper Volta, 67–69
  France, views of in, 131–134
  Zambia, African, 97, 99–100,104, 122–124
  Zambia, white settler, 95–96, 98–101, 103–104
Agriflora (Zambia), 106–110, 113, 122–125, 206
Agro-ecology, Burkina Faso and Zambia, 21
AIDS, 8, 118–119
Anglophone commodity network
  as case study, 20–23, 27–29
  tribal nature of, 216
Appelation d'origine controllée (AOC), 54–55, 57
Appert, Nicolas, 43

Audit
  culture, 202, 204, 221
  "explosion," 28
Audits, supermarket supplier, 12, 27, 116, 198–202

Baby vegetables,
  French importers of, 158
  symbolism of, 197
  Zambia's production of, 21, 95–96, 107, 109, 124
Best practice, codes of, 27–28 *See also* standards
Bobo-Dioulasso, 12–13, 67–71
Bové, José, 26, 166
Bovine spongiform encephalopathy (BSE)
  African origins theory of, 8
  in Britain and continental Europe, 6–7, 115, 133,155, 211
  Creuzfeldt-Jacob disease (CJD), 6–7, 211
  in the United States, *viii*
Brand names
  of African export products, 87, 215
  of British activist organizations, 188, 192
  as guarantee of food purity and quality, 45, 172–173
  corporate efforts to protect and promote image of, 96, 155, 169, 175, 209, 215
  French importers' lack of, 162, 214
Brillat-Savarin, Anthelme, 50
Britain
  Agricultural Act of 1947, 172–173
  agro-food activism in 167–169, 177–178, 181–193
  Competition Commission, 176

Britain (*continued*)
consumer cooperatives in, 44–45
countryside preservation in, 7, 22, 48,
167, 169, 188
food adulteration in, 38–41
food culture, changes in late 20th
century, 176–177
Food Safety Act, 1990, 29,174
food scares in, 6–7, 174, 178
media coverage of supermarkets in, 178–
180
Policy Commission on the Future of
Farming and Food, 171
Sale of Food and Drugs Act 1875, 41–42
ties to former African colonies, 57
British South Africa Company (BSAC), 98–
99
Burkina Faso
agro-ecology, 21
Bobo people, 81
comparison with Zambia, 20–22
colonial Upper Volta, 64–70
contract farming, 73, 79–80
development aid in, 62, 74–75, 87–89
economic statistics, 23
foodways in, 70, 90
forced labor in, 66–67
introduction of French vegetable
gardening in, 61
map, 65
meanings of exporting work in, 86–91
Mossi people, 76, 81
Mossi Plateau, 66
postcolonial green bean schemes in, 70–
73
"protecting" peasant producers in, 89–91
women produce traders in, 71, 90
Burnett, John, 43–44

Campaore, Blaise, 74
Canned food, 37, 38, 43, 52, 154
Canning, food, as "imperial technology"
Carrefour, 136, 137–138, 154, 171
Category management. *See* supply chain
management
Chefs
celebrity, in Britain, 176, 178–179
French, 49–51

Child labor, 118–119, 155–156, 170, 184,
186
Christian Aid, 184–185, 187
Civilizing mission, 30, 49, 61, 96–97
CODEX, 220
COLEACP, 114
Colonialism
British, in southern Africa, 96–98
French, in West Africa, 16, 63–66
Commerce, sociable, 25–27 See also *Halles*
Commodity networks, transnational
comparative research on, 18–23
culture and nature in, 9–12
See also Anglophone commodity
network, francophone commodity
network
Commonwealth Development Corporation
(CDC), 106
Confederation Paysanne (CP), 26, 48, 132–
133
Contract farming, 14, 73, 90
Consumers
knowledge about food and farming, 133,
160, 170, 178
research on, 132, 133, 140, 177, 210
See also power, consumer buying;
shopping
Convenience foods, consumer demand for,
129, 140–141
Cookbooks, French, 51–52
Cooperatives,
agricultural, 53, 61, 71, 76,80, 122–124
consumer, 44–46, 172
Copperbelt, 93, 97, 101–102
Copper industry, Zambian 103–105
Corporate paternalism, 96,101, 109–110,
207–208
Creuztfeldt Jacob Disease (CJD), 6–7
Cuisine
Britain's polyglot, 17, 55
French, claims to superior, 49–51
See also foodways
Culture
corporate, food manufacturing 53
as explanation for inequality, 217
within transnational commodity
networks, 9–10
See also audit culture, power

Cultural economy
   analysis, 9, 16, 216–18
   Burkinabé intermediaries' work in
      transnational, 63
   of corporate food sourcing,170
   of French food retailing, 129
   of vegetable exporting in Zambia, 96

Department of Environmental and Rural
   Affairs (DEFRA), Britain, 171
Development
   aid in Burkina Faso, 62, 74–75, 87–89
   aid to private sector in Zambia, 109, 123
   economic, in rural France, 49, 56
   strategies, non-traditional, 13–15
Dole France, 136, 157, 158–159
Due diligence, 15, 116, 174, 178, 199

England. See Britain; United Kingdom
Escoffier, Auguste, 50–51
l'Etats Generaux de l'Alimentation
   (EGA),127
Ethical trade, 118–119, 196, 206. 219 See
      also Ethical Trading Initiative
Ethical Trading Initiative (ETI), 114, 183–
   187, 192, 198, 206
EUREPGAP, 114,116,175, 198
European Union (EU), 7–8, 14, 155, 165,
   174, 199
Expertise
   lack of, in Zambian horticultural industry,
      109, 112
   merchants', 42, 130, 148, 151, 213
   peasant, 133
   See also métis
Export company managers, Zambia 120–121
Exporters, Burkinabé
   meanings of work, 88–89
   relations with French importers, 84–86
   relations with growers, 79–80, 84–86

Fair trade, 177, 183, 187, 188, 192–193
Fairtrade Foundation, 192, 193
Famine, 36, 37, 56–57, 67, 70, 211
Farmers markets See markets
Food
   as unique commodity, 9–11
   in debates over colonial expansion, 35–37

Food adulteration
   in Britain, 38–41, 44
   France, 39–40, 53
   Lancet report, 40–41
   legislation to combat, 38–43
Food-borne disease, 5–7, 38, 47
Food canning, 43
Food globalization, 33–34, 167–168
Food miles, 167, 168, 218
Food packaging. See packaging, fresh
   produce
Food provisioning. See food supply
Food quality
   as assured by product packaging and
      brand image, 45
   as defined and achieved in Burkina Faso
      green bean export trade, 63, 80–83, 88
   French consumers' ideas about, 135, 140
   French vs. British methods of controlling,
      16–17
   standards and audits, 27–28, 58, 198–201
Food safety
   British consumers' declining concerns
      about, 211
   norms, culturally specific nature of, 220
   political and moral nature of, 38
   smallholder production and, 203–204
   Zambia Export Growers Association
      (ZEGA) code, emphasis on 115
   See also standards
Food Safety Act, Britain's 1990, 29,174
Food safety legislation
   adulteration and, 38–43
   British supermarkets' response to, 174–
      175
   European, 7–8, 155, 165, 174, 199
   institutional framework of modern, 46–
      47
Food scares
   consequences for Africa, 8–9
   definition, 5–6
   effects on French food supply, 133–4
   late 20th century, 6–7
   media role in Britain's, 178
   undermining public trust in government
      and science, 7, 174, 190, 211–212
Food security, 72, 81–82. See also famine
Food Standards Agency (FSA), 211

Food supply
    Britain, nineteenth century quality of, 43
    France, changes in, 129–130, 137–142,
        165–166
    French consumers' attitudes, 133–134
    hypermarkets' growing control over, 141–
        142
Foodways
    agrarian change and, 55
    Britain's national, 55
    Burkinabé, 70, 90
    colonial, 37, 61, 68, 103
    consolidation of French national, 49–55
    definition, 47
    differences between French and British,
        17–18, 48–49
    imperial roots of European, 56, 219
Forced labor, colonial Upper Volta, 66–67
France
    Agence Francaise de Developpement
        (AFD), 74–75
    anti-adulteration legislation, 42
    chain stores, early, 45–46
    consumer cooperatives, 45
    consumers'attitudes about food
        supply,133–134
    cooking courses and cookbooks in 19th
        century, 51–52
    economic statistics, 23
    l'Etats Generaux de l'Alimentation
        (EGA),127
    food adulteration in, 39–40, 53
    hypermarket expansion in, 139–140
    ideal of rural nature in, 132–133
    ideal of sociable commerce in, 25, 27
    peasant agriculture in, 52–53, 131–132,
        164
    peasant associations in, 42, 53
    rural development in, versus in Africa, 56
    shopping patterns in, 138
    ties to former African colonies, 57–58
    top ten vegetable and fruit imports, 17
    See also Halles; Rungis
Francophone commodity network, 10, 19,
        63–64
    as case study, 10. 12–15, 18–20, 212–214
    cultural norms of anglophone and, 29–31
    role of trust and friendship in, 130–131

Fraud, growth of mass market in France
        and, 53–54
French beans see green beans
Fresh fruits and vegetables (FFV)
    global value chain analysis of, 16
    top ten imports into France, 17
    top ten imports into United Kingdom, 17
Friendship
    in francophone network, 130–131, 162,
        164–165, 213–214
    between growers and exporters, Burkina
        Faso,79–80, 84–86
    See also trust

Gallot, Yves, 162–166
Gastronomy, 19th century Paris, 49–50
Gender
    equity, workplace assessments of, 28,
        186
    livelihoods, 69, 130
    See also women
Genetically modified (GM) food, 211–212,
        216–217
Genetically modified organisms (GMOs),
        opposition to, 7, 127, 132–133
Geographic indication labels, wine, 54. See
        also Appelation d'origine controllée
        (AOC)
Germ theory, 43
Governance, food
    British supermarkets' role in, 11, 22, 28–
        29, 169–170, 177–178, 208–209, 215,
        220–221
    media and non-governmental
        organizations' role in, 180–181
    See also neoliberalism
Globalization
    British critics of, 167
    cultural analysis of, 216
    French concerns about, 127
    intermediaries' roles in, 24–25, 128, 152
Globalized food economy, 4–6, 9, 14–15
Green beans
    Burkina Faso exports, 3, 13–14, 15, 61–
        62, 70–73, 76–78
    French preferences in, 137
    Kenyan 13, 14, 15–16, 17, 61, 202–203
    symbolism of, 197

HACCP (Hazard Analysis and Critical
    Control Point) 174
Halles, les
    importers and their suppliers, 146–147
    mandataires, 143, 146
    neighborhood of, 143–144
    relocation to Rungis, 148–149
    social atmosphere, 143–145
    traders' knowledge of products at, 147–
    148
Haricot vert. See green beans
Hoof-and-mouth disease, 7
Horticulture. *See* Zambia, corporate
    horticulture in
Hygiene
    and colonization debates, 36–37
    early chain stores emphasis on, 45
    European Commission, standards of food
    and crop, 9
    Zambian packhouse 117–118
    See also standards
Hypermarkets
    Carrefour, 136, 137–138, 154, 171
    domination of French fresh produce
    retailing, 141–142
    expansion, 139–140

Importers, fresh produce
    British, 194–196, 200
    French, at *les Halles*, 146–147
    French, large-scale, 152–157
    French, relations to Burkinabé exporters,
    84–86, 212–213
    French, small scale, 160–161
Institute for International Environment and
    Development, 187
Intermediaries, 5, 13, 18, 24–31, 42, 61–62
    anglophone, 156, 170, 181, 194, 209, 215
    Burkinabé agro-entrepreneurs as, 64, 74–
    75, 78, 91
    French, 128, 130
    Technological, 11–12
    See also exporters, importers,
    wholesalers
International Labor Organization (ILO),
    185, 220
International Monetary Fund (IMF), 31, 104
Irrigation, 13, 66, 68–72, 122–123, 165

Kaunda, Kenneth, 103–105
Kenya
    exporters' "learning tour" to, 88–89
    Guardian story about horticultural
    industry in, 210
    as leading African green bean exporter,
    13–17, 61, 74
    as "success story" of non-traditional
    export development, 15
    restructuring of horticultural sector in, 15–
    16, 120, 202–203
    white settlers in, 35, 95, 103

Labels
    distinguishing "fair" and "ethical"
    products, 183, 187, 193
    as information source, 5, 180
    Soil Association certified organic, 190–193
Labor
    child, 118–119, 155–156, 170, 184, 186
    family, 72–73, 123, 202
    forced, in Upper Volta, 66–67
    organizing, in Copperbelt 102
    shortages, Northern Rhodesian settler
    farming, 100–101
    Zambian horticultural industry, 108–110,
    111
Liberalization, economic
    Burkina Faso, 14,73–74
    Zambia, 95, 105
    See also structural adjustment
Livingstone, David, 97–98
Local food, 25–26, 167, 218–220
London, 45, 93, 103, 105, 211
Lusaka, Zambia, 93, 97

Mad cow disease. *See* Bovine spongiform
    encephalopathy (BSE)
Mali, 15, 74
Malnutrition, 104
Mandataires 143,146
Mangetout, BBC documentary, 179–180
Marché Internationale de Rungis See
    Rungis
Markets
    farmers' 25–26, 218–219
    outdoor, in France, 138–139
    See also Halles; Rungis

Marks and Spencer, 140, 173, 176, 189
McDonalds, opposition to, 26, 48, 129, 133, 166
Media, popular
  and British supermarkets, 22, 29, 193–194
  fueling food scares, 178, 215
  role in shaping British food knowledge and politics, 178–182
  Zambian export companies' concerns about, 21,110
Mennell, Stephen, 132
Métis, 26–27, 85–86, 147, 181, 204, 222
Miller, Daniel, 210, 219
Ministry of Agriculture, Food and Fisheries (MAFF), 6–7
Mintz, Sidney, 58, 217
Missionaries, role in agricultural development, 69–70
Modernization
  of rural France, 48–49, 56
  of West African agriculture, 65, 74, 129
  theory, 111
  white settlers as political opponents of, 111
Moral economy, 11
Moral geographies, 182, 210
Multiples. *See* British supermarkets
Multi-site research, 18

Native Reserves, colonial Zambia, 99–100
Networks. *See* actor-network theory;
  commodity networks, transnational
Neoliberalism, 28, 169, 174, 181, 198, 215, 221
Non-governmental organizations (NGOs)
  audits and, 181, 201,
  neoliberal governance and, 169–170
  relations with media, 22–23, 177–182, 193
  supermarkets'efforts to cope with demands of, 195, 209, 215
Non-traditional export commodities, 13–15, 57, 87, 214
Northern Rhodesia *See* Zambia
Nutrition, 36, 47, 177

Organic
  food production, French views of, 134
  movement in Britain, 48. *See also* activism, agro-food, Soil Association standards, 190–192
  vegetables in Zambia, 124
Ouagadougou, Burkina Faso, 3–4, 61, 68, 70
Outgrowers, Zambia, 111–114. *See also* agriculture, white settler

Packaging, fresh produce
  British supermarkets' preferences for, 173
  French attitudes towards, 136–137
  Zambian industry of, 21, 107–108, 175
Paris, 49–50, 52–53, 138, 142–144 *See also Halles,* Rungis
Patronage relations, 53, 63, 156, 163–164, 213
Peasant
  agriculture in France, 52–53, 131–132, 164
  Burkina Faso's policies to "protect," 64–67, 89–91
  disappearance of in Britain, 55
  French confidence in, 133–34,164
  See also Confederation Paysanne, smallholders
Pesticide residue laws, harmonization of, 8–9
Pesticides
  British supermarkets' concerns about, 170, 174–175, 200, 204
  in Burkina Faso, 71, 80, 82–83
  in Zambia, 116, 118, 123
Postcolonial
  power, 30–31 170–171
  relations between Europe and Africa, 30–31
  studies, 30
Power
  consumer buying, 139, 183, 217–218
  exporters, 84–85
  postcolonial, 30–31, 170–171, 214,
  structural, 58–59, 212, 217–218

Preservation, food canning, 43
Pure food movement, 41, 44–46

Quality. *See* food quality

Race to the Top (RTTT), 189–190
Race, characterizations of, 36, 103, 156–157, 161 *See also* stereotypes
Rationalization
   agricultural modernization and, Burkina Faso 74
   supply chain management (SCM) and, 195–198
Retailers. *See* hypermarkets; supermarkets
Rhodes, Cecil B., 98
Risk
   British supermarkets' handling of, 170, 194, 196, 203
   colonial expansion and, 35, 58, 98
   diversification as a means of managing, 77, 82–83, 213
   French import firms' handling of, 129–131, 156, 165
   government failures to address, 6, 127
   inherent in agriculture and eating, 10
   posed by expanding market economy, 49, 53, 59
   posed by export fruit and vegetable production, 15, 70, 113
   trust and friendship as protection against, 11, 13, 165, 214
Rungis market
   changes in produce wholesaling at, 149–152
   market "in search of a soul", 149, 150
   relocation from *les Halles*, 148–149
   research at, 19–20

Sainsbury's, 45, 155,171, 175–176, 189, 191
Sale of Food and Drugs Act of 1875 (SFDA), Britain, 41–42
Salmonella, 6, 115
Sankara, Thomas, 72–74
Science
   as basis for standards, 220
   colonialism and, 35–37, 56, 58

food adulteration and, 40–44
food scares and authority of, 7, 191, 212
gastronomic culture and, 34, 51
Selection, 162, 163
Shopping
   ethical vs. moral, 210, 219
   France, changing patterns of in, 137–140
Sinclair, Upton, 38
Slow Food, 7
Smallholders. *See also* peasant
   British retailers' concerns about, 202–205
   Zambian horticultural industry's recruitment of, 122–124
Social responsibility, corporate 28, 169, 189–190. *See also* ethical trade
Soil Association (SA), 23, 190–193, 195. *See also* organic
Southern Rhodesia. *See* Zimbabwe, colonial
Space-time compression, 11–12
Stakeholder capitalism, 180, 181
Standards
   aesthetic, enforcement of in Burkina Faso, 84
   aesthetic, French produce trade's 137, 148, 213
   British supermarket, 15–16, 28–29, 93–95, 175, 198–202
   characterizing anglophone network, 27–28
   food safety, 29, 114–118, 164, 200–201, social welfare, 15, 21, 94, 114, 118–119. *See also* Ethical Trading Initiative
   Zambian horticultural industry's, 114–122
Stereotypes 29–30. 48, 63, 81, 131, 161, 213, 221–222 *See also* race, characterizations of
Strathern, Marilyn, 178
Structural adjustment, 74–75 See also liberalization, economic
Succarsales, 45–46
Supermarkets, British
   audits, 116–117, 198–202
   competition between, 175–176. *See also* Race to the Top
   control over suppliers, 22, 270,194–202
   ethical mission of, 210

Supermarkets, British (*continued*)
  fresh produce retailing, 173
  gatekeeper role of, 174
  influence over British foodways, 171–2
  Kenya's fresh produce exports to, 15–16
  media coverage of, 22, 178
  non-governmental organizations (NGOs)
    as stakeholders, 180–181
  predecessors of, 45
  standards, 28–29, 94–95, 198–201, 215,
    222
  store brand products, 173–174
  supplier performance, measures of, 205–
    206
  ties to TV cooking shows, 179
  value added freshness, promotion of 174
Supermarkets, French
  dominating French fresh produce
    market, 141–142
  food safety demands, 155
  See also hypermarkets
Supply chain management (SCM), 27–29.
    194–198, 206–208, 215–216 *See also*
    supermarkets, British

Taste
  cultural distinctiveness of, 14, 25, 37
  French cultural identity and, 34, 49–52,
    135–136, 141, 213
  globalized, 14
Terroir, 49, 54
Tesco, 167, 176, 179–180, 183, 189, 199,
    210, 221
Traceability, vii, 8–9, 12, 15, 27, 29, 199–
    200, 203
  in Burkina Faso, 83–84
  in France, 134, 155, 221
  in Zambia, 116–117, 123
Trade. *See* commerce; commodity networks;
    markets
Transparency 28, 201, 221
  tyranny of, 201–202, 209–210
TransZambezi Industries (TZI), 106–107
Trust
  Burkinabé growers' and exporters'
    cultivation of, 76, 79, 83, 85
  consumer, in supermarkets, 174, 189,
    190
  cultural identity as basis for, 10
  importance to perishable food trading, 11–
    12, 13
  public, in government and scientific food
    safety measures 7, 174, 190, 211–212
  organic food and, 190–191
  quality assurances based on, 26, 30
  role in British supermarket supply chain
    "partnerships," 116, 121–122, 202, 209
  role in francophone network, 130–131,
    146–147, 154–155, 213–214

UCOBAM (formerly UCOVAM), 71–72, 80
United States Agency for International
    Development (USAID), 87–88, 123
Upper Volta. *See* Burkina Faso

Wal-Mart, 114, 137–138, 171
Weber, Eugen, 48–49, 56
White farmers. *See* agriculture, white settler;
    outgrowers
Wholesalers, fresh produce
  British supermarkets' circumvention of,
    173
  Burkinabé women as, 13, 68, 70–71, 77–
    78
  French, at Rungis, 149–152, 157, 159–
    160
Wiener, Martin, 169
Wines, 54–55
Wolf, Eric, 217
Women
  in Burkina Faso fresh produce trade, 13,
    68, 70–71, 77–78
  in France's paid workforce, 140
  in Zambian horticultural industry, 111–
    112
  19th century domestic science courses
    for, in France, 51–52
  See also gender
World Bank, 13–16, 30, 57, 64, 74–75, 87–
    88, 104
World Trade Organization (WTO), 9, 14,
    15, 218, 220

York Farms (Zambia), 106, 108–110, 124–
    125, 206

Zambia
case study comparison with Burkina
Faso, 20–22
colonial Northern Rhodesia, 98–103
copper price collapse 1975, 104–
105
company-driven development in 98–99,
101–103
corporate horticulture in, 95, 105–111,
124–125. *See also* corporate paternalism
"detribalization" in, 102–103
distinction between corporate and white
farmer enterprise in, 100–102, 110–
111
economic statistics, 23

genetically modified (GM) food
controversy in, 211–212
liberalization in, 105
map, 97
outgrowers in, 111–114, 118–121
smallholder production in, 122–124
Zambia Export Growers Association
(ZEGA), 109, 114–118
Zimbabwe
colonial, 57, 98–103
horticultural industry in, 17, 77, 107, 111,
179, 195, 202, 207–208
political unrest in, 20–21, 95, 101, 110,
120–121, 207–208
Zola, Emile, 142